Decolonization Models
for America's Last Colony

Decolonization Models for

America's Last Colony:

Puerto Rico

Ángel Collado-Schwarz

Radio interviews with
Francisco Catalá-Oliveras and Juan Lara

SYRACUSE UNIVERSITY PRESS

Copyright © 2012 by Syracuse University Press
Syracuse, New York 13244-5290

First English Edition 2012

12   13   14   15   16   17   6   5   4   3   2   1

Originally published in Spanish as *Soberanías exitosas: Seis modelos para el desarrollo económico de Puerto Rico* (Puerto Rico: La Voz del Centro, 2008; 3rd ed., 2010).

∞ The paper used in this publication meets the minimum requirements of the American National Standard for Information Sciences—Permanence of Paper for Printed Library Materials, ANSI Z39.48-1992.

For a listing of books published and distributed by Syracuse University Press, visit our Web site at SyracuseUniversityPress.syr.edu.

ISBN: 978-0-8156-0963-6

Library of Congress Cataloging-in-Publication Data

Collado Schwarz, Ángel, 1951–
   [Soberanías exitosas. English]
   Decolonization models for America's last colony : Puerto Rico : radio interviews with Francisco Catalá-Oliveras and Juan Lara / Ángel Collado-Schwarz.—1st English ed.
      p. cm.
   "Originally published in Spanish as Soberanías exitosas: Seis modelos para el desarrollo económico de Puerto Rico (Puerto Rico: La Voz del Centro, 2008; 3rd ed., 2010)."
   Includes bibliographical references and index.
   ISBN 978–0-8156–0963–6 (pbk. : alk. paper) 1. Puerto Rico—Economic policy.
2. Decolonization—Puerto Rico.   3. Economic development—Puerto Rico.
4. Decolonization—Case studies.   5. Economic policy—Case studies.   6. Economic development—Case studies.   7. Catalá Oliveras, Francisco A.—Interviews.   8. Lara, Juan, Dr.—Interviews.   I. Catalá Oliveras, Francisco A.   II. Lara, Juan, Dr.   III. Title.
   HC154.5.C6313 2010
   330.97295—dc23   2012000613

Manufactured in the United States of America

"This much needed English edition underlines the sad political history of Puerto Rico, presents its recent past inadequate economic results and its current calamitous situation, and argues vigorously and convincingly for resolving its colonial status. Drawing on examples of six comparable nations, the author makes a strong case for sovereignty that would allow the people of this island to achieve their full and long awaited potential. While there are economic clouds over the world at this time, small states may still have special opportunities for advancement and Puerto Rico demands close attention."

—JAMES WOLFENSOHN, president, World Bank, 1995–2005

"In both Washington and San Juan the high hopes and constructive ambiguities of the creators of Commonwealth in the 1950s seem to have run their course and may no longer be sustainable. The initial high hopes have been followed by the serial disappointments of recent decades. Yet they have rarely been accompanied by constructive new thinking. An exception is this provocative book by Ángel Collado-Schwarz. He combines a bold vision with a fresh approach, both to the island's current problems and to its potentially prosperous future."

—THOMAS L. HUGHES, former US assistant secretary of state
and former president of the Carnegie Endowment for International Peace

"This is an important work which connects the collapse of the Puerto Rican economy with the island's unresolved political relationship with the United States. It analyzes the success of six other small economies as models for lifting Puerto Rico out of its downward economic spiral. Must reading for any American concerned about US management of its five remaining territories."

—AMBASSADOR PETER R. ROSENBLATT, Washington lawyer and
former president Carter's personal representative in negotiations to
terminate the US trusteeship over Micronesia, the Marshall Islands, and
Palau, and to establish their free association with the United States

"This book has the audacity of taking up one of the most difficult questions faced by humanity: What makes a country and its people prosperous? It searches for answers not in abstract theory but in concrete experiences. How did Ireland do it? How did Slovenia, Israel or Singapore do it? How can Puerto Rico achieve the same levels of development as countries that were poor until a few decades ago and today are examples for the rest of the world? The answers are sketched in these pages full of pleasant conversation, revealing facts, and surprising conclusions. This book should be obligatory reading for those who believe that Puerto Rico's future should be more prosperous than its past."

—MOISÉS NAÍM, PHD, former editor in chief,
Foreign Policy (Washington, DC); columnist,
El País (Madrid)

Ángel Collado-Schwarz is the founder and chairman of the Fundación Voz del Centro, a cultural nongovernmental organization, and the producer and host of the radio program *La Voz del Centro*, which has aired more than four hundred programs since 2002 in Puerto Rico, New York, and Chicago over Univision Radio (www.vozdelcentro.org).

Born in Puerto Rico in 1951, Collado-Schwarz holds a doctorate in contemporary Latin American history from the Universidad Complutense in Madrid. He also holds a master's in business administration from Syracuse University and studied at the University of Puerto Rico, the New School in New York, the Center for Advanced Studies on Puerto Rico and the Caribbean in San Juan, and the Instituto Universitario Ortega y Gasset in Madrid.

He worked for many years in the communications industry at the international level, establishing a regional communications network, which he directed from Puerto Rico, with operations in eighteen Latin American and Caribbean countries as well as in New York City, Los Angeles, and Miami. He was also a member of the board of Saatchi & Saatchi Worldwide (London) for more than two decades.

The founder and president of the Marine Conservation of Culebra Foundation and the Richard Wagner Association of Puerto Rico, Collado-Schwarz was also the chairman of the board of the University of Puerto Rico Press and is a member of the Advisory Board of the Maxwell School, the Board of Trustees of Syracuse University, and the Barenboim-Said Foundation.

Collado-Schwarz has published four books: *Voces de la cultura 1* (2005), *Voces de la cultura 2* (2006), *Voces de la cultura 3* (2007), and *Soberanías exitosas: Seis modelos para el desarrollo económico de Puerto Rico* (2008). His forthcoming book is on the Cold War, Truman, and Puerto Rico. He also writes a regular column in Puerto Rico's principal newspaper *El Nuevo Día*.

Why Conclude Puerto Rico Is Still a Colony?

▸ United States laws apply to the Puerto Rican people without their consent.

▸ United States laws can override provisions of the Commonwealth Constitution.

▸ The President of the United States and executive appointees negotiate treaties and take other actions which affect Puerto Rico without consulting it.

▸ Through the unilateral grant by Congress of diversity jurisdiction, United States courts decide cases involving strictly local matters of law.

▸ There is no equality or comparability of rights between United States citizens residing in Puerto Rico and those domiciled in the States.

▸ Congress assumes that it can unilaterally exercise plenary powers over Puerto Rico under the territorial clause of the United States Constitution.

▸ The United States government contends that sovereignty over Puerto Rico resides solely in the United States and not in the people of Puerto Rico. . . .

▸ Even if courts eventually hold that there is now a binding compact and that this compact encompasses the Federal Relations Act, the consent extended by the Puerto Rican people in 1950 when accepting Law 600 in a referendum is over-broad. Consent to the unrestricted application to Puerto Rico of all federal laws, past and future, does not thereby erase the colonial nature of such an arrangement. A slave's consent to bondage does not make him a free man. . . .

▸ Puerto Rico plays no role in the life of the international community, either directly or indirectly as a participant in the decisions by the United States.

▸ Commonwealth status as it is at present does not meet the decolonization standards established by the United Nations.

> —JOSÉ TRÍAS MONGE, M.A. and LL.B. Harvard University; S.J.D.
> Yale Law School. Attorney General of Puerto Rico, 1953–57; Chief Justice
> of Puerto Rico, 1974–85.

From José Trías Monge, *Puerto Rico: The Trials of the Oldest Colony in the World* (New Haven, CT: Yale Univ. Press, 1997), 161–63.

Contents

PART 4 : *Newspaper Columns by Dr. Ángel Collado-Schwarz*

Maps

Introduction to the 2011 English Edition

The year 2011 began with dictators being deposed in Tunisia and Egypt, turmoil in the Middle East, and accompanying cries for democracy. The United States is paying attention to the world's trouble spots, yet it is failing to conduct a reality check regarding its territory (colony) since 1898, located in its own backyard, the Caribbean.

I am referring to the unincorporated territory of Puerto Rico, "which belongs to but is not part of the United States," as defined by the US Supreme Court in the Insular Cases of 1922, and which is in a social and economic freefall.

Article 3 of the US Constitution states that Congress has plenary powers over its territories. Puerto Rico is ruled by the US Senate Committee on Energy and Natural Resources and the House of Representatives Committee on Natural Resources.

The Senate committee states the following about the relationship between the United States and Puerto Rico:

> The newly acquired insular areas—Puerto Rico and the Virgin Islands in the Eastern Caribbean, and American Samoa and Guam in the Pacific— which possessed unique geographic and cultural characteristics, were valued primarily for their strategic importance. They did not fit the traditional mold of the States. In a series of decisions rendered by the U.S. Supreme Court in the early 1900's, the offshore territories, except Hawaii, were classified as unincorporated, a term distinct from previous territories destined to become States.[1]

1. US Senate, Committee on Energy and Natural Resources, available at http://energy .senate.gov/public/index.cfm?FuseAction=About.History.

xiv ▸ 2011 Edition Introduction

The laws that affect Puerto Rico are approved by a US Congress in which Puerto Rican citizens have no voting rights. Is this democracy?

Federal judges, appointed by someone not elected by Puerto Ricans, rule the daily life of the territory (colony). Puerto Rico's legal system is integrated with the US federal judicial system, so federal laws prevail over local laws.

The federal judges intervened in the 2004 gubernatorial elections to decide which candidate had won. In February 2011, they jailed the president of the Puerto Rico Bar Association for failing to post a fine on a gag order in a case against the association. In a democracy, judges either are elected or are appointed by elected officials.

The jurist and former chief justice of the Supreme Court of Puerto Rico, José Trías Monge, affirms throughout his book *Puerto Rico: The Trials of the Oldest Colony in the World* that the unilateral power of Congress to legislate for Puerto Rico is not consistent with the principle of government by mutual consent.[2]

Over the past decades, Puerto Rico has been dominated by two political parties in various power-sharing permutations. Over the same decades, the situation in Puerto Rico has deteriorated drastically. The problem is not who is driving the car; the problem is the car itself—that is, the colonial situation in Puerto Rico.

At present, Puerto Rico is facing its worst economic moment. The unemployment rate has rocketed to almost 20 percent. The Economist Intelligence Unit estimated that the economy shrank 3.6 percent in 2010. According to the Central Intelligence Agency's *World Factbook*, for economic growth Puerto Rico ranked 214th in the world (out of 216) in 2010; indeed, it estimated that the economy shrank by 5.8 percent—an even worse performance than that of Haiti, which ranked 213th.

Also in 2010, only 36 percent of the Puerto Rican workforce was employed. Ten years earlier the figure had been 40 percent. In 2000, the

2. José Trías Monge, *Puerto Rico: The Trials of the Oldest Colony in the World* (New Haven, CT: Yale Univ. Press, 1997).

Puerto Rico Electric Power Authority had 1,986 industrial clients; ten years later the figure was 808.

Puerto Rico's public debt is almost equal to its gross national product; in other words, it is almost as great as the country's annual economic product. Rampant criminality is eroding Puerto Rican society. In 2011, the crime rate is heading toward an all-time record. Drug trafficking is the main cause of criminality, and drugs are being smuggled into a country whose borders are controlled exclusively by the federal government in Washington, DC. Domestic violence is destroying the Puerto Rican family. According to the *International Report on Violence Against Women,* published in 2010 by the Queen Sofia Center in Spain, Puerto Rico has more domestic murder victims per capita than any other country in the world.

A colony lacking a plan for what it might be as a nation cannot possibly solve its own economic and social problems. How is Puerto Rico to address its problems as long as sovereignty resides in Washington, where the US Congress has plenary powers over Puerto Rico?

Puerto Rico lacks the powers to create its own economic model tailored to its own situation. By contrast, Singapore, with the same population but no natural resources and one-fourteenth the area, led the world in economic expansion in 2010 with almost 15 percent growth.

Puerto Rico needs to integrate itself with the global economy by maintaining strong relations with the United States while developing new ones with the European Union, China, India, Latin America, and the rest of the world.

This English edition of *Soberanías exitosas* aims to bring the issue of Puerto Rico's decolonization to the rest of the world. In the globalized twenty-first century, there is no room for colonies.

In 2010, I stated at the hearings on Puerto Rico held by the United Nations Special Committee on Decolonization that as a result of colonization Puerto Rico was in the midst of its worst economic and social crisis, facing the dire challenges previously described. I emphasized that those looming issues will not be resolved while sovereignty remains with the United States. I called for the referral of Puerto Rico's situation to the

General Assembly and for a constitutional assembly to be formed as a decolonization mechanism.

On June 21, 2010, the United Nations Department of Public Information issued a press release titled "Special Committee on Decolonization Passes Text Urging General Assembly to Consider Formally Situation Concerning Puerto Rico: Draft Resolution Calls on United States to Expedite Island's Self-Determination."[3]

The release stated:

> The Special Committee on Decolonization approved today a draft resolution calling on the Government of the United States to expedite a process that would allow the Puerto Rican people to exercise fully their right to self-determination and independence, and for the General Assembly formally to consider the situation concerning Puerto Rico, which the world body had not formally taken up since the Territory's removal from the list of Non-Self-Governing Territories in 1953.

Pleading their case before the Special Committee on Decolonization— known also as the "Special Committee of 24"—more than thirty petitioners called for the international community to recognize the territory's colonial status and for both the United Nations and the United States to acknowledge a Puerto Rico constitutional assembly as a valid procedural mechanism for decolonization.

Is a sovereign Puerto Rico a viable option in the global economy of the twenty-first century? In an effort to answer that question, this book reviews the case studies of six countries with roughly the same population as Puerto Rico that succeeded economically and socially after achieving sovereignty: Singapore, Slovenia, Ireland, Israel, New Zealand, and Estonia. During the recent global economic crisis, some have done better than others. According to the Economist Intelligence Unit, Singapore performed better than expected, with a 15 percent growth in 2010, whereas Ireland encountered a major economic crisis, with growth of −0.4 percent. The other four models—New Zealand, Israel, Estonia, and Slovenia—had

---

3. Available at http://www.un.org/News/Press/docs/2010/gaco13209.doc.htm.

growth rates between 1 and 5 percent in 2010. Their performance was not related to their sovereignty, but rather to their respective governments' economic policies.

This book incorporates radio interviews with two prominent economists, Francisco Catalá-Oliveras and Juan Lara, aired by Univision Radio in Puerto Rico and New York in 2007. Although some of the facts in those interviews are of that year, updated tables are provided as of December 2011 in part 3, "Comparative Tables." The third edition includes updated statistics, new forecasts, and additional columns. This English translation has added a brief history of Puerto Rico; introductions to the interviews, written by the guest economists; the most recent statistics and forecasts; additional columns; and suggested reading lists.

Introduction to the Third Edition (2010)

So far as Porto Rico was concerned, that was to belong to us, and it was, therefore, competent to do with respect to franchises there whatever we might deem best. . . . With respect to Porto Rico, we had no specific pledge to redeem, but we had a general duty to govern that people in accordance with the spirit of our institutions, although outside constitutional restrictions and limitations, that it was deemed unwise if not impossible to apply there. . . . Porto Rico belongs to the United States, but it is not the United States, nor a part of the United States.

—SENATOR JOSEPH B. FORAKER,
Notes of a Busy Life

The United States does not suffer from the inexperience of Porto Rico in self-government, but Porto Rico suffers from the inexperience of the United States in governing others.

—FÉLIX CÓRDOVA-DÁVILA,
Resident Commissioner, Puerto Rico, 1928

[T]hree decades after the establishment of the new status of "association" with the United States, there is a widespread consensus that the Commonwealth of Puerto Rico, in its present form, has reached a dead end, that a radical restructuring of this relationship with the United States is imperative if the island is to solve the difficult economic and social challenges that it faces in the 1980s.

—JORGE HEINE,
Time for Decision: The United States and Puerto Rico

[US provisions for independence] . . . are enacted in recognition of the unique relationship between the United States and Puerto Rico, to affect a smooth and fair transition for the new Republic of Puerto Rico with a minimum of economic disruption, and to promote the development of a viable economy in the new Republic of Puerto Rico.

> *The definition of the independence option in The Puerto Rico Referen-*
> *dum Act, S. 244, Sec. 313, January 23, 1991, [is] endorsed by the Governor of*
> *Puerto Rico, Rafael Hernández-Colón, all the political parties of Puerto Rico*
> *and President George H. W. Bush.*

The unceasing debate about the island's political status and the uncertainty about its future is [*sic*] sapping Puerto Rico's strength to stand on its own feet and deal with its severe economic problems. Keeping Puerto Rico in a state of subjection does not serve any perceivable United States interest and is seriously out of line with developments in the rest of the world.

—JOSÉ TRÍAS MONGE, *Puerto Rico: The Trials of the*
Oldest Colony in the World

These quotations dramatize how perspectives on Puerto Rico's colonial status have evolved over the past 112 years: from a classic colony to one with limited powers of self-government and finally to acceptance that there is a colonial problem and that a sovereign Puerto Rico is possible.

The first two editions of *Soberanías exitosas* achieved unprecedented sales among books on the topic at hand, which reaffirms that the people of Puerto Rico want to explore other options, given the deterioration of the economic and social model with which they are burdened today and given the lack of real options.

Following the publication of the first two editions of this book in 2008 and 2009, the world economy has suffered its worst crisis since the Great Depression. All of the world's countries have been affected by that crisis in one way or another. [See the interview "Successful Sovereignties," which took place in 2009 and was added to the third edition.] However, while sovereign countries are reinventing themselves, taking advantage of the economic crisis, and investing in the future, as Singapore has done by opening three new universities, Puerto Rico has reduced the budget of the University of Puerto Rico to the detriment of that island's future. Spanish banker Emilio Botín recently said:

Investment in education is the most effective medium-term bet to advance toward more open, more socially balanced, and more economically dynamic societies. . . . In economic times as complex as the ones we are experiencing, we need to state clearly that society . . . will not be able to face the challenges posed by growing globalization of the society of knowledge if our universities and their researchers do not assume a greater role. . . . Higher education is one of the main forward-looking investments in any country.[1]

Just before the turn of the new century, Puerto Rico lost its tax advantages when the federal exemptions it enjoyed were terminated. Then, between 1985 and 1988, when it tried to substitute Japanese investors for the US investors who had benefited from Section 936 [of the US Internal Revenue Code], the United States blocked that initiative owing to other priorities dominating the US-Japan relationship, in particular the import of Japanese autos. Around the same time, with the implementation of the North American Free Trade Agreement, Puerto Rico lost its advantage of exclusive access to the US market. The current colonial status, with the limitations imposed by the colonial power, has not allowed Puerto Rico to establish an economic model that would relieve the devastating effects of these events and open its way into the new century.

The twenty-first century has also begun with a marked deterioration in the quality of life in Puerto Rico. Lack of opportunity for our young people recently graduated from our excellent universities has forced them to emigrate.

Just as the sixteenth century was ruled by Spain, the seventeenth by Holland, the eighteenth by France, the nineteenth by Great Britain, and the twentieth by the United States, the twenty-first century is destined to be controlled by the country with the highest population in the world: China.

The strength of Chinese civilization, which is more than 1,000 years old, was witnessed by the world during the 2008 Olympic Games in Beijing

---

1. Emilio Botín, president of Banco de Santander, speech given at the Universidad Pública de Navarra, November 12, 2008.

and was seen again with the 2010 World Expo in Shanghai. Yet Puerto Rico cannot establish diplomatic or commercial relations with China, nor can it benefit from links with the country that has replaced the United States as the principal investor in Latin America and the Caribbean. Instead of creating jobs with the new investors of the twenty-first century, we are compelled to beg for additional US federal funds even while successful sovereign nations are strengthening their commercial relations with China, the European Union, the United States, and India.

China, which holds 24 percent of the US public debt (making it the principal holder of that debt), has proposed that a new international currency replace the US dollar. Though China is not immune to the world crisis, the United Nations has recently projected that its economy will continue to grow through the present recession.

Americans have been much more affected by the current recession than the people of other developed countries, for they lack strong social programs such as universal health care and widespread public transportation. Those other countries have generous benefits for people who lose their jobs, and the state provides free, high-quality healthcare and education. Public transportation is excellent, and medicines and food can be had at reasonable prices.

Countries of roughly the same size as Puerto Rico have also been adversely affected by the world crisis. Six of them are discussed in this book. Despite the recent world economic downturn, however, all six remain remarkable models, with situations markedly superior to that of Puerto Rico.

Of the six economic models discussed in this book, the two most affected by the current deep recession are Singapore and Ireland. According to Nobel laureate economist Paul Krugman, their crises are the result of having followed and exceeded the American strategy by launching themselves into the new world of deregulated global markets. Both countries are applying the power inherent in their sovereignty to correct the situation based on their alliances with China, the European Union, and the United States.

[The table "Growth of Real Gross Domestic Product" in the "Comparative Tables" section shows] the Economist Intelligence Unit's projection of the economic-growth figures for Puerto Rico, Singapore, and Ireland.

Sovereign countries have the power to make the decisions that serve their citizens best; they also possess the tools to overcome their crises. A territory or colony must wait for the colonial power to send additional remittances to solve the crisis.

Puerto Rico's stock exchange is the repository of most local capital. Dramatically reflecting the island's situation is the Puerto Rico Stock Index. In December 2003, that index was $14,637; in 2007, it was $4,606; in February 2010, it was $1,641.

The principal strategy of the revolving-door governments in the unincorporated territory of Puerto Rico has been to increase public debt and dependence on the colonial power. Because Puerto Rico lacks sovereign power, it cannot devise a new economic and social model based on job creation and high quality of life.

The tiny nation of San Marino on the Italian peninsula, with 30,000 inhabitants and its own passport (having rejected that of the European Union), is the oldest sovereign state in the world. It has twice [Puerto Rico's] per capita income and a growth rate of 4.3 percent—a far better record than our own shrinking economy. San Marino's successful sovereignty should be another source of inspiration for a successful Puerto Rico in the twenty-first century.

The US House of Representatives Committee on Natural Resources has jurisdiction over Native Americans, fisheries, geological studies, water supplies, national parks and forests, mineral resources, military battlefields and cemeteries, and insular possessions, which include the unincorporated territory of Puerto Rico. On October 8, 2009, the committee issued Report No. 111-294, in which it described Puerto Rico's current status as "hybrid" (one definition of which is "the product of elements of a different nature"), formed from elements characteristic of territories, states, and sovereign nations.

The report states that the US Supreme Court has established that Puerto Rico is an unincorporated territory and that incorporated territories are those destined to become states of the union, whereas unincorporated territories can become sovereign nations.

The report stresses that the Territorial Clause of the Constitution grants Congress plenary powers over its territories. It says that Congress, in exercising its powers, can treat Puerto Rico differently from the fifty states, the District of Columbia, and the rest of the territories—that is, as it sees fit.

The report notes that Puerto Rico does not enjoy full democracy because it does not vote in congressional or presidential elections; in other words, Puerto Ricans do not have the right to vote for those who pass and implement laws affecting citizens in the territory.

The committee admits that during the first two decades of the twentieth century, federal laws imposed on Puerto Rico placed limitations on elements of self-government that had been in effect when Spain owned the island (Autonomic Charter, 1897).

In 2005, the President's Task Force on Puerto Rico's Status submitted a report that underscored that the United States has the power to give away Puerto Rico to another country. That report was issued under George W. Bush's Republican administration. Later, under Barack Obama's Democratic administration, a Democratic Congress issued a report conveying a similar message regarding Puerto Rico's current status.

The House of Representatives report noted that over the years there had been attempts to alter our hybrid status. The most recent effort was in 1998, when it was proposed that the Commonwealth of Puerto Rico be developed as a nation associated with the United States.

The report, however, also indicated that initiatives to develop commonwealth status with expanded powers for the island were not practicable: "Proposals for such a governing arrangement have been consistently opposed by federal authorities in the executive and legislative branches, including this Committee, on both constitutional and policy grounds. Nevertheless, this hybrid proposal continues to be promoted in Puerto Rico as a feasible status option. Such proposals have resulted in misinformed and inconclusive referenda in Puerto Rico in July 1967, November 1993 and December 1998."[2]

---

2. *Report by the President's Task Force on Puerto Rico's Status* (December 2005), 6, available at http://www.whitehouse.gov/sites/default/files/uploads/Puerto_Rico_Task_Force_Report.pdf.

All of this confirms what many of us in Puerto Rico already know—that no matter how many plebiscites ratifying development of commonwealth status we may hold, the colonial power will not act on them.

"Commonwealth" is a hybrid status that was created by the US Navy in the context of the Cold War—a status that has lost its validity in the twenty-first century. Yet the colonial power has no intention of revising it.

Statehood is available to Puerto Ricans, but not to Puerto Rico. We Puerto Ricans have available fifty states where we can individually attain statehood.

Hybrid status in the twenty-first century is the cause of our economic and social problems and of our severely debilitated quality of life. As long as Puerto Ricans deny that simple fact, we will never overcome our country's crisis.

This is a historic moment for Puerto Rico, a moment when we may finally be able to resolve our colonial status, which has lasted for more than five hundred years. The rejection of the statehood option by the United States; the US Navy's exit from Puerto Rico; and the freefall of the island's economic and social structure have left Puerto Rico with a single real option: sovereignty, with its two possible forms of decolonizing political status—free association or independence. Both would involve continuing harmonization with the United States but would also be suitable for maximizing opportunities with China, the European Union, and the rest of the world.

Puerto Rico today is still under the Territorial Clause of the Constitution of the United States, which assigns to Congress plenary powers over our country. This provision makes Puerto Rico a territory or colony no matter what we call it (the "Commonwealth of Puerto Rico" or "Free Associated State," for example). Once we place ourselves outside the clause, we will stop being a territory or colony and will achieve sovereignty, with two possible political options: free association or independence. Attaining sovereignty will insert us into the new century's globalized world alongside 192 sovereign nations that have chosen pragmatism.

Sovereignty cannot be wished into being with a magic wand. Just as with the six economic models presented in this book, turning a sovereign country into a successful model takes effort, sacrifice, tenacity, and perseverance. Puerto Rico has an extraordinary workforce and is in a better position than the six countries discussed in this book were in when they attained sovereignty. All that is lacking is the will in Puerto Rico and in Washington, DC, to do what must be done.

As the Chinese philosopher Confucius (551–478 BC) said, "If you know what to do and do not do it, then you are worse off than before."

Introduction to the First Edition (2008)

> In the second half of the twentieth century, the emergence of scores of
> new states has made international politics and economics truly global
> for the first time in history. At the same time, technology has made it
> possible for nearly every country to participate in events in every part
> of the world as they occur.
>
> —DR. HENRY KISSINGER, foreword in
> Lee Kuan Yew, *From Third World to First:*
> *The Singapore Story, 1965–2000*

The changes in the twenty-first century are even more dramatic than
those mentioned by Henry Kissinger in the second half of the twentieth
century. In 1945, the United Nations had 49 sovereign states as members;
by 2008, it had 192 member states.

The decolonization process began formally in 1941 with the Atlantic
Charter signed by US president Franklin D. Roosevelt and British prime
minister Winston Churchill. As countries evolved from their territorial
or colonial status and attained sovereignty, many achieved economic and
social success. This book examines six countries from around the world
that are similar to Puerto Rico in population and size. Two of these countries—New Zealand and Ireland—achieved sovereignty before the Second World War; two others—Israel and Singapore—did so after the war.
All four have maintained close relations with their former colonial power,
Great Britain. The other two countries, Estonia and Slovenia, achieved
sovereignty as a direct result of the dismemberment of the Soviet Union
in 1989. Each of these six cases is different, and each offers superb lessons
for Puerto Rico in the twenty-first century.

Professor Lester Thurow of MIT inspired this book when in a speech delivered in Puerto Rico in the early 1980s he recommended that we study Singapore as an economic model for Puerto Rico. Later on, during a visit I made to Singapore, a professor of economics from that country's principal university remarked that his own country had made use of Puerto Rico's model. Yet at the end of the twentieth century, while Singapore was entering the world of biotechnology, Puerto Rico—given the impossibility of developing its own political and economic model—was taking the road of dependency on US federal welfare.

Lee Kuan Yew, the founder of Singapore, in his book *From Third World to First: The Singapore Story, 1965–2000* (New York: Harper, 2000), discusses his country's development in a way that can inspire Puerto Rico in the twenty-first century. From its beginnings as a Spanish colony, Puerto Rico was a military stronghold because of its geographical location. Early in the nineteenth century, military strategist Admiral Alfred Mahan made Puerto Rico part of his plans whereby the US Navy would control the world's oceans.

In 1898, as a result of the Spanish-American War, Puerto Rico was ceded to the United States in the Treaty of Paris. In that treaty, it was established that "the civil rights and political status of the native inhabitants of the territories hereby ceded to the United States shall be determined by the Congress" (Article IX). Spain, here, was ceding Puerto Rico to the United States in violation of the Autonomic Charter that it had granted the island in 1897. The US Constitution grants Congress absolute power over the territories: "The Congress shall have power to dispose of and make all needful rules and regulations respecting the territory or other property belonging to the United States" (Article 3).

The Insular Cases of the US Supreme Court (1922) define Puerto Rico as a unincorporated territory that belongs to the United States but is not a part of it. The Insular Cases were very recently ratified unanimously by the Supreme Court in *Boumediene v. Bush* (553 U.S. 723 [2008]).

A combination of the Atlantic Charter, Puerto Rican nationalist activism, and the prevailing political realism of the Cold War led the United States to allow Puerto Rico to elect its own governor, and many of the vestiges of a classic colony were eliminated through the establishment of the

Commonwealth of Puerto Rico in 1952. The new status had the uncondi-tional support of the military, economic, and government structures of the colonial power to develop a successful economic model that might coun-terbalance the Communist bloc in the Cold War. The new political status, the Commonwealth of Puerto Rico, fulfilled its objective. But Puerto Rico's sovereignty, as in the case of other territories, continues to reside in the US Congress and not in the people of Puerto Rico. Puerto Ricans have neither a vote in Congress nor an embassy in Washington to defend their interests.

After the Cold War, with the geopolitical theater shifting to the Mid-dle East, Puerto Rico no longer had a military use. And when the Puerto Rican people manifested their strong opposition to the US Navy's pres-ence, the navy abandoned its operations area on Vieques and closed the important Roosevelt Roads Naval Base.

In the 1990s, the US government repealed the tax exemptions granted under Section 936 of the US Internal Revenue Code—exemptions that had made Puerto Rico the pharmaceutical capital of the world. The companies slowly began to establish new operations with other patents in countries, such as Ireland, that could offer greater benefits. The Puerto Rico economic model grew weaker and now relies mainly on federal handouts. Less than one-third of the Puerto Rican population is employed, and those people are having to support the rest through their work and the taxes they pay. Put another way, 32 percent of the island's inhabitants support all the rest. Dependency has eroded the people's dignity and is the source of many of the social maladies affecting Puerto Rico.

Puerto Rico froze institutionally in the 1950s. To face the twenty-first century, it needs to thaw, to open itself to the world, and to explore its options. It needs to build a vigorous economy like those of the countries discussed in this book and to launch the new economic model it will require in order to take hold of the powers that come with sovereignty.

Puerto Rico's current political status does not allow it to enter into trade agreements with other countries, to participate in international forums, or to use the most efficient and cost-effective commercial ship-ping. Puerto Rico likewise cannot determine what immigrants or how many immigrants will become a part of its society.

Puerto Rico as a nation is different from the United States, with a distinct culture, language, and character. For more than one hundred years, the United States has consistently made it clear that annexation of Puerto Rico is not desirable for the colonial power. The other territories that were destined to become states were incorporated territories; Puerto Rico and the Philippines were established as unincorporated territories because from the beginning there was no intention of annexing them as states. The United States has given no sign whatsoever of wanting to make Puerto Rico an incorporated territory, which is the first step toward annexation.

As recently as 1989, a US Senate committee rejected a bill calling for a plebiscite in Puerto Rico because it was not comfortable with granting a petition for statehood, if that were to be the result of the consultation process. So it rejected the bill even though it had been passed by the House of Representatives, was supported by all local political parties, and had been proposed by President George H. W. Bush.

Because statehood is not a real option, the two remaining options for Puerto Rico are to continue with the current model as a territory, with Congress holding full powers, or to achieve a status in which sovereignty rests with the people of Puerto Rico at the same time that it maintains a close relationship with the United States, where nearly four million Puerto Ricans now live.

Puerto Rico can implement the best strategies of the six sovereign countries discussed in this book. In the twenty-first century, natural resources and territorial extension are no longer the primary elements required for development. Instead, the most important factor for a country is its human resources. Puerto Rico has no competition in the quality, diversity, and proficiency of its human capital. Over the centuries, Puerto Ricans have consistently reached the top internationally in most disciplines. Puerto Rican educator Eugenio María de Hostos and the Spanish thinker José Ortega y Gasset are the only two Hispanics who appear among the fifty great educational thinkers of all time. Dr. Ramón Emeterio Betances was one of the most famous physicians in Paris during the last years of the nineteenth century. Painter Francisco Oller taught Paul Cézanne and later introduced Madrid to impressionism.

Puerto Rican military men, such as General Antonio Valero, fought alongside Simón Bolivar in the Venezuelan War of Independence, and Juan Rius-Rivera and Pachín Marín stood out in the Cuban War of Independence.

In the twentieth century, Puerto Ricans were present in almost all fields throughout the world: tenor Antonio Paoli performed in the world's great opera houses, and José Ferrer, Rita Moreno, and Benicio del Toro were awarded Oscars in Hollywood.

Justino Díaz performed at the opening of New York's Metropolitan Opera and at the John F. Kennedy Center for the Performing Arts in Washington, DC. In 2008, Benicio del Toro received the Best Actor Award at the Cannes Film Festival.

In sports, there are exceptional [Puerto Rican] athletes in baseball and golf; the [Puerto Rican] Olympic basketball team is outstanding; and a Puerto Rican physician has climbed Mount Everest. Puerto Rico makes its presence felt on the International Olympic Committee. Puerto Ricans have formed part of important boards of directors of private corporations and nongovernmental organizations and have managed multinational companies and one of the principal US labor unions.

A Puerto Rican heads the Greek and Roman Art Department in one of the world's major museums, the Metropolitan Museum of Art in New York. Our performers win the highest honors in popular music. Marta Casals headed the principal music center in Washington, DC. Less well-known Puerto Ricans have held prominent positions in important orchestras, multinational corporations, not-for-profit organizations, and universities.

Among all these heroes, the most symbolic and inspiring for the twenty-first century is Orlando Figueroa, born and raised in Puerto Rico, who directs the National Aeronautics and Space Administration's Solar Systems Division and Mars Exploration Program. A Puerto Rican is responsible for conquering the planet Mars for humanity.

Puerto Rican talent, which is much more substantial and abundant than Puerto Rico's small size would suggest, is recognized internationally. The most important element of a country is its human capital, which can solve any problem in life. Puerto Rico has been and still is disproportionately endowed with a wealth of talent, which with focus, discipline, and perseverance will constitute the key to success.

For Puerto Rico to make the most of its extraordinary human resources, it must solve the problem of its political status. A country based on dependency cannot face the demands of the twenty-first century. The key to success for Singapore, New Zealand, Israel, Ireland, Slovenia, and Estonia has been their remarkable human resources, which, with the necessary powers, have been able to set goals, formulate master plans, and enter into strategic alliances.

Despite its geographical limitations and mix of cultures, Singapore has succeeded. It has been able to build skyscrapers while becoming a tropical paradise by planting more than a million trees. A country as distant as New Zealand has also succeeded. Estonia, despite its small population, isolated language, long colonial history, and totalitarian past, has succeeded as well.

Ireland, many of whose people had to emigrate to find opportunities, is slowly displacing Puerto Rico as the pharmaceutical capital of the world. Despite being constantly at war and facing internal political problems, Israel has transformed its desert into successful farmland and become self-sufficient in food. Slovenia, with a small population, has embraced free trade and achieved the success it desired.

Based on a platform of sovereignty, Ireland, Estonia, and Slovenia have joined the European Union, and Singapore and New Zealand are part of the British Commonwealth.

This book analyzes and weighs how each of these six countries found economic and social success after achieving sovereignty. I have visited them all and have seen how they represent possible scenarios for Puerto Rico in the twenty-first century.

General Note

The six "country interviews" in this book were conducted in early 2007, just before the global financial crisis began. Therefore, in this edition we append this brief note about the impact of that ongoing crisis on the six countries.

To our knowledge, no one has argued that sovereignty insulates countries, especially small ones, from the effects of business cycles and financial crises. If large countries are sensitive to such things—indeed, they are usually the epicenters of them—small countries, which tend to have very open economies, are clearly affected as well.

The interviews in this book do affirm, though, that institutional and technological change has released development policies from the fetters of economic scale. Small economies today can have much greater diversity in production, foreign trade, and sources of investment than was possible in the past. The economic vitality of many sovereign countries of modest scale should help to lay to rest the myth that small countries are powerless against global economic buffeting. Size is not an impediment to development. Weak institutions and political impotence clearly are.

Francisco Catalá-Oliveras
Juan Lara

PART 1

A Brief History of Puerto Rico

The Caribbean island of Puerto Rico, located between the Greater and the Lesser Antilles, has a rich history. It has been populated for almost 6,000 years. The native population that the Europeans found when they discovered the island had come to it from the east coast of what is today Venezuela and the island of Trinidad in successive migrations. They were Arawaks—an ethnic group found throughout South America as far south as northern Argentina. These people, distinct from the first inhabitants of the Caribbean, had developed an agriculture based on cassava (or manioc) as well as other technologies, such as the canoes that allowed them to move from one island of the Antilles to the next.

The pre-Hispanic population of Cuba, Hispaniola, Puerto Rico, and the Caribbean in general had adapted well to their environment and were self-sufficient and fairly numerous. It is estimated that there were half a million Arawaks in the Caribbean, most of them on Hispaniola and Puerto Rico. They were not as "developed" as other New World indigenous peoples—for example, in Mexico, Central America, and the Andes. Even so, the Taínos—as the natives of Puerto Rico were called—had organized themselves into *cacicazgos*, groups of clans under the leadership of a chief or cacique, that controlled large amounts of land on the islands.

Puerto Rico was discovered for the Europeans by Christopher Columbus in 1493 during his second voyage while he was sailing from the Lesser Antilles to the northern coast of Hispaniola, where he had left a small contingent of crew members on the first voyage. He found that the natives had destroyed the fort his people had built on Hispaniola. The encounter between the Spanish colonists and the native peoples was not a peaceful one. On the contrary, from the very beginning the colonists had to wrest control by force, and a great demographic disaster followed owing to high mortality rates among the native population.

At the beginning of the sixteenth century, the island of Hispaniola was the center of Spanish operations in the Americas. From there—and especially from the city of Santo Domingo on the south coast of Hispaniola—the Spaniards explored and conquered Cuba and Puerto Rico as well as other islands. Expeditions were launched to Mexico and to both North America and South America from the Caribbean islands. During that first stage, Castile was the only European monarchy exploring the Americas, except for the Portuguese, who eventually established a presence in Brazil. The other European countries did not arrive on the scene until almost a century later, though from very early on European pirates posed a threat to Spanish trade routes and settlements. By the first decade of the sixteenth century, the Spanish conquistador Juan Ponce de León had gained a foothold in Puerto Rico (which the Taínos called "Boriquén") and had founded two settlements there: one on the northern coast that would eventually be named "San Juan" and another on the southwestern coast called "San Germán." Taíno resistance led to very strong repression in 1511.

At first, the colonial economy was based on the mining of precious metals, using the native people as either slaves or forced laborers. Livestock was also an important activity: the early colonists left livestock on the islands so that they could provision themselves on subsequent voyages. This first phase of colonial society and economy did not last long, for there were no large mineral deposits in the Caribbean; even so, the native population declined dramatically within a few years of the Spaniards' arrival.

The conquest of Mexico and Peru—both of which had vast mineral resources and large indigenous populations organized into empires— would have a powerful impact on the Spanish colonies in the Caribbean. But until those conquests happened, the effort to establish colonies in the Caribbean lost momentum soon after it had started. The building of settlements stopped, and migration from Spain decreased, for the new continents proved a stronger draw for settlers. Spain was faced with the problem of how to maintain its population in Puerto Rico and to generate economic activities that would make its presence on the island viable. It could not allow its island colonies to be depopulated, for the trade routes linking Spain with its holdings on the mainland passed through the Caribbean. Along those routes, growing amounts of gold and silver— especially the latter—flowed into Spain, and exports destined for the colonial markets flowed out, with Seville controlling this trade.

Thus, from very early on the history of Puerto Rico was conditioned by the geopolitical and strategic needs of the Spanish Empire, which required a strong sentinel at the entrance to the Caribbean. San Juan became that sentinel. It was a fortified city, part of a network of garrison cities protecting the Spanish Empire's trade routes. This strategic function was reflected in the autocratic forms of government that characterized Spanish colonial dominion over the island.

Puerto Rico and other Caribbean possessions were treated as a line of defense for the empire and particularly for the Viceroyalty of New Spain. The governors appointed by the Crown bore the title "captain-general"; with very few exceptions, they were military officers, and their functions were largely military. It is noteworthy that Puerto Rico was attacked on various occasions from the sixteenth to the eighteenth centuries by powers hostile to Spain and that for a brief time in 1596 San Juan was under British rule.

The Captaincy General subordinated civil matters to military ones and excluded the local population from participating in government. The colonial government concentrated power to a high degree. For example, the captain-general was the highest judicial officer in his territory, and his decisions could be appealed only before the Audiencia Real (Royal Court) in Santo Domingo.

In the sixteenth century, the Crown sought alternatives to mining, which was in decline, in the hope of halting the colony's population decline and stimulating the stagnating economy. Thus, it supported the development of sugarcane plantations to sustain the colonial economy. This industry was based on the labor of African slaves. By the early seventeenth century, sugar was one of Puerto Rico's main exports. However, sugarcane on its own could not generate enough fiscal resources to make the colony self-sufficient. The abundance of land and the government's weak control over the island's interior led to the development of a peasantry—subsistence farmers who contributed nothing to the fiscal base of the Spanish government. By now, smuggling was becoming widespread, even through the capital itself. It was possible to evade the controls of the colonial authorities, who themselves were often in league with the smugglers. Thus, the empire found itself having to subsidize its administrative and military apparatus in San Juan with funds transferred from the Viceroyalty of Mexico, known as the *situado mexicano*. These funds allowed, among other things, the fortification of San Juan and the maintenance of a garrison. Other Caribbean cities of strategic value also received such transfers of funds.

By the seventeenth century, Spanish authority over its American and Caribbean colonies had been greatly weakened. At the same time, Spain was being challenged by other colonial powers such as Holland and England. When the Spanish Crown passed into the hands of the Bourbon dynasty, there was an effort to promote economic and administrative reform, to modernize the empire, and to stop the erosion of colonial power. The occupation of Havana by the English in 1762 and the military threat to San Juan made reforms a matter of urgency. New policies stimulated the export economy based on tropical products such as sugar, coffee, and tobacco. Settlement was encouraged, and the population increased as new towns were founded. By 1802, most of Puerto Rico's 163,192 inhabitants were white or mulatto, with nearly 30,000 blacks (both free and enslaved). Also by this time, a strong sense of identity had arisen among Puerto Ricans— an identity that would grow stronger as the nineteenth century wore on. This strong sense of identity has been a distinctive trait of Puerto Ricans ever since, one that has outlasted political loyalties and contingencies.

From 1776 to 1825, several revolutions led to the fall of the traditional colonial powers in America. The Revolutionary War that resulted in the United States; the French Revolution, with all its effects in America; the Haitian Revolution; and the wars of independence in Latin America weakened the presence of the European colonial powers in the Americas until colonies remained only in the Caribbean and in Canada. Spain lost its American empire, retaining only two Caribbean colonies: Cuba and Puerto Rico. These islands became the bases from which Spain tried to counter pro-independence rebellion. Spain also increased its control over these island remnants of its empire in order to prevent the rise of anti-slavery and emancipation rebellions of the sort that might be inspired by events on the North American mainland and in Haiti.

This need to increase control suggests why Spain's approach to ruling Puerto Rico during the nineteenth century was highly autocratic, allowing very little space for democratic participation by Puerto Ricans, who were clamoring more and more loudly for greater freedom and political participation. Also, as the century went by, the strength of a new power, the United States, was gathering as it gradually became more and more important commercially and culturally for the Spanish colonies. This growing US importance, too, eroded Spain's control. In 1868, Spain grew even more concerned as it faced an armed rebellion in Cuba, which led to ten years of bloody repression. Almost simultaneous uprisings took place in several cities in Puerto Rico during 1868, one of them since immortalized as "El Grito de Lares" (the Lares Uprising). All were repressed. These uprisings were the only attempt by Puerto Ricans to confront Spain militarily. With the revolutionary path closed, Puerto Ricans expressed their claims for greater liberty through a strong autonomist movement with a liberal orientation that by the end of the century became a majority.

The liberal reforms that took place in Spain during the nineteenth century were never fully applied in Puerto Rico; the colonies were treated as exceptions. In 1824, in the context of the crisis of the Spanish Empire in America, the governor was granted absolute authority over the island; his absolute powers were known as *omnímodos* and were analogous to the powers of the commander of a besieged fortress. Puerto Rico was excluded from the various constitutions that were being developed in Spain. With the Constitution of 1869, Puerto Ricans were permitted to organize political parties, and there was a brief period of respect for public freedoms that lasted until 1874. The restoration of the monarchy cut short that experience, so Puerto Ricans never enjoyed full democratic rights and liberties, not even those granted at different times to their fellow citizens in Spain. And the population had to face periods of great political repression, such as what would come to be remembered as the "Terrible Year," 1887.

On November 25, 1897, shortly before the Spanish-American War erupted, with one eye on the deteriorating situation in Cuba and the other on the growing might of the United States, Spain decreed a widespread political reform known as the "Autonomic Charter." This reform was a belated attempt to quench the flames of rebellion in Cuba, to address the claims of autonomists in Puerto Rico, and to prevent the United States from intervening. This new law, issued as a Royal Decree, went further than the demands of the autonomists and was the most advanced document of any regarding a Caribbean colony until after the Second World War. The degree of self-government it granted Puerto Rico was much greater than what the United States has been willing to concede in the present day. Moreover, the charter would not be subject to amendments except by the initiative of the Puerto Rico legislature.

But the charter was never fully implemented, for the Americans defeated the Spanish during the war of 1898. The American military now occupied the island under the command of General Nelson Miles, who came ashore at Guánica on the island's southern coast.

Though the Spanish-American War had its immediate causes in the Cuban war, the United States delayed negotiations for a peace treaty until it occupied Puerto Rico, which it saw as of great strategic value for its eventual control of the Caribbean Sea. In annexing Puerto Rico, it acquired an entire people, one with its own culture formed over several centuries, one with a strong identity that had been affirmed during its conflicts with Spain. By 1899, when a census was conducted, the population was approaching one million, dispersed in seventy-seven urban clusters whose populations ranged in size from 45,000 (San Juan) to 704 (Culebra). Therefore, in 1898 the United States confronted for the first time the challenge of governing an overseas colony with a population that was not assimilable culturally and that did not want to integrate politically. As of this day, Puerto Rico is "the oldest colony in the world."[1]

Most Puerto Ricans responded to the end of Spanish rule and the beginning of American rule with hope for political and social improvements. The United States was perceived to be a republic that enjoyed great material progress and civil liberties. And General Miles promised in a proclamation that the advantages of an "enlightened civilization" would be bestowed on Puerto Rico. Quite soon, though, it was evident that such expectations would not be fulfilled. Influenced by the US secretary of war, Elihu Root, the Americans established new colonial institutions that severely restricted Puerto Ricans' political participation. These institutions were patterned after the British "Crown colony" model.

After two years of a military government that laid the foundation for the new colonial order, the US Congress approved the Foraker Act, which stipulated a new form of government for Puerto Rico. According to that law, the governor of Puerto Rico and his principal executive officers would be appointed by the president. The same law created an Executive Council with eleven members, all appointed by the president; it would be one of the legislative bodies. Puerto Rican elected representation was limited to a Chamber of Delegates of thirty-five members, which could not pass laws without the Executive Council's concurrence. The judges of the Supreme Court of Puerto Rico were also to be appointed by the US president. This arrangement greatly concentrated power in the executive branch in Washington, thus breaching the US constitutional principle of separation of powers. Furthermore, it did not extend US citizenship to Puerto Ricans, who until 1917 remained "natives" or "citizens" of Puerto Rico.

There was an obvious lack of correspondence between the US Constitution and the form of government established for the new overseas colonies of the American Empire. Those contradictions were resolved in a series of cases decided by the US Supreme Court between 1901 and 1922 known as the "Insular Cases." In 1901, the important *Downs v. Bidwell* (182

1. From José Trías Monge, *Puerto Rico: The Trials of the Oldest Colony in the World* (New Haven, CT: Yale Univ. Press, 1997).

U.S. 244) case was decided. Justice White argued that Puerto Rico was "foreign in a domestic sense." According to these Supreme Court decisions, the US Constitution was not fully applicable to the new territories because they were not an integral part of the United States, but only "belonged" to the United States and thus came under the plenary powers of Congress. That colonial judicial doctrine is still in effect.

In 1917, American citizenship was granted to Puerto Ricans over the opposition of the island's resident commissioner, Luis Muñoz Rivera. Also, Puerto Ricans were given stronger powers of self-government. That year's reforms, under the Jones Act, also addressed some of Puerto Ricans' political demands in order to ensure their loyalty in light of the American involvement in the First World War. During that conflict, military conscription was established for the first time. Just as the Spanish had, the Americans assigned great strategic importance to the new colony, particularly as part of US defense of the recently opened Panama Canal. Another factor in all this was Germany's interest in establishing a presence in the Caribbean. (At this time, the United States also acquired the US Virgin Islands from Denmark.)

Under the Jones Act, the governor continued to be a presidential appointee, but a bicameral legislature was created for Puerto Ricans, comprising a nineteen-member Senate and a thirty-nine-member House of Representatives. Both chambers were to be elected locally. However, the governor and the US president could veto any law passed by the Puerto Rican legislature. In other words, US citizenship had not extended full political rights to the islanders.

The first three decades of the twentieth century were not concerned solely with political changes in the colonial relationship. There were also great economic and social transformations, supported by the government. The most important were the rapid expansion of the sugar industry and the stagnation of traditional coffee production, which was based in the mountain municipalities in the center of Puerto Rico. From one end to the other, the island became in practice a single-crop producer of sugar and sugarcane, particularly in the coastal municipalities. There was a flow of American sugar capital to Puerto Rico as well as to other Caribbean countries, and there was a wave of migration toward the coastal zone that contributed to the country's urbanization.

In its expansion phase, this sugar model meant material progress, but after the First World War, when beetroot production in Europe recovered, difficulties began to arise. By the 1930s, the model had shown that it was unable to generate employment for the growing labor force or to continue as the island's core economic activity. The imposition of a sugar quota by the United States hindered production growth, and the sugar industry came to be perceived as the source of poverty, stagnation, unemployment, and other social maladies.

The decade of the 1930s was therefore one of crisis for the single-crop, absentee-capital, colonial model established by the United States at the turn of the century.

In 1931, Bailey W. Diffie and Justine Diffie published the powerful book *Porto Rico: A Broken Pledge,* which declared that the United States had failed to fulfill its promise of political and economic improvement for the island. They wrote: "Porto Rico is at once the perfect example of what economic imperialism does for a country and of the attitude of the imperialist towards that country. . . . Porto Rico can hope for no relief under the existing system."[2]

Theodore Roosevelt Jr. was the first governor to criticize the American colonial policy in Puerto Rico, of which his father had been one of the architects.

At the time, other Caribbean societies besides Puerto Rico were showing a high degree of political instability. Those years were marked by popular discontent with the economic and political structures then prevailing.

There was a revolution in Cuba in 1933, and uprisings were taking place throughout the English-speaking Caribbean. In Puerto Rico, the economic depression resulted in a dramatic increase in unemployment and a decline in living conditions, which led to widespread labor unrest.

2. Bailey W. Diffie and Justine Diffie, *Porto Rico: A Broken Pledge* (New York: Vanguard, 1931), 220.

Pro-independence sentiment grew in both moderate and radical versions, and support rose for the Nationalist Party, headed by Pedro Albizu Campos.

The Franklin D. Roosevelt administration dealt harshly with the crisis in Puerto Rico. The president named Robert Gore as governor—a very poor choice. Also, between 1934 and 1939 he appointed General Blanton Winship to repress the discontent. In 1935, violence erupted, during which Nationalists were killed as well as the American police commissioner. The Federal Bureau of Investigation, under the personal supervision of its director J. Edgar Hoover, implemented an aggressive plan to criminalize the independence movement, imprisoning its leaders in federal jails.In 1937, nineteen Nationalists were massacred in Ponce, and more than one hundred were wounded. Winship had allied himself with the sugar interests, which meant that the New Deal reforms were postponed on the island. At the same time, though, there was an attempt to stabilize the social situation by investing large amounts of federal funds through the Puerto Rico Reconstruction Administration. These funds eventually were much larger than the budget of the Government of Puerto Rico itself, and the new government programs generated more jobs than the sugarcane industry as a whole.

At no time during these years did anyone seriously consider recognizing Puerto Rican sovereignty or integrating Puerto Rico into the United States as a state of the union. It was thought that Puerto Rico, like Panama, had great strategic value and should be retained, especially at a time when the political situation in Europe was deteriorating.

However, by 1939 the Roosevelt administration was beginning to revise its policy toward Puerto Rico. It withdrew from the island key figures such as Winship and Ernest Gruening, the Reconstruction Administration director. Admiral William D. Leahy, a close associate of Roosevelt, was appointed governor of Puerto Rico in 1939, which allowed a new reform movement to win the 1940 elections: the Popular Democratic Party (PDP), under the leadership of Luis Muñoz Marín. The party leaders originally favored independence for Puerto Rico, and they addressed Puerto Rico's colonial status during the 1940 campaign. However, Muñoz decided that the issue of relations with the United States would not be solved through general elections, but rather by a separate plebiscite.

The years of the Second World War saw enormous economic and social transformation in Puerto Rico and were decisive in forming the Puerto Rico of the postwar era. Despite the scarcity caused by the submarine war, the Puerto Rican economy grew rapidly, stimulated by large investments in defense as well as by rum exports. The war also contributed to the modernization of Puerto Rican society by encouraging internal migration. Thousands of soldiers were recruited from rural areas, which drew women into the workforce. There was a notable increase in work building large infrastructure projects. At the same time, the reforms favored by the PDP and Governor Rexford G. Tugwell were implemented. Tugwell, a member of Roosevelt's "Brain Trust," had been appointed governor in 1941.

After the war, two interrelated processes occurred: the massive immigration of thousands of Puerto Ricans to cities in the eastern United States and the investment of US manufacturing capital in the island's growing light industry. As a result of immigration, there were now more Puerto Ricans in the United States than in Puerto Rico itself. The island's rapid economic growth during the 1950s and early 1960s made it a model for material progress. During the Cold War, the United States enjoyed a positive image among Puerto Ricans.

But the war also postponed any reform of colonial relations between Puerto Rico and the United States. The Atlantic Charter had created great expectations that after the conflict decolonization would begin. During the war, meetings had been held between Puerto Rican leaders and officials in Washington to explore decolonization options. But in the context of discussions of a bill by Senator Millard Tydings, the US Armed Forces, especially the navy, expressed their opposition to any process that would lead to independence or to acknowledgment of Puerto Rican sovereignty. The onset of the Cold War was used to justify maintaining the status quo, though important political changes in relations with the United States were made.

The first important change in the postwar era was the appointment in 1946 of the first Puerto Rican governor, Jesús T. Piñero, and the passage of the Elected Governor Act. In 1948, for the first time, Puerto Ricans voted for their governor. Luis Muñoz Marín was elected by an overwhelming majority.

In 1950, a revolution erupted in several municipalities, culminating in assassination attempts on Muñoz Marín in San Juan and on President Harry S. Truman in Washington. Persecution of the independence advocates escalated, and hundreds were jailed with or without due process. These events, demands by the local government, and international pressure forced the US government to grant in 1952 some elements of self-government under a new Puerto Rico Constitution approved by the people of Puerto Rico and later revised by the US Congress. These measures allowed greater self-government but did not alter the basic fact that Puerto Rican sovereignty continued to reside in the US Congress. Several attempts by the PDP to broaden Puerto Rico's sphere of power were unsuccessful. In a plebiscite held in 1967, the level of support that the existing arrangement still had was confirmed, but so was growing support for statehood, attributable to the effect of the increase in welfare funds to the island.

Since the Truman administration (1945–52), there has been no major change in political relations between Puerto Rico and the United States. Several plebiscites have failed to bring about any juridical changes in the relationship. Congress has refused to commit itself to any binding process that might obligate it to grant statehood to Puerto Rico if so requested.

The PDP's hegemony ended in 1968 owing to divisions within the party. A new statehood party, the New Progressive Party, emerged and has been rotating power with the PDP ever since. This statehood party dramatically increased the dependence on federal welfare; implemented the federal minimum wage, thus eliminating a competitive advantage to attract investment; lobbied for the elimination of federal tax incentives for the pharmaceutical industry; and positioned statehood as the culmination of a welfare society with the war cry "Statehood is for the poor people."

The end result is that Puerto Rico has become more and more dependent on the US federal government, which exercises growing power over all aspects of Puerto Rican life. Puerto Ricans have ever less control over key aspects of their society. This concentration of power at the federal level has paradoxically been accompanied by a profound political, economic, and social crisis in this Caribbean colony. The model that led to industrial growth, first based on light manufacturing and then on high-tech industries, has been exhausted for several decades now.

The economy has deteriorated radically to a level that cannot be attributed solely to the current economic recession. Sovereign neighboring countries, such as the Dominican Republic, have continued to grow, whereas Puerto Rico has fallen back economically. Crime and violence have grown to unprecedented levels and are out of control. Government corruption has grown worse, with one political scandal after another. The country has no means for responding to the huge changes in the world economy, for formulating new development strategies, or for providing answers to the great challenges posed by the crisis in the colonial structure. The road to statehood is a mirage that only serves to generate support for certain political sectors. Sovereignty for the Puerto Rican people has become imperative both for the United States and for the people of Puerto Rico to set this society's course toward social progress, democratic freedom, and renewed economic recovery.

The *Report by the President's Task Force on Puerto Rico's Status* of March 2011 states that Puerto Rico can become the Singapore of the Caribbean.[3] Singapore is a country that has no natural resources, is fourteen times smaller than Puerto Rico, and has almost the same population. What transformed that country was the conversion from a colony to a sovereign country.

---

3. *Report by the President's Task Force on Puerto Rico's Status* (December 2005), available at http://www.whitehouse.gov/sites/default/files/uploads/Puerto_Rico_Task_Force_Report .pdf.

PART 2

Interviews

Successful Sovereignties

Decolonization Models for America's
Last Colony, Puerto Rico

Interview aired on La Voz del Centro, *Univision Radio Puerto Rico and New York, September 8, 2009.*

ÁNGEL COLLADO-SCHWARZ: Paco, I would like you to summarize Puerto Rico's current economic situation.

FRANCISCO CATALÁ-OLIVERAS: As we can see in the news we read every day, Puerto Rico's current economic situation is critical, so much so that I do not think it should be classified as a recession or a depression—it is even worse. However, let us assume for a moment that it is a recession or depression. In fiscal year 2007, the gross national product of Puerto Rico—that is, the production and income of Puerto Rico residents, whether owners, entrepreneurs, or salaried employees—contracted 1.2 percent. In fiscal year 2008, it contracted 2.8 percent; in fiscal year 2009, which ended this past June 30, the contraction was 5.5 percent. A subsequent revision reduced this percentage to 3.7 percent. This is the Puerto Rico Planning Board's data. If we were to add the already evident contraction registered during the current fiscal year (2009–10) to the three years mentioned, the accumulated percentage of contraction would be approximately 10 percent. In other words, productive activity and the income that Puerto Ricans received declined 10 percent in real terms. Such a situation, by any standards, is more than a recession, which is defined as a contraction sustained for two consecutive quarters. Here we have four consecutive *years* of contraction. It might be classified as a depression.

17

Let's also take into account that during this whole first decade of the twenty-first century Puerto Rico's economy has been slow, and the unemployment rate has remained at two-digit levels. The most recent Planning Board report in the month of July places the unemployment rate at more than 16 percent. For the decade as a whole, the labor-participation rate—that is, the number of persons who are able to work and are employed or actively seeking a job—is approximately 45 percent of that portion of the population. So more than 50 percent of the people sixteen years and older are not even in the labor market. This applies to the entire decade.

And there is more. If we go back to the 1970s and look at economic-growth indicators from that decade to this day, we see that during this whole long period the economy of Puerto Rico grew very modestly every year—at around one-third the rate at which it had grown in the previous period, during the 1940s, 1950s, and 1960s. This means that we are confronting an economy that has been exhausted for some decades now. It is in this context of exhaustion that the recession or depression has occurred.

Also relevant is the fact that this recent recession or depression started in Puerto Rico before the credit crisis, the financial crisis, which then turned into a recession in the United States and in the world. The key date accepted by the Planning Board itself for the start of the recession is March 2006, so our recession came first and has been aggravated by that of the United States. And the exhaustion of Puerto Rico's economy also preceded, by many years, the recession in the United States and in the world.

ACS: To what do you attribute this situation, Paco?

FCO: To many things, but I believe that the one that stands out is this: the world has changed, and Puerto Rico resists the change. Here we talk about change, about globalization and international treaties, but nothing is done in that regard.

When Puerto Rico was industrializing in the 1950s, it had practically no competition. Moreover, in the 1960s the number of international treaties could be counted on the fingers of one hand, and there were fingers to spare. Today, there are hundreds [of treaties]. The world is an interactive network of different jurisdictions, nations, and states, and Puerto Rico does not participate in that interactive network; it has stayed behind.

ACS: In other words, Puerto Rico's economic model is broken.

FCO: Yes. It is not in harmony with the norms that govern the economic dynamics of the world.

ACS: We can say that the measures taken by our revolving-door administrations have not worked. It has been like giving an aspirin to a person with terminal cancer, no?

FCO: Exactly. The welfare and recovery funds that come from the United States produce no structural changes in Puerto Rico. They simply help one sector of the population keep up or increase certain levels of consumption in particular periods. But they are not being used to fix the root of the problem, which is of an institutional nature.

ACS: Are you talking, say, about the assistance received some years ago from the administration of President George W. Bush and the aid being sent at present by the administration of President Barack Obama?

FCO: Correct. It should be noted that a couple of years ago Bush's assistance amounted to more than $1 billion for Puerto Rico. That sounds massive. However, though [the aid] came at the same time as the contraction of the Puerto Rican economy, it did not prevent the contraction. Why? In the first place, because the contraction of the local economy is larger, the strength of the contraction is greater than the effects of the recovery funds, so the economy continues to contract. Second, such recovery funds are not meant to alter the economic structure or institutional base of Puerto Rico's economy. As a consequence, the problems continue to worsen.

ACS: Besides these economic problems in Puerto Rico, it is also important to take into account that Puerto Rican capital has evaporated during the past years, particularly on the Puerto Rico Stock Index, which comprises most local banks. Wealthy families have lost a significant percentage of their fortunes. Another sector that has been affected is that of the employees of financial institutions, most of whose retirement plans are based on the value of the shares of their employers. How can we assess the effects of that situation?

FCO: In regard to that particular subject, we are still in the eye of the hurricane. It is more closely linked to the American and world recessions. The financial debacle has been very serious. There are several reasons for this. Some claim that although the US Federal Reserve System eventually took action, the fact that it delayed taking steps helped precipitate the recession. But notwithstanding the role played by the Federal Reserve System, it was speculation with a whole series of financial instruments based on very weak structures—such as mortgages, which themselves depended on rates based on inflated prices—that led to the collapse.

The Puerto Rican banking system, which itself is involved in what is occurring internationally—but mainly in the United States—has felt the effects of this collapse directly. The market value of the shares of such banks—in particular the banks established in Puerto Rico, Puerto Rican banks—has declined dramatically. For their shareholders, this has meant substantial losses. How much will it all add up to? Right now I cannot answer that question. How will they recover? That will be determined by the market, but so far the process has been very slow. I assume that over time there will be some recovery, though we may also see—and I would not be surprised if we did see—the sale of some of those assets.

ACS: Paco, one of the most important economic statistics is the unemployment rate. Job creation should be a priority for the government. As you were saying, in the 1940s and 1950s [unemployment] was one of the most important issues. However, it is estimated that the unemployment rate will be 16 percent for 2009. What is the effect of such a rate, and why is job creation so important?

FCO: [The unemployment rate is important] for several reasons. The first reason is that unemployment is quite simply a form of unutilized resources. If you have unutilized resources, you are not using your potential to its full capacity. When I say "unutilized resources," I mean, for example, unused capital, manpower, and agricultural land. Puerto Rico is weighed down by idle, unutilized resources, so here we have a production potential that is not being developed. That is the first problem.

The second problem is a human problem. When people are laid off, their self-esteem crumbles—understandably so because they are unable to generate an income to support themselves and their families. This low self-esteem degrades human beings. In the end, it diminishes the productive resource, which is not a capital asset or a plot of land, but, I repeat, a human being. The loss is huge.

The third problem is antisocial behavior and criminality, both of which, obviously, are associated with the problems of unemployment. Social problems are intensified by unemployment and economic problems.

ACS: Unemployment has a social effect on new generations. For example, an unemployed and depressed father becomes a terrible model for his children, and this has psychological effects on them. Unemployed people in general overload the public systems. For example, there are those people who have medical insurance paid for by the employer. When they lose their jobs, the government has to solve their health problems. The same thing happens with education. There are many parents who had their children in private schools but lost their jobs and no longer had the income to pay for those schools, so they had to move their children into the public-education system. In other words, unemployment overloads the services delivered by the government.

FCO: Yes, unemployment is extremely costly for government and for the economy in general. I would say it is the central problem in Puerto Rico, the root cause of a whole series of other problems, not only economic, but social and psychological as well.

ACS: Paco, one of the reasons given to justify the layoffs of public employees is that Wall Street investors demand that these local government employees be laid off so that the bonds issued by the Government of Puerto Rico won't be given a negative credit rating. Other people say that the government simply has too many employees. What do you have to say about these arguments?

FCO: In this matter, there is kind of an objective reason and also a subjective one. Let's first talk about the second reason, the subjective element, which is easier to define. I believe that the present government is ideologically biased in favor of private enterprise over public enterprise, so, for ideological reasons, it wants to reduce the size of government. That is the subjective or ideological aspect.

Then there is the objective element. Moments ago I mentioned that after the 1970s the Puerto Rican economy began to wear out. Growth indicators dropped noticeably, and unemployment increased. What was done to compensate for all that? The exhausted Puerto Rican economy began to depend on three essential variables.

One, federal transfers increased during that decade. This was when the nutritional assistance program and federal scholarship programs began.

Two, in an attempt to compensate for economic inactivity, the government increased its spending, financing this [spending] mainly with more debt, but without revising its tax base.

And three, it applied Section 936 [of the US Internal Revenue Code], which had been established by law in the 1970s mainly as a tool to attract US companies. This mechanism allowed companies to repatriate their revenues to their headquarters in the United States without having to pay taxes.

But not even with these three powerful instruments—increased government spending, the rise in federal transfers, and Section 936—was the economy able to achieve the growth it expected. That's because none of these instruments was *designed* with that objective. So Puerto Rico's economy did not grow at the same rate as it had during the 1950s and 1960s; it instead declined dramatically. What happened?

The debt, which at the time [in the 1970s] was 20 or 30 percent of gross national product (GNP), is now almost *equal* to GNP. Add up the debt of the central government, the public corporations, and the municipalities, and it is virtually equal to the entire GNP of Puerto Rico. As a consequence, the government's debt-issuing capacity is no longer what it used to be. Here we have an objective problem that the current government has to deal with. And how does it want to deal do that? By reducing spending. But it should also reform the tax base; instead of imposing higher and more onerous taxes, which would have a negative effect, it should *broaden* the tax base.

ACS: Paco, regarding unemployment and its effects, some figures on retail sales were published recently. It is interesting that in 2009 retail sales were $2.74 billion, less than in 2008, when they were $2.78 billion.

Another negative effect produced by unemployment is that young graduates in Puerto Rico, whose higher-education system is excellent, have to leave Puerto Rico for lack of job opportunities. The Puerto Rican taxpayer is paying for their education, but when the engineers from the [University of Puerto Rico] Mayagüez campus and the doctors from the Medical Sciences campus in Río Piedras finish their degrees, they have to leave Puerto Rico because there are no jobs here.

FCO: There you have two issues, you see: one about the migration of talent and the other—the first one you mentioned—about a slowdown in retail spending. With regard to retail sales, something fascinating is happening in Puerto Rico and the United States. First, as you correctly point out, when unemployment increases, the capacity to spend decreases. Second, there is another phenomenon—one that cancels out in part the positive effects that might result from funds from the federal reconstruction and reinvestment legislation, commonly known as "Obama funds"—and that is the psychological factor. People see that things are tough, and they say, "Wait, let me be a little more conservative with my spending." And maybe they try to save some money and pay down their debts. Puerto Ricans, at a personal level, are heavily indebted. Their savings reduce the amount of money in circulation.

Another problem we have is the migration of talent, as you mentioned. It's sad because the University of Puerto Rico makes an extraordinary investment, as you stated, in graduating doctors from the School of Medicine and engineers from the Mayagüez campus, to mention only two obvious examples.

We should be proud of this investment, and we should continue to make it, but we lose a considerable part of it through migration. It is something we need to solve, and we have the mechanisms to do so. For example, medical students years back had more opportunities in Puerto Rico to do their internships. Then some fifteen years ago there was a movement to privatize facilities and implement health-care reform, and the opportunities to do internships locally became scarce. Today, many students graduate from the Medical Sciences campus and go directly to internships in the United States. Once they finish, they receive job offers there, and it turns out to be more expensive for them to return to Puerto Rico.

ACS: Add to this the fact that when these medical interns leave, they do not perform the important task of working in emergency rooms, helping solve Puerto Rico's health-services problem.

FCO: Right. [Those] interns [who stay here] begin to pay back—some of them more than they should—the investment made in them by the people of Puerto Rico.

ACS: An important sector in our economy is the construction industry. It has become more important than it really should be owing to the collapse of the manufacturing industry. The situation is made worse by the lack of a land-use plan. Moreover, one of the government's strategies has been to streamline the permit-procurement process for construction projects, thinking that doing so will solve the sector's problems. There is a consensus that our permit processes are obsolete and should be made more efficient. Even so, the sector's problems will not be solved simply by changing processes. We must also consider that there are no buyers for the housing units being built, that construction costs are much higher, and that no financing is available. It is worth noting that sales of cement, which is necessary for construction, have been declining. In 2007, total cement sales amounted to $3.21 billion; in 2009, they came to only $2.03 billion. What do you have to say about this?

FCO: Construction is probably the industry that has been most affected by the credit crisis because it depends so heavily on financing. The impact of tight credit is twofold: the builder of a housing unit or other structure needs to find financing, and so does the buyer. The restrictions that both parties are encountering in the credit markets are having a dramatic effect on the industry.

But there are two other elements we must also examine. First, the construction industry should be considered a support industry, not a primary industry. In support of what? In support of manufacturing, services, electric power, and water supply. Once you make it a primary industry, it makes no sense; it loses its direction. Here in Puerto Rico, it had been becoming a key industry, and we have seen yet another phenomenon: sometimes things that ought not to be built are built, and other times things are built where they should not be built. For example, houses and apartments are built for which there is no demand because of their high cost. But meanwhile there is a high demand for affordable housing, which is not being built. That is the paradox we face here. To reduce costs, projects are sometimes built in valleys suitable for agriculture; they are sometimes even built in flood-prone areas. And when that happens, we are killing a productive resource, which is the land. That should not be—construction is not meant to kill productive resources by spreading cement on agricultural fields.

So construction must, first, be conceived as a support industry, and, second, it must be governed by rules that enable the rational use of our resources. To achieve that, it is imperative that we develop a land-use plan.

ACS: [For the] interviews I conducted with you and Juan Lara [in 2007] on economic models for Puerto Rico, we chose six countries similar in size to Puerto Rico, some in terms of population and others in terms of physical size. In those interviews,[1] we talked about the success of these six models, but their economies were affected by the economic crisis afterward, as were all the other economies in the world. How have these countries managed their economic crises compared to Puerto Rico?

FCO: We have to admit that all of them have felt the crisis because it has been widespread. However, we find two differences between those countries and ours. The first is that in economic terms they were in a much sounder economic position [going into the recession] than Puerto Rico was. Subtracting from one hundred is not the same as subtracting from fifty. The second difference is that they had and still have the fiscal and monetary tools to engage in the economy through their governments—tools that Puerto Rico does not have. We can see that clearly.

The two least-affected countries, for different reasons, have been Israel and New Zealand.

In 2009, the Israeli economy was stagnating: it grew only 0.6 percent. Compare that to the 5.5 percent contraction in the case of Puerto Rico. Israel has forecast growth of 2.7 percent for 2010. It is already coming out of the economic crisis. It was hardly impacted at all. Why? Because it rapidly implemented a relaxed monetary policy—that is, it moved more quickly to loosen credit than other countries did. And it was lucky in that endeavor—or, better said, it was bold.

New Zealand was not much affected, but for other reasons. In its case, foreign investment and linkages with the rest of the world were not as

1. These interviews appear in part 2 of this book.

intense as for other economies. They weren't absent, but they weren't so intense. This factor somewhat isolated New Zealand from the recession. Did it feel it? Yes, it did. Its contraction in 2009 was on the order of 0.6 percent—again, relatively low. It is already anticipating recovery in 2010 and 2011. So these two countries did not feel the crisis directly.

Singapore did feel the crisis. Having an extraordinary export platform, its exports were affected to the same degree as the countries to which it exports products themselves felt the widespread recession. Also, Singapore has a considerable financial sector, so the impact on Singapore was more dramatic, but its reaction was just as dramatic as the impact. Singapore's GNP *grew* in 2008. For 2009, [the Singaporeans] anticipated a reduction of 8 percent, but it was only 2.1 percent. For 2010 and 2011, they are already anticipating a recovery. But what happened in Singapore? Faced with the crisis, the government took drastic measures: it injected nearly $14 billion into the economy, a truly massive amount. Note that this is more than double the amount of the so-called federal recovery funds assigned to Puerto Rico, which are between $5 billion and $6 billion, and obtaining those funds depends on whether recipients qualify for them or not. But what makes Singapore different from Puerto Rico here is not only quantity, but *quality*. [The latter factor] has two aspects: first, the origin of the funds.

The origin of the funds in Singapore is entirely internal. Therefore, the priorities for using the funds are determined by Singapore and no one else. Where did they get the funds? Let us remember the teachings from the biblical account of Joseph: store wheat in the good years so that you can use it in the bad years. Singapore has its reserves, extraordinary public savings that arise from three sources: corporate savings, personal savings, and governmental savings. In this case, [the funds came] mainly from governmental savings. The analysis issued by *The Economist*'s [Economist] Intelligence Unit states that Singapore still has reserves that can be used in the future if necessary. So what is the origin of these funds? Internal resources. They do not come from a relation of dependency.

The other qualitative aspect that differentiates Singapore from Puerto Rico involves the *use* of the funds. Singapore has used the money mostly to stimulate productive activity. That is, it tells an enterprise, "Do not lay off a single employee. If you do, you will not qualify for the subsidy I will give you or for the tax exemption that I gave you." In this way, Singapore has not stimulated the consumer directly to spend money and thus in turn to stimulate indirectly the productive apparatus; rather, Singapore has stimulated the productive entities *directly*. Also, it does so to get ready, as [the Singaporeans] put it, for the recovery.

For example, they are conducting a project in the three new universities supported by the government. One of them is part of a consortium with MIT in the United States. They are guiding the three universities to prepare Singapore's labor force for new technologies, the development of new products, and new research lines. I think this is fundamental. Singapore has been highly active in establishing new research laboratories in the pharmaceutical industry. This is an industry that has been undergoing many structural changes at the global level and in which many patents have been expiring, adversely affecting several sectors initially. Singapore has been very agile in this whole process. It is an extraordinary phenomenon.

Of the countries with successful sovereignties, Slovenia, Ireland, and Estonia have been perhaps the most affected by the crisis.

In Slovenia, the economy grew 3.5 percent in 2008. (In Puerto Rico, there was no growth.) For 2009, the contraction anticipated for that country was estimated at 7.6 percent. Then, in 2010 and 2011 a recovery is expected. When the economic crisis began, Slovenia was already part of the European Union (EU), but it was not yet in the Euro Zone, which it has entered just recently. The government has increased public spending. It has applied the Keynesian strategy of increasing public spending to compensate for the contraction caused by the recession, so it has not used drastic tools, but rather a very conventional increase in public spending. It had the reserves and the borrowing capacity to do so because public debt in Slovenia had been managed very efficiently in the past.

Of the countries being discussed here, Ireland and Estonia have been most affected by the crisis.

In Ireland, the construction industry—which collapsed across the whole world—had become a very important industry, and its collapse in Ireland was as profound as the importance it held there. (In Spain, this industry was also greatly affected by the contraction.)

Also, Ireland had been too aggressive in its planning strategy. It created kind of a bubble, which burst with this crisis. In this [aggressive strategy], it was strongly influenced by its former colonial power, Great Britain, which suffered a serious impact from the recession in its construction industry and most of all in its financial sector.

The Irish financial sector was too exposed to the US and European sectors, and that exposure affected it dramatically. (Singapore's financial sector was linked to other [sectors] to a degree, but it was also isolated in regulatory terms, which allowed it ample agility.)

So in Ireland we have two serious issues: the effects of the recession on the construction industry and the effects on the financial sector. The 7 percent contraction forecast for 2009 will probably extend into 2010, when the contraction is projected to be 1.9 percent. Then, for the year 2011, some recovery is anticipated based on a series of measures that are already being taken. The Irish are even discussing whether to nationalize their commercial banking system. Another measure being considered is an increase in public spending. Meanwhile, unemployment has increased and is now in the vicinity of 12 percent. Of course, Ireland is encountering this situation with a very high per capita income—one of the highest in the EU, if not *the* highest—and this will cushion to some degree the effects of the recession.

Estonia's case is different. It is a very small country, a neighbor to Russia, with a little more than one million people. That it is near Russia is Estonia's first problem. The difficulties confronted by Estonia with regard to its commercial traffic and its oil supply have generated political tensions with Russia. This situation is part of the recessionary crisis. In addition, Estonia is a very open economy, currently with a relatively conservative government, and of the six successful sovereignties discussed here it has been the one most strongly affected by the recession. Contraction for 2009 there was forecast at nearly 14 percent, which would be equivalent to the contraction in Puerto Rico if we combined the contraction in [Puerto Rico] over the past four years. The contraction may extend, though moderately, into 2010. In 2011, recovery is expected.

But in Estonia they are doing something interesting: they are taking concerted action with other eastern European countries. For example, the contraction and economic crisis registered in Latvia, its neighbor to the south, were equally strong. What did Estonia, which was in better shape, do? It joined with the Czech Republic and other eastern European countries to finance Latvia's recovery policy. So in the case of these eastern European countries, the concerted actions they have taken, whether part of the EU or not, have been remarkable.

There have been ongoing discussions between the EU's western and eastern countries regarding those separate concerted actions because there have been some differences between the two groups with regard to their responses to the recessionary crisis. In Estonia and the other eastern European countries, the response has been to generate greater stimulus—they needed it the most—and to coordinate actions with one another. This [approach] has made them quite interesting within the framework of that fascinating experiment that is the EU—if we can still call it an experiment after the success it has had.

ACS: Like all the world's countries, the six models [discussed] in *Soberanías exitosas* have been affected by this economic crisis, given that we live in a global economy. However, those six have certain characteristics that distinguish them from us. First, they all entered the crisis in a much sounder economic position than the one we were facing in Puerto Rico, which had been in freefall since the 1960s, though temporarily aided by Section 936. Also, as sovereign countries, they have the necessary tools to manage their economies. The first thing that stands out is that they had nation building in mind. Each of the six countries had a structured economy and the tools to face the crisis. That has not been the case in Puerto Rico; because of its colonial relationship with the United States, the economic tools are controlled by Washington, not us. Paco, what would the economy of a sovereign Puerto Rico be like?

FCO: To dramatize how far behind we are, how we are lagging behind, I will begin to answer your question with something said more than fifty years ago by Gilberto Concepción de Gracia, the founder of the Puerto Rico Independence Party in 1946: "The system of free nations is what makes the world one. It is universal coexistence based on reciprocal, mutual, and equal rights."

In other words, sovereignty means holding the instruments with which to become part of the world's dynamics. The world is a series of jurisdictional spaces: regions, nations, groups of nations. Within these spaces, a jurisdiction is in a certain sense a resource, an economic resource. The world is an interactive network, one that is becoming more tightly bound in terms of trade, but also in terms of culture, the environment, and labor standards. It is extraordinary. And to develop in this world, one must understand that true development means two things: [first,] more access to goods, articles, and services and, [second,] the reduction of wrongs.

The wrongs are unemployment, criminality, alienation, and environmental pollution. So access to goods and the reduction of wrongs are what true development provides. To use a jurisdiction fully in this interactive world, one *must* have a certain number of capacities, such as the ones detailed in the literature on development in small countries. These capacities are a series of powers. They are not absolute because nothing is absolute, but they enable a country to enter that interactive world.

The first of these capacities is power over the financial sector. The second is power over imports and exports—that is, over trade. The third is power over the taxation system. The fourth is power over natural resources. The fifth is power over transportation and communications, which is essential because all exchanges between jurisdictions rest on those two sectors—which, by the way, have experienced a revolution in the modern world. The sixth is power to enter into international treaties—not only commercial treaties, but also tax, environmental, labor, and cultural treaties. All of this enriches interaction with other countries while adding value to one's own country, to human life, and to citizens. This is sovereignty.

ACS: I would add the power over immigration.

FCO: When I said power over imports and exports, I was thinking mainly about merchandise, but that really includes production and human factors.

ACS: Is it important to have the power to determine who can enter Puerto Rico?

FCO: Yes, and that does not necessarily convert Puerto Rico into an ethnocentric or xenophobic country or any such thing.

ACS: On the contrary. And in terms of Puerto Rico's current economic situation, what thoughts would you share with us? If Puerto Rico were a sovereign country today, how would it be handling this economic crisis?

FCO: Let's use the examples we discussed earlier and analyze what those countries have done and what we should do with the powers we have mentioned.

I believe that Puerto Rico should generate production at three levels: for domestic consumption, for export, and for regional services.

Let us examine the second. We might turn Puerto Rico into an export platform because we are in a quite privileged maritime trade zone. What do I mean when I say an "export platform"? In Puerto Rico, we have been building—we have already practically built—the Port of the Americas. I mention it because it already exists. I am not making it up. It is in Ponce. To use that port to its fullest potential, we need two of the powers already mentioned: power over transportation and power over trade. We must have the power over transportation because we need to be able to decide which ships we want moving in and out of that port. If a ship from the port of Amsterdam or Rotterdam arrives with the intention of docking at the port of Ponce on its way to the United States, we want that to be possible; and if that ship wants to stop over here on its way to Costa Rica, we want that to be possible, too. But the US cabotage laws prevent it, especially in the case of transportation between Puerto Rico and the United States. But elimination of the cabotage laws would not be enough. We need the power to enter into commercial treaties because it is through such treaties that trade routes are defined.

We must have the power to set up value-added operations—a subject often mentioned—to stimulate production in Puerto Rico and the transshipment of certain goods that can be further processed here and so have a higher value in other markets.

We might also mention a third point: a regional center for services. We would resemble Singapore in this regard. When I say "regional," I am thinking of all of Latin America. We would become part of a center to which we can contribute agricultural technology, veterinarians, resources from the Mayagüez campus, legal services, graphic-design services, translation services (let us capitalize on the connections we have had with the United States), film production, financial services, tourism, health services, information technologies, and flexible production systems—a new technology that utilizes a common base of resources to produce different things. The simplest example is the furniture industry. Today, with a series of industrial computers, you can produce beds as well as living-room furniture. You can use the same facilities and tools to produce different things.

But all of this must be given shape by a set of treaties, certainly taking into account—I think this would be essential for Puerto Rico—two outstanding economic centers: the EU and Asia, both of which we have neglected so far.

ACS: In Asia, we have China, which is set to become the most important economy in the world. China has established a strong presence in the Caribbean and Latin America, which offers a great opportunity for a sovereign Puerto Rico. India is also one of the largest economies in the world. *New York Times* columnist Thomas Friedman recently suggested that the United States should be attracting more engineers from Bangalore with the objective of developing a second Silicon Valley. Indian engineers helped launch the first Silicon Valley, working with technology firms such as Microsoft, Apple, and Intel. A sovereign Puerto Rico, with powers over immigration, might adapt Friedman's idea and attract engineers from Bangalore to complement the work of our engineers at the University of Puerto Rico at Mayagüez. We might create a Center of Excellence and earn a position at the international level. This would keep many of our recently graduated engineers from having to leave Puerto Rico to find work.

Another sovereign model that we discussed [in the country interviews] is Israel. A sovereign Puerto Rico might develop its agricultural sector to achieve food self-sufficiency, which Israel has done. But the situation of our farmers today is so poor that we are actually importing plantains from the Dominican Republic.

Israel also has plans to achieve self-sufficiency in energy production. Puerto Rico might establish a long-term plan to do the same. We have the right climate to do so.

FCO: Certainly. With regard to food, I think that feeding the population is not only imperative, but also fundamental as a security strategy. I have always thought that Puerto Rico can do much more. For example, it might link its agricultural development to the development of a food-processing industry, which might be oriented not only toward the internal market, but also toward exports. Of course, it might turn out that Puerto Rico's agricultural production would not be sufficient for a food-export industry. But if we imported raw materials such as fruits and grains to augment our local production, that would stimulate agriculture and the establishment of an industry that would export to Europe and even to Asia. You can import raw materials from the Dominican Republic or Latin America without necessarily having to export them all back to those markets. You export to where there is a market. It is a very complex network of linkages.

We should not forget that there are three emerging economies (as they are called in some circles) that today are key in the world. The first and most often mentioned is China; the second is India, which is also growing—you just mentioned both; and the third emerging economy is Brazil. None of these three shows any signs of having felt the recession. Given that they are so large, we must target them. Otherwise, we will remain isolated. Sovereignty is a means to make the world one. There should be no question about that.

I think the subject of food is interesting in the case of Israel because it is not a country with great agricultural resources. Perhaps its food self-sufficiency has come about for a wrong reason, which is war, but in our case it may be for a right reason. The Israelis have shown that it is possible to achieve this kind of self-sufficiency even when the land is inhospitable. I think that Puerto Rico's agriculture can be developed more easily. Here we have good soils. But we need to halt the invasion of productive lands by developers as soon as possible. We are not going to develop by planting houses in the valleys. In that regard, we must take advantage of the great potential that urban centers have to rejuvenate themselves, something we have also neglected.

ACS: I believe that what we need is a master plan to structure a nation, an economic plan. We have the land and the sea, so it is absurd to have restaurants in Culebra serving frozen seafood. But we do not have a plan to provide incentives to our fishermen or to develop a fishing industry as such. In the case of energy, Puerto Rico has the sun available all year long, but it does nothing with it. Countries such as Germany and Spain, without having this resource available all year, maximize the sun's use.

FCO: I also think that sovereignty should be undertaken with intelligence and imagination. Nothing kills imagination more than being subordinate and dependent. Achieving sovereignty will be an extraordinary opportunity to use the imagination that has lain dormant in us for years. When we get the chance to enjoy sovereignty, we will assume the responsibility for exercising it with freedom and imagination. To do so, we will need to eradicate the culture of dependency. That is the challenge of sovereignty.

ACS: Another "industry" that is hardly ever discussed is culture. Our performers, who have been negatively affected by the crisis, should have an important presence in the media. However, we lack the power to grant licenses to the electronic media, which is something that all sovereign countries are able to do. Instead of showing imported soap operas, we should be able to develop such programs using local talent, thus creating jobs for our performers.

FCO: A moment ago we were talking about the migration of talent, and we mentioned doctors. Puerto Rico might be a regional center for health services to fight cancer and other diseases. Our Cardiovascular Center should be used to its full potential and be developed further. The much talked about Cancer Center is an initiative of the University of Puerto Rico. Through it, we have the opportunity to develop a state-of-the-art regional center for health services.

ACS: In this interview, we have discussed how sovereignty is the most important element if we are to achieve Puerto Rico's economic development. The current model, in use since the 1970s, is in decline, and we cannot see light at the end of the tunnel. Our present condition is the result of our colonial relationship with the United States, a relationship that does not provide us with the tools to create a nation-building plan, with a progressive economy to generate a high-quality life. The six economic models we discussed [in the country interviews] have faced their economic problems effectively because they are sovereign countries and possess the powers to overcome crisis.

Singapore

An island fourteen times smaller than Puerto Rico, with a similar number of inhabitants.

—ÁNGEL COLLADO-SCHWARZ

Singapore in 2010

Population:	5 million
Territory:	1,000 square kilometers
Population density:	7,252 per square kilometer
Gross domestic product (GDP):	$208.8 billion
Gross national income (GNI):	$203.4 billion
GNI per capita:	$40,070
Unemployment rate:	5.9 percent (2006–2009)
Internet users:	70.1 per 100 people

Source: World Bank, *World Development Indicators* (Washington, DC: World Bank, 2011).

Updated Comments

Singapore's average rate of real GDP growth was higher than 7 percent between 2004 and 2007. Growth slowed to a mere 1.1 percent in 2008, and a sharp contraction was expected in 2009 owing to the financial crisis. Thanks to an expansionary fiscal policy, however, the actual contraction was less than predicted—only –2.1 percent. The fiscal push and a rebound of exports led to outstanding growth in 2010: 14.5 percent. Meanwhile, the unemployment rate has remained quite low. It is currently (2011) only 2 percent of the labor force, which is basically frictional unemployment. The Economist Intelligence Unit forecasts 5 percent average annual growth for 2011 to 2015.

> Francisco Catalá-Oliveras
> Juan Lara

Interview

Interview aired on La Voz del Centro, *Univision Radio Puerto Rico and New York, April 22, 2007.*

ÁNGEL COLLADO-SCHWARZ: The first time I had contact with Singapore, to evaluate it as a possible model for Puerto Rico, was more than twenty years ago at a conference held at the Bankers Club in Hato Rey sponsored by a committee headed by Teodoro Moscoso, Antonio Luis Ferré, and Rafael "Papi" Carrión. On that occasion, Lester Thurow, a professor of economics from MIT, was invited to be the guest speaker. In the forum, Professor Thurow talked about Singapore as a model for Puerto Rico. Months later I visited Singapore and met with the director of the Department of Economics of the University of Singapore, and we also talked about Puerto Rico. She remarked that Singapore had used Puerto Rico as an economic model when it established and launched [its own] new economy. When I reflect on where Puerto Rico got off track, I see that the turning point was when we chose to take the road of welfare and dependence on federal transfer programs. Whereas Singapore explored new opportunities in biotechnology, Puerto Rico was taking the easy road—welfare dependency.

Paco, let's give our radio listeners some background on Singapore.

FRANCISCO CATALÁ-OLIVERAS: For the benefit of our audience, Singapore is an island nation off the southern tip of Malaysia, to the north of Indonesia, on the Malacca Straits connecting the Indian Ocean with the Pacific. It has built a train and road link to Malaysia. Its size changes because [the Singaporeans] reclaim land from the sea, but it is roughly 640 square kilometers, which makes it one-fourteenth the size of Puerto Rico.

Singapore has a population of 4.3 million, which gives it a population density sixteen times higher than Puerto Rico. It can be thought of as a city-state, although this was not always so.

When adventurer Thomas Stanford Raffles established a colonial post there at the beginning of the nineteenth century, Singapore was a fishing village with just two hundred inhabitants. That post thrived, and Singapore gradually transformed itself into a port city similar to others in Asia, Latin America, and Africa. For many years, that was its role, without becoming an example of outstanding development.

In the 1950s, with the disintegration of the British Empire, Malaysia achieved independence, and Singapore became part of the Malaysian Federation. Then in 1965 it detached itself from the federation and became a sovereign state. That was when Singapore's experience truly became interesting.

ACS: During the period in 1965 that you mention, one of the important elements in the refounding of Singapore was its leadership. [It] had an extraordinary leader who is still living, Lee Kuan Yew. His son is the current prime minister. Some people simplify Singapore's achievements, attributing them to the quasi-dictatorial powers of the founder of modern Singapore. Would you care to comment on this?

FCO: If it depended on the doings of dictators, the whole world would be developed because we have certainly had our share of dictators in many different geographical regions. Singapore is formally democratic, but there is no question that it has a somewhat authoritarian political culture. We have to keep that in mind. It has a parliamentary system that has long been under the control of a dominant party, the People's Action Party.

Lee Kuan Yew was Singapore's prime minister from 1959 until 1990. Then there was a transition, and Goh Chok Tong, a member of the same party, became prime minister, holding that post until 2004. That year the country's administration passed to Lee Hsien Loong, who is the son of Lee Kuan Yew, who still acts as a kind of minister emeritus. In fact, though on in years, he is still a member of the cabinet. The elder Lee was an energetic leader.

In Singapore, labor unions and cooperatives have been sponsored in great measure by the state, so there are strong links between the cooperative system—composed of many cooperatives, mostly consumer cooperatives, managed by labor unions—and officials in the government. However, it seems rather simplistic to reduce the explanation for Singapore's economic dynamism to simply a consequence of its authoritarian culture.

ACS: I agree with you. I have heard people here in Puerto Rico say that "Singapore works because it is a dictatorship." That is not correct. There were dictatorships without development in Santo Domingo, under Rafael Leonidas Trujillo, and in Nicaragua, under Anastasio Somoza.

FCO: Singapore has dozens of trade treaties that other countries might have and that some *do* have. There is an institutional agility in Singapore, but it cannot be explained as a function of a man such as Lee Kuan Yew.

ACS: Paco, what was Singapore's formula for success?

FCO: I believe that right at independence Singapore set its goals and then adjusted them on a continuing basis. It diagnosed each situation and said, "Now for this problem we need to do this." If that did not work, [the Singaporeans] did something else: "For that other problem we need to do that." Quite simply, they connected each problem to a series of institutional mechanisms to solve it—solutions that might seem obvious now, but that at the time may not have been.

For example, in 1965 or even before, when Singapore was part of the Malaysian Federation, it established one of the first economic plans, with the assistance of a team from the United Nations. A Dutch economist headed the development of the plan. Ah, that's another thing! [The Singaporeans] sought talent everywhere and brought it to Singapore. That time it was a fellow named Albert Winsemius, a Dutch economist. The problem they had then was unemployment. They began by protecting infant labor-intensive industries. This strategy more or less characterized the Singapore of that decade. Later on, in the 1980s and 1990s, the picture changed, and [it] achieved full employment.

Singapore currently has 2 percent unemployment,[1] but it is "frictional unemployment." That term refers to the circumstances of people who graduate from university and start looking for a job. While they are looking, they register as unemployed. Or it may refer to people who have a job, become unhappy in that job or have some sort of situation with it, and leave it for another. Those things are frictional unemployment. Singapore has had periods with higher unemployment; it experienced a recession in the late 1990s and early 2000, but it has since overcome [that recession].

So around the 1980s, Singapore[ans] said, "No, wait. We are going to make the development of high value-added sectors, such as machinery and electronics, a priority." Then they began placing enormous emphasis on engineering and technical careers. They also began to strengthen education dramatically, as they did other areas that had not been so important in the 1970s, when industry was labor intensive, and the workforce lacked the sophistication needed for the new industries they were promoting. In the 1980s, the new industry was developed mainly through external human capital and the establishment of multinational companies. That has changed, and the change is interesting.

Then they said, "Oh my, it seems that the first plan, designed to solve unemployment, has resulted in a labor shortage. Unemployment is no longer the problem; now it is a lack of workers." So they developed a plan to increase productivity through education. They began moving in the direction of a whole range of new currents in biotechnology and pharmaceuticals, where the biological sciences play a major role. More recently, however, since the 1990s or perhaps earlier, Singapore's indicators have been those of a developed country—that is, in education, health, and per capita income. It had more than double the per capita income of Puerto Rico. However, [its leaders] began to notice certain vulnerabilities—for example, the enormous

1. For data after 2007, when the interview was aired, see the table "World Bank Statistics" in part 3, "Comparative Tables."

influence of the multinational companies on the economy, especially on export activity, where the US market was preeminent; the high share of reexportation compared to internal production; and the high dependency on oil. Another vulnerability factor was that 50 percent of the drinking water that Singapore consumes is imported from Malaysia.

How did they tackle those vulnerabilities? Regarding the influence of the multinationals, they did several things. First, they stimulated local capital. Singapore's savings rate is 40 percent of national income. That is a huge savings rate. To a certain degree, it is forced saving. For example, in Puerto Rico public employees are obliged to save through the Commonwealth Employees Association. In Singapore, there is an obligatory social-savings fund that is used to channel resources to the principal productive activity.

With that capital, [Singapore's leaders] began to emphasize the establishment of national Singaporean enterprises, many of them undertaken by the state, others [by] private [individuals or companies]. They also promoted participation in foreign enterprises. That is, they began to foster joint ventures between the state of Singapore and foreign enterprises, and they began to establish Singaporean enterprises in foreign countries, with two objectives in mind: to locate natural resources and to open export markets.

Another strategy they implemented was to promote the establishment not only of multinational subsidiaries but also of multinational headquarters in Singapore. You might say, "Well, General Motors is not going to move to Singapore." And that is right, but recently established enterprises based on new technology—young enterprises that are still experimenting—certainly *can* establish their headquarters in other countries with relative ease. And Singapore began to provide these enterprises with incentives to do so, which was quite clever, which caused the GDP and the GNI to come closer together. That is, the repatriation of capital gains did not take away so much income from the country because it was balanced by the repatriation of capital gains by the enterprises Singapore had elsewhere and by repatriation of capital gains to multinationals with headquarters in Singapore. That is different from what has happened in Puerto Rico.

ACS: Paco, it was not just the multinationals that had their headquarters there. Other companies established their regional headquarters in Singapore as well. Corporations relocated to that country, especially after China took over Hong Kong in 1997.

FCO: That is correct. Also, they established export platforms in Singapore for different markets, not just a single market. That is another thing: vulnerability, depending on just one market. To [Singapore's leaders], that [sort of dependence] is a vulnerability. For example, they measure vulnerability as a percentage of exports. If the percentage of exports to a single market is very high, they begin to worry because if something happens to that market, it will affect Singapore's economy.

They were concerned because exports to the United States amounted to between 15 and 16 percent of their total exports, which is nothing out of the ordinary. [By contrast] in the case of Puerto Rico, exports to the United States are 90 percent of the total. So [the Singaporeans] increased their exports to other countries. They did not reduce the absolute amount of exports going to the United States, but they reduced the relative weight of that factor. What markets have they increased lately? Well, their principal market continues to be Malaysia, to which they send around 14 percent of their total exports. Another market that has been gradually increasing, for obvious reasons, is China, but they keep [their exports to] it between 10 and 15 percent of the total.

Here we have to be careful. Hong Kong's economic statistics are generally kept separate from mainland China's. When you add the statistics of Hong Kong and mainland China together, they represent approximately 20 percent of Singapore's total exports. But we are talking about China, which is a giant.

So [Singapore] practice[s] export diversification, so much so that in their efforts to diversify several years ago they signed a number of trade agreements concurrently with Malaysia, Japan, and New Zealand and on our side of the world with Chile to the south and the United States and Mexico to the north—a great variety of trade agreements to diversify both the import and the export markets, to reduce vulnerability.

Singapore depends heavily on oil imports from the Middle East. That dependency is the most difficult factor to mitigate, but [it is] trying to develop alternative sources of energy. By the way, Puerto Rico, which should also take that road, has expressed its intention to do so through its Electrical Power Authority.

Singapore has also been dependent with regard to water. [The Singaporeans] have centuries-old treaties with Malaysia, with terms of one hundred years, but they do not depend solely on them. They have lately been making an effort to desalinize water from the sea because depending on a single market to obtain half their drinking water is clearly a vulnerability.

So diversification on all fronts is Singapore's [leaders'] key mechanism for reducing vulnerability. Note that they identify their weaknesses factor by factor. They identify each one and ask, "What are we going to do about export concentration? What are we going to do about reexportation?" They itemize each challenge one by one and say, "This is our strategy." Then they implement [that strategy].

The definition [of a challenge] is simple, and the strategy [for addressing it] is simple. Of course, to operationalize it all is complex, but the beauty lies in the simplicity of the diagnosis and of the strategy developed to solve the challenge.

ACS: Singapore is an island but is almost joined to the Malay Peninsula. The distance between the two countries is very short. Every morning ships arrive with workers from Malaysia, who spend the day working in Singapore, and each night they return to their homes in Malaysia.

FCO: Maybe that is why in the 1950s and 1960s it was logical to think that Singapore was part of the Malaysian Federation—as it once in fact was—not only because of its geographical proximity, but also because of the workforce you are referring to, which I find very interesting. We must also point out that the Port of Singapore is one of the busiest in the world. Every ten minutes a ship arrives or departs from it. It is truly an extraordinary operation. Singapore has also become a source of expertise in many fields: in technology, port construction, and management as well as in the legal field.

At the general headquarters of the World Trade Organization in Switzerland, Singapore has many people, and though its influence [in that body] bears no relation to its size—its influence is quietly much greater—it often effectively represents not only Singapore's interests, but also Asia's.

This gives Singapore more power than it would have on its own if it represented its interests exclusively.

ACS: Another interesting fact is the composition of Singapore's population, something that in another country might be a huge problem. Its population is composed of different Malaysian groups as well as Indians, Chinese, and [native] Singaporeans. Yet all of these groups work in harmony despite their ethnic, cultural, and religious differences. You can walk through a neighborhood and find a Buddhist temple and a Hindu temple, and they all practice their own religion in harmony with the rest.

FCO: That is right—their ethnic, cultural, and religious pluralism is remarkable. Imagine, they have Christians, Muslims, Hindus, Confucians, and others—all coexisting. It is extraordinary.

ACS: Paco, let's talk about how Singapore, with so little land, has been able to develop its agriculture.

FCO: When you examine the statistics for Singapore, you might think that there is no agroindustry because [it is] a powerhouse in exporting manufactured products, financial services, and other products. But [the Singaporeans] have developed what they call "agrotechnology parks" because they feel that to call them "farms" would be an exaggeration. In these agrotechnology parks, they produce poultry, eggs, fish, vegetables, and different fruits, and the production is modest. However, for some products, such as orchids, Singapore is an important world supplier. Also, its research centers do not just do manufacturing research: they are pioneers in molecular agrobiology. [Singapore also has] research centers dedicated to agriculture, which allows [it] not only to develop [the] agrotech parks, but also to export services related to agricultural research. Such a small country!

Compared to Singapore, Puerto Rico would seem to be an agricultural giant with the land it has. Yet if there is anything we underestimate here, it is agriculture, whereas in Singapore they do not underestimate production in *any* field. I would say they do not underestimate or overestimate; they assign the exact value to everything.

ACS: On a recent trip to Singapore, I visited the botanical gardens, which cover a large expanse of land. It is hard to believe that an island fourteen times smaller than Puerto Rico can have such extraordinary botanical gardens. It is the result of good planning.

Singapore has a construction industry. [The Singaporeans] erect buildings, but, obviously, most housing is vertical rather than horizontal. As a result, they have maximized protection of their natural resources and green areas. Even the University of Singapore, whose structures and site are very much like our own University of Puerto Rico, is located in an area that, though it is not a botanical garden, gives the impression that it is. An interesting fact is that the University of Singapore's School of Public Administration is named for Lee Kuan Yew, and it is the only instance in which the founder of the new Singapore has agreed to have an entity or structure named after him. This exception highlights the importance he has always assigned to public administration.

FCO: There is no question that Singapore's public administration is among the most efficient in the world and the most honest. Also, the University of Singapore is closely linked to all the economic strategies we are discussing. For example, not long ago I read that when Singapore signs its trade treaties—the most recent I know of are with Chile, Mexico, the United States, and Japan—it establishes university teams that simulate with models how each trade treaty will affect Singapore's economy. Then the teams monitor each treaty to determine empirically what its real impact has been. First, they anticipate the results, then they closely monitor the process. So there is a very tight relationship between Singapore's educational framework and these strategies. It is not merely a matter of preparing technical workers; education has been tied closely to the government's entire decision-making process.

ACS: Paco, what you mentioned earlier is important, that in Singapore they engage in a kind of stock taking: they assess their strengths and weaknesses, then outline a strategic plan for social and economic development. For example, as we just mentioned, they have assigned a high priority to infrastructure. Singapore is now the principal airport in Asia after Bangkok and is one of the most important in the world. So, you may ask, how can so small an island without beautiful beaches have such a vibrant tourism industry? Well, very easily. [The Singaporeans] laid out the infrastructure and built convention centers; they attracted tourists [by means of] conferences and conventions, without the need for beaches because [they were offering] business tourism.

Another important thing is that Singapore [has been made] an air and marine transshipment hub. Singapore Airlines is considered the best airline in the world. In all the rankings in all the tourism magazines, Singapore Airlines ranks number one.

FCO: It is extraordinary—Singapore is one vast loading dock. To give you an idea, Singapore's imports and exports exceed those of India, Brazil, and Russia. We are talking about countries with hundreds of millions of inhabitants. India alone has almost one billion inhabitants. This does not mean that all those exports are produced in Singapore. The country acts as a transshipment port for a number of other markets. It is really phenomenal.

Now, something you just mentioned is very important: How do they diagnose and find solutions—for example, to a structural problem?

When Singapore became independent, it had a housing problem. There is a motto that summarizes Lee Kuan Yew's purpose: "Building a nation presupposes housing the population." What did [Singapore's leaders] do? They increased the population living in government-built housing from 9 percent in 1960 to almost 90 percent today. How did they finance the construction of that public housing? They established the Central Providence Fund, which is a kind of social-security program. With those savings, they began construction, which is subsidized; that is, it complements the workers' salaries. If a worker wants to buy a property, he or she is financed through the providence fund or social fund. Singapore's culture and policies are very much against welfare systems that encourage dependency. There *is* a welfare system, but it does not foster dependency. So they created the fund, and today 90 pecent of Singaporeans live in government-built housing. They solved the housing problem, but in a very particular and well-planned fashion.

ACS: Local corporations, such as Singapore Airlines, are public corporations, and anyone can buy shares in them; they are listed on the Singapore Stock Exchange. The government owns a significant block of shares in the airline but does not control it—the board of directors does.

FCO: Yes, the role of government is very unusual. Besides the central bureaucracy that we were discussing a moment ago, which is highly efficient, [Singapore] also [has] state enterprises. The government participates in private enterprise through what are called "statutory boards." In this way, companies and government are linked, but those firms are managed privately. Singapore also has a rather important cooperative sector.

So if Singapore[ans] need a multinational company for one kind of activity, a national enterprise for another, a joint venture for another, and a cooperative for yet another, they know how to set these things up because they are very much aware that no single form of enterprise is appropriate for all activities. Some activities will require one kind of enterprise, others a different one. [Singapore has] that kind of institutional flexibility.

ACS: That is important because the strong capacity to adapt to any circumstance is a significant factor in Singapore's success. For example, when China assumed its role as a global player, Singapore knew it could not compete, so it developed ways to harmonize its strategies with those of China.

FCO: That is correct. As you may recall, several years ago there was a recession in Asia, especially in Japan, where there was a financial crisis, and [then] that [health] "epidemic"—if my memory serves, its acronym was SARS—also affected Singapore. For the first time in many years, Singaporeans took a big economic jolt, but they adjusted immediately. They began attending to the new information-management industry. They activated their trade treaties and signed new ones. They did it all immediately, with extraordinary agility, to the degree that for the past year, 2006, they were already growing at more than 7 percent in real terms. And speaking of economic growth, I should mention that during the 1960s and 1970s Puerto Rico's per capita income was higher than Singapore's, yet today it is two times lower, which illustrates Singapore's extraordinary dynamism relative to our economy.

ACS: How do you explain that dramatic change in Puerto Rico's position in relation to Singapore, from a better position to the current position, which is so much worse?

FCO: I believe that Puerto Rico committed itself to a model, and then the time came to set it aside, but [Puerto Rico] never did. What was the model? Puerto Rico made a very simple bet. After the Second World War, the only industrial economy still standing was that of the United States. Europe had been destroyed by the war, and Japan also. China was not on our radar; it was too distant. Puerto Rico bet on bringing in investment from the United States and in exporting to the United States. That was the whole bet. And [that bet] is still on in spite of globalization [and] even though the world has been transformed. Now the privilege of access to the US market is not what it once was.

The United States has opened up. US capitalists are interested in investing in other countries and exploring new markets, not necessarily in order to export to the United States, though that market is still strong, especially in the case of China, which exports a great deal to the United States.

China has opened up. It now has a strong economy. Europe is extraordinarily dynamic. [Here in Puerto Rico] we have stayed with the old model, even though the world has changed. Singapore has not. Singapore has changed in concert with the changes that have occurred in the world.

ACS: A study conducted by the Brookings Institution and the Center for the New Economy states that the problem with federal transfers and food stamps is that they motivate people in Puerto Rico not to work. That is odd because—as I stated earlier—during my visit to the economist at the University of Singapore more than twenty years ago I realized that the key moment at which Singapore and Puerto Rico took different paths was when Puerto Rico decided to increase federal transfers and establish an economy based on dependency, on federal assistance, whereas Singapore was entering the world of high technology and sophisticated finance. Puerto Rican politicians rushed into a competition to see who could bring in more federal funds. The most successful resident commissioner in Washington was the one who was able to attain the most federal assistance funds for Puerto Rico.

FCO: I would put it another way, which complements your theory without contradicting it. Puerto Rico has created a culture of dependency that is inhibiting. Simply put, Puerto Rico leaned back and did not even consider exploring institutional forms. There are two good examples, and you just mentioned one: food stamps. The other is Section 936. Section 936 was a special mechanism to attract US capital [by exempting it from taxation]. Because it existed and worked, Puerto Rico chose to rely on it and to do nothing else. We operated as if on autopilot and did not explore institutional forms. Note that in both cases we are talking about institutional mechanisms that originated elsewhere. Section 936 is part of the US Internal Revenue Code. The food-stamp benefit is a US federal government program. So we decided to delegate exploration of institutional forms to the United States, and we did not do it for ourselves.

After Section 936 disappeared, what did we say? "We have to find another provision in that Internal Revenue Code, another section that can protect us." I believe that for years the culture of dependency has been inhibiting the exploration of institutional forms, which go hand in hand with economic development. That is, economic development needs exploration of institutional forms—exploration and invention. When I say "institutions," I mean ways of doing things: standards for coordinating work, for harmonizing production processes, and for drafting trade treaties. When I talk about institutional agility, I am talking about all of these. Puerto Rico does not have institutional agility, nor is it searching for [such agility]—it just leans back.

ACS: To that we must add elements such as the US maritime cabotage laws. Our colonial status does not allow us to explore the possibilities.

FCO: Correct. In that regard, we have the famous example of the attempt by the Rafael Hernández-Colón administration to enter into a trade agreement with Japan. The US Department of State said no, and that was that.

ACS: Paco, let's compare Puerto Rico's statistics with those of Singapore.

FCO: Before we go into that, let me tell you that I was looking at some statistics in *The Economist* of March 3, 2007. It publish[es] an indicator [it] call[s] the "Capital Access Index" that summarizes the performance of some fifty-six financial variables indicating how easy it is for a country to raise financial capital relative to other countries. Then [it] rank[s] the countries. The best place in the world to raise capital is Hong Kong, which as you know is part of China; the second is Singapore; the third is the United Kingdom; the fourth is Canada; and the fifth is the United States. These are 2005 rankings. Look what league Singapore is playing in—the big league.

Singapore has somewhat more than 4 million inhabitants, and as we said earlier, it is one-fourteenth the size of Puerto Rico. It has 6,708 people per square kilometer; Puerto Rico has 428. [Singapore's] population density is sixteen times higher than Puerto Rico's. The fact that Singapore is playing in the big league should get us thinking. Here in Puerto Rico, I hear many folks say, "Ah, no, Puerto Rico is too small. Ah, no, Puerto Rico has too many people. Ah, no, Puerto Rico is. . . ." We seem to use any imaginable excuse to justify the culture of dependency and subordination. I believe we have to discard that argument in light of the Singapore example and the example of a number of other countries, some of which we will be discussing later. But Singapore is certainly playing in the big league.

ACS: Paco, some people think that enterprises in Puerto Rico cannot be as successful as their counterparts in Singapore. I do not share that view. The best example is the Banco Popular de Puerto Rico. The Banco Popular, an institution founded when we were still part of the Spanish Empire, has successfully entered the US banking market to become the principal Hispanic bank in the United States.

FCO: That's right. I believe that Puerto Rico has well-prepared people, and where we do not have them, we can train them, as Singapore has done. If we do not have the technicians in a particular area, we can train them.

Two or three years ago some extraordinary discoveries were made about the human genome. What did Singapore do? It immediately contracted some of the US scientists who participated in that research, and [now] a couple of them [are] doing research in Singapore. *That* is institutional agility.

There is another example that I think is dramatic for Puerto Rico. Puerto Rico's GNI is a little more than $50 billion. That is the total income of all Puerto Ricans taken together, whether they are property owners, capitalists, or workers. When you add it all up, you get somewhat more than $50 billion. In 1996, that GNI did not increase because we had a recession; in fact, it shrank.

In Singapore, the GNI is more than $100 billion, twice as much. Last year it grew 7.7 percent. And this is *real* growth, after inflation. Both the GNI and the production level in Singapore are double ours, and they are growing at levels as high as 6 percent, 7 percent, even 8 percent, whereas Puerto Rico, in its best recent years, has grown 3 percent in real terms. Obviously, as time passes, we are falling farther behind in terms of production and income. As time goes by, we will be farther and farther behind economies such as Singapore's. We need to be alert to be able to compete.

We talk about competence, we say that we will compete with Ireland and compete with Singapore, but we are certainly not competing.

ACS: Unfortunately, we lack the power to develop an advanced or forward-looking economic model. That is our biggest limitation. For example, you are talking about how Singapore recruited scientists from all over the world to go work there and to contribute to its economic model. Here, because Puerto Rico has no power over immigration, we cannot even grant tourist visas. Immigration policies are set by Washington, which has its own valid priorities. But Puerto Rico's priorities are not the priorities of the United States.

FCO: That is indeed correct. Here is another example: Singapore has if not the busiest port in the world, at least *one* of the busiest, which serves as the port of entry and departure for many countries. Puerto Rico is constructing the so-called Ponce Port of the Americas, but [that port will be] governed by US cabotage laws. When a ship arrives from Europe with cargo, it cannot continue on to the United States because the law requires that US-flag vessels transport all cargo from Puerto Rico to the United States. This makes it very difficult to design trade agreements. Another example: Singapore has diplomatic missions in more than 160 countries. In 40 of them, where [Singapore is a] principal trading partner, [it has] what [it calls] "economic intelligence units" attached to [its] embassies to study those economies, learn from them, and assess how [it] can trade with them more effectively. Those economic intelligence units are scattered all around the world. Puerto Rico, in contrast, does not have a single economic intelligence unit or even a single diplomatic mission anywhere because it cannot. So how are we to compete with someone who has tools at hand that we cannot have? It is like wanting to plant seeds with one's bare hands while the competition is using a hoe.

ACS: Paco, let's summarize Singapore's development process. From being an English colony, how was it able to become a country that, as you have pointed out, competes in the same league as the United States?

FCO: I recently read an author, Johnny Sung, who asks and answers that very question. In a book published in 1996, he sets out to explain Singapore's development in terms of what he calls the "missing link," which

Singapore found. The missing link is a workforce focused on fulfilling certain development goals.

For example, in the 1960s Singapore decided that its workforce should be employed in building a manufacturing base; then by the late 1960s, the workforce was concentrating on value-added industries; by the 1990s, it was focusing on reducing vulnerability, as we discussed earlier. Now, in the 2000s, it is focusing on a global endeavor that takes world dynamics into account and that aims to diversify Singapore's economy as much as possible—though it is in fact already fairly diversified, both in terms of its production profile and services and in terms of its export and import efforts.

Two variables have been fundamental in Singapore, variables that must be viewed as a synergy. One of these variables is an enterprising government, which has formulated these plans. But for plans to be carried out, the people must be involved, so that enterprising government must be accompanied by a working class who knows and acknowledges that the plans are good and who identifies with them. That is, the people must see the concrete benefits they will receive if certain development goals are achieved—goals that once met can be translated into concrete benefits in health, wealth, and housing. (As we noted earlier, the government housing program in Singapore has been extraordinary.)

In this way, benefits for the working class are directly linked to the achievement of public goals. These goals are not defined in terms of the profits of certain private entities, which obviously set up shop in Singapore with profit in mind. Rather, the government of Singapore attracts those entities in order to further certain public goals: "I want you here, and you will generate profits, but what I want is to export to China or export to the United States, or I want to have a production line that I did not have before and cannot generate here, but you have it. And that will generate such and such a public benefit for me." [Singapore's leaders] connect what would apparently be exclusively private goals with public objectives, and they persuade the citizens to recognize such public objectives as their own. This generates amazing work dynamics that are really difficult to emulate if you lack that whole cauldron of institutional tools and those links with the world. In Singapore, they learn from the world with extraordinary speed.

Notice how they establish those links. Here in Puerto Rico, we sold the telephone company to a US enterprise, and the money from the sale was placed in a fund under the Puerto Rico Infrastructure Financing Authority, supposedly to help improve the deteriorating water infrastructure. Quite frankly, from the day of the sale until this day I have yet to see great advances in our water infrastructure, and there has been even less progress with respect to the government retirement plan, which was the other objective and which has an $11 billion deficit.

What did Singapore do? Singapore privatized. It sold part of its telephone company, and what did it do with the product of that sale? It invested it in the European telephony industry. That is called being globally linked. Why did [the] Singapore[ans] invest in European telephony? Because they want to have some clout in European telephony—to acquire knowledge, transfer technology, and strengthen their connections with the industrial and research apparatus of Europe, the United States, and Asia. Among all economies, Singapore may be the one that is best connected to the world. This explains how a country so small can occupy such a large economic space, transcending its territory—how it can have what the Singaporeans call "multidimensional space." I did not make up that term—it is used by all of Singapore's political agents: *multidimensional space.*

They say that their space is the world. They place exports and imports in the world and establish enterprises with Singaporean capital in the world. They invest in European telephony and in whatever other activities they like because their space is the world. And by defining the world as their economic space, they achieve concrete development of their national territory because, of course, they are highly aware of what that national territory is.

ACS: Paco, if you were a consultant from Singapore, using Singapore as a model, what would be your three principal recommendations for Puerto Rico?

FCO: First of all, we must establish an enterprising and efficient government. This will require an extraordinary change in Puerto Rico's political culture.

Second, we must diversify commercially. We must get connected to the world. We must find ways to enter into trade agreements. Without trade agreements and the agility to negotiate them, we cannot compete in today's economy; it is impossible.

Singapore, for example, attracts European and US investors and tells them, "Look, I will give you an edge." The investor can say, "Look, I am not interested in your market because you have only 4 million people. I am interested in China's market, which has more people than I can count." "Ah, well, hold on, I have this agreement with China, or I can negotiate this agreement with China, and that will allow you to use me as an export platform to China." Puerto Rico certainly does not have this kind of agility. We have the Latin American market right here, and we have turned our backs on it. We turn our backs to the European Community. We sent a mission to China, but people do not know what will come of it, what agreements are possible. So my second piece of advice would be to get that agility.

And my third piece of advice is to think seriously about changing the culture of dependency. It is a tumor that needs to be extracted, radically extracted.

ACS: Singapore is a small island, one-fourteenth the size of Puerto Rico, with the same population as Puerto Rico and with many different cultures coexisting on that small territory. Yet it has achieved extraordinary growth in per capita income, from lower than Puerto Rico's to far higher. Singapore has a parliamentary government, as do almost all other democracies in the world. With sovereignty as its foundation, it is a splendid model for Puerto Rico in the twenty-first century.

Suggested Reading on Singapore

Lee Kuan Yew. *From Third World to First: The Singapore Story, 1965–2000.* New York: HarperCollins, 2000.
———. *The Singapore Story.* Singapore: Prentice Hall, 1998.
Mahbubani, Kishore. *Can Asians Think?* Singapore: Marshall Cavendish, 2010.

Slovenia

A European country that achieved sovereignty in 1991. With half the population of Puerto Rico, it has one of the highest growth rates in the world.

—ÁNGEL COLLADO-SCHWARZ

Slovenia in 2010

Population:	2 million
Territory:	20,000 square kilometers
Population density:	102 per square kilometer
Gross domestic product (GDP):	$46.9 billion
Gross national income (GNI):	$49.0 billion
GNI per capita:	$23,860
Unemployment rate:	5.9 percent (2006–2009)
Internet users:	69.2 per 100 people

Source: World Bank, *World Development Indicators* (Washington, DC: World Bank, 2011).

Updated Comments

The Slovenian economy grew at an excellent pace during 2004–7, averaging better than 5 percent. In 2007, before the financial crisis, real GDP increased 6.8 percent. It grew also in 2008, albeit at a reduced rate of 3.5 percent. The global recession's impact was felt during 2009, when exports and output declined sharply. Real GDP declined 7.6 percent that year, and unemployment rose significantly, to more than 10 percent. There was a mild recovery in 2010 that did not improve the employment picture noticeably. Moderate growth of between 2 and 3 percent annually is projected for 2011–15. Some structural and fiscal reforms are expected to stimulate investment, especially foreign investment, which so far has played a limited role in Slovenia's economy.

Francisco Catalá-Oliveras
Juan Lara

Interview

Interview aired on La Voz del Centro, *Univision Radio Puerto Rico and New York, March 18, 2007.*

ÁNGEL COLLADO-SCHWARZ: Slovenia is one of the most recent countries to achieve sovereignty. Paco, let's give our radio listeners some background on Slovenia.

FRANCISCO CATALÁ-OLIVERAS: Certainly. Slovenia is not well known in Puerto Rico, though I believe a Puerto Rican played on the Slovenian basketball team. Now Puerto Ricans are playing basketball all over Europe. Slovenia is a country with only 2 million inhabitants. That is why its experiences turn out to be enlightening for Puerto Rico—because it is a small country.

ACS: Two million is half of Puerto Rico's population.

FCO: However, Slovenia has more than twice our territory—nearly 20,000 square kilometers. Slovenia borders Italy to the west, Austria to the north, Croatia to the south and southwest, and Hungary to the northeast.

It is on the border of what I would call old western Europe and eastern Europe, referring not so much to its geographical position, but rather to a political one: this border divided capitalist Europe from socialist Europe.

From the Second World War on, Slovenia was part of the Yugoslav Federation under the government of Josip Broz Tito, Marshal Tito. The federation was made up of Croatia, Macedonia, Montenegro, Bosnia-Herzegovina, and Serbia, in addition to the autonomous provinces of Kosovo and Vojvodina. In 1990, [ten years] after Tito died, a referendum was held, and the Yugoslav Federation began to fall apart. Some 86 percent voted for the independence of Slovenia.

ACS: Paco, before talking about Tito's death, explain what happened with regard to the Iron Curtain and the fall of the Soviet Union at the end of the 1980s.

FCO: Yes, that is pertinent. First, we must distinguish Yugoslavia from the rest of the countries that made up Europe, socialist eastern Europe. Yugoslavia was the only country that liberated *itself* from the Nazis, through the actions of Tito's Partisans and not through the intervention of the Soviet army, which never entered Yugoslavia. From the beginning, that gave Slovenia a certain degree of political independence, and major differences arose between Tito and Joseph Stalin.

The first distinction we have to make is that from the very beginning Yugoslavia established less-strained political and economic relations with the West, with western Europe. The second distinction is that Yugoslavia was something of an artificial state, composed of a number of very different nations with different languages and even different alphabets. Some used the Latin alphabet, as we do, whereas others used the Cyrillic alphabet. Besides this, its peoples—the Serbians, the Croatians, the Slovenians, and so on—practiced different religions, and each of them had a strong national identity. These differences moved the country to remain relatively decentralized so that even though [it] had a central economic plan, [it] granted more prerogatives to the governments of these republics in the federation than was characteristic of other countries of eastern Europe or even of the Soviet Union.

So [it] gradually established what was called a "policy of self-management by workers." However, the prerogatives granted to workers under this policy were often counteracted by the decisions taken by the central government. At times, the intervention of the Communist League, as the Yugoslavian Communist Party was known, was more decisive. So the worker self-management policy oscillated between the poles of centralization and decentralization.

During the 1980s, the Soviet bloc and the Yugoslav Federation began to weaken. Also, Tito, whom some called "the only Yugoslav"—because the rest were Serbians, Croatians, Macedonians, and so on—had died in 1980. Of course, during that decade, the Soviet bloc continued to grow weaker, both economically and politically, until the great fragmentation of the 1990s, the breakup of the Soviet Union after Mikhail Gorbachev's period in office. Naturally, this event caused explosions in eastern Europe—in Poland, Hungary, Yugoslavia, and the Baltic countries.

Yugoslavia was not the only country to break up. Czechoslovakia, for example, split in two, into Slovakia and the Czech Republic. The division in Yugoslavia was bloodier than in other places. We all remember the Kosovo War.

One of the most developed republics while the Yugoslav Federation still existed was Slovenia. Keep in mind that it had borders with Italy and Austria. Historically, it had always been westernized, if I may use the expression. Initial conditions count, and Slovenia's were not so bad. It was in that context that [Slovenia] held the 1990 referendum, and independence won out—a sentiment that had been latent in the Slovenian people since the Second World War.

ACS: We must note once more that at that time the Soviet Union itself was breaking up. From it, several new republics arose: Ukraine, Belarus, the three Baltic countries, and Muslim countries to the south. Soviet hegemony had ended. You mentioned that the Soviets had never had much influence over Tito. By this time, they had even less.

FCO: I would say it went from little to none.

ACS: Going back to the 1990 referendum, that was when Slovenia decided to become an independent nation.

FCO: Correct. And so did Croatia at the same time. Then in 1991 [Slovenia] faced the intervention of the Yugoslav army, which by then was a sort of coalition of Croatians, Macedonians, Bosnians, and Albanians, who were really not that interested in war, which was fortunate for Slovenia. In fact, the Yugoslav army was so reluctant to go to war that the army disintegrated and was replaced by the Serbian army, the one that later started wars in other parts of the old Yugoslavia. But that moment favored Slovenia, and thanks to the mediation of the European Union (EU), the Brioni Agreement was signed between the Yugoslav Federation, or what was left of it, and Slovenia, ending the war.

The Brioni Agreement is interesting. The prime minister of the Republic of Slovenia said that it had been written with "constructive ambiguity." No one knew for certain what the treaty said. It stated that the implementation of Slovenian sovereignty would be delayed for three months, but it did not detail what would happen at the end of those three months. What happened was that Slovenia declared its independence and managed to make it stick and that a new constitutional order was established. What makes the case of Slovenia so interesting is that at that time [in the early 1990s] it was experiencing a series of extraordinary transitions. In a way, all human beings in all societies are always in transition because we all change and all societies evolve. But radical ruptures too often occur. In this particular case, the Slovenians were having to deal with extraordinarily radical transitions. Look how many mutations were taking place at the same time.

Slovenia had to transform itself from a member of a federation into an independent republic and from a socialist economy into a market economy. Now that it had left the Yugoslav Federation, it would have to develop its own bilateral trade treaties. After that, it would have to gain admittance to the EU. And, finally, it would have to change its currency, from the Yugolav dinar to the newly minted Slovenian tolar. Later, in January 2007, it would move yet again from the tolar to the euro. All of these changes were required by the circumstances. And on top of all this, it would have to negotiate with the Yugoslav Federation and its creditors regarding what share of the Yugoslav Federation's external debt would be [Slovenia's] responsibility. This financial transition, which was necessary to obtain international credit, took from 1991 to 1996.

ACS: How were [the Slovenians] able to manage such huge transitions?

FCO: With great wisdom. They managed to do it, first, because they had powerful internal consensus. Some theorists postulate that when countries have many diverse nationalities and much regional and economic diversity in their income distribution or income levels, it is difficult to achieve consensus. Slovenia, a fairly well-integrated society with sufficient consensus (the vote in favor of independence, as we saw, was 86 percent), was able to establish a coherent policy on all fronts. [It] managed to get technical expertise from the World Bank. Note here that Slovenia was the first eastern European country to transform itself from a recipient of World Bank aid into a donor country, and today it is still a donor country. It did that in only twelve or fourteen years, which is extraordinary. At the moment, Slovenia has a per capita income of $14,800, quite a high figure. (All the figures I am quoting are from 2004, and I am using the World Bank as the source so that comparisons will be possible.) When we calculate per capita income in terms of parity of purchasing power—a technical device used by the World Bank that adjusts per capita income to what a Slovenian citizen can purchase in goods with one dollar, so parity means that he can buy with one dollar [in Slovenia] what can be bought with the same dollar in the US market—when this adjustment is made, the $14,000 in Slovenia—I am talking US dollars—is equivalent to $20,730 in our market.

ACS: What natural resources does Slovenia have?

FCO: Mineral resources. That is why Slovenia's siderurgical and metallurgical industries are fairly well developed. That is why [it] export[s] a great deal of machinery—even construction machinery—and of course machine parts. A big share of its exports is related to manufacturing because Slovenia has a relatively well-developed metallurgical industry. That is one of its strengths.

ACS: And what about the service industry?

FCO: That is also very well developed. The population is well educated, a quality that dates back to the Yugoslav Federation. It was always a well-educated population, and their services in communications and even in the financial sector are fairly well developed. That is why they managed to make their financial transition relatively quickly.

As an indirect indicator of this sophistication, let me point out that in Puerto Rico there are 234 Internet users for each thousand inhabitants. Slovenia has 545 users per thousand inhabitants. This is an indirect indicator, but it still gives us a good idea of the people's sophistication.[1]

ACS: When Slovenia was part of the Yugoslav Federation, it had a Communist system of government. It was not a Western country, and it did not have a market economy. How [was it] able to make such a dramatic transition to a market economy?

FCO: The key was the plurality of its constitutional order. It is most interesting. [The Slovenian] system reflects liberal, socialist, democratic, and corporativist influences. Why liberal? Remember that it share[s] borders with Italy and Austria, so [it has] always had links with western Europe—which is where the liberal influence comes from. [The Slovenians] established a liberal parliamentary democracy with the classic separation of church and state and protection of human rights, although they also retained an extraordinary array of social benefits from socialism. In addition—and this is the most interesting point—their orientation was toward worker self-management.

"Worker self-management" means that workers participate in managing the enterprise. When privatization took place in Slovenia, it was not done as it was elsewhere, but rather through a process by which the workers themselves took control of the enterprises—something with which they already had experience. That is why foreign investment in Slovenia is less than in other eastern European countries—not nonexistent, but comparatively less. This is so because Slovenian entrepreneurial management has been the protagonist in this process. I find it interesting that [the Slovenians] did not totally discard the old order. They incorporated liberal democracy but retained self-management socialism.

In addition, they have had corporativist influence. Where there is no self-management, but there *are* workers' associations, Slovenians tend to

---

1. For data after 2007, when the interview was aired, see the table "World Bank Statistics" in part 3, "Comparative Tables."

set up coordinating bodies in which employers, workers, and public agencies or the government participate.

So it has been a rather pluralistic order, one that has enabled Slovenians to remain stable and to make many transitions at once.

ACS: It's impressive that such a small country—as we mentioned, it has half the population of Puerto Rico—has in just a few years been able to make so many transitions: economic, political, social, and even administrative, whereas in Puerto Rico we drown in a glass of water though we have had the same currency for one hundred years and the same type of government for fifty-something years. How has Slovenia been able to make all these transitions simultaneously?

FCO: Frankly, it surprises me, too. Such an achievement must be due to a great many factors. First among them, I imagine, was that Slovenia did not think of the change as a total break with its past. It kept worker self-management, for example, or at least some institutions related to self-management, inherited from its socialist past. It incorporated parliamentary democracy but retained social benefits. It was not a complete break with the past.

A second element that I think was important in facilitating these transitions was that because Slovenia was on the border between the West and the East, and Yugoslavia always had a somewhat independent relationship with the Soviet Union, [Slovenia] managed to maintain its cultural ties—in the broadest sense of the expression—with western Europe. It never lost cultural contact with those countries. And supporting such contact was the fact that for many years Yugoslavia was practically the number one supplier of immigrants to western Europe. Yugoslavian immigrants, especially Slovenian immigrants, were vital to the Yugoslav Federation's foreign-exchange reserves. I think those elements synergized to facilitate the transitions.

To that I believe we must add the enormous consensus among Slovenians, evidenced in the vote of 86 percent in favor of independence and then of more than 80 percent in favor of joining the EU in 2004. However, such a broad consensus also allowed for political diversity. If we were to characterize Slovenia's political orientation, we would have to say that it is pluralist, with a prevailing social-democratic current.

ACS: How have [the Slovenians] been able to harmonize politically the extremes on the left and right that must have emerged, especially without Slovenia's having a democratic tradition? Yugoslavia did not have democracy: it had Tito's dictatorship. Today, as in many other countries of the old Soviet bloc, there are still a Communist group supporting Tito's positions and another group that is capitalistic. When you say "pluralist," are you referring to the existence of many political parties?

FCO: Yes, there are several parties, and that has led to a parliamentary form of government, which often encourages multiple parties and the formation of governing coalitions. In Spain, we see this clearly. But in addition to that, we must consider that Slovenia was never characterized by extremes, not even in the years before it became the independent republic that it is today. It was a relatively conservative society, strongly Catholic, rather homogeneous in terms of ethnicity, and it always gave the impression of being a reluctant member of Tito's regime. I believe that reluctance caused all of these transitions to be well received by the vast majority of Slovenians.

ACS: Your point about Slovenia's having a parliamentary system is an important one, especially in the context of Puerto Rico, where there is much discussion about replacing the present bicameral legislature with a unicameral one. Like most of the world's democracies, Slovenia has a parliamentary system in which the executive branch arises from the legislative branch. (For anyone who wants to learn more about this subject, I have published a column in *El Nuevo Día* in which I compare the presidential system with the parliamentary system. It can be accessed at www.vozdelcentro.org.) Unfortunately, we, like the United States, do *not* have a parliamentary system, as do most democracies in the world.

FCO: True. Sometimes on television we can watch a Spanish or British parliamentary session while [Prime Minister] José Luis Rodríguez-Zapatero or Prime Minister David Cameron is making a presentation. In both parliaments, representatives of the opposition parties are able to stand up and debate, refute, what the majority leaders have said. A very intense, rich interaction develops from this—something that is unheard of in presidential regimes, where the president acts almost like a grand emperor.

ACS: Paco, is Slovenia's economy an open economy—that is, [does it] have foreign investment?

FCO: Yes, it is an open economy, but as I was telling you, local capital has been predominant. Slovenians began trading with the world through a network of bilateral treaties, which they negotiated very ably. The first thing they did was establish a foreign-affairs ministry. But, in addition, they did not commit to just one market—something that is very characteristic of these small countries—which I find interesting. It is totally different from the Puerto Rican experience. For example, 90 percent of Puerto Rico's total exports by value go to the United States. By contrast, Slovenia's biggest market is Germany, to which it exports only 20 percent by value. You might say, "Ah, but maybe they export 80 percent to the EU." In fact, they export between 50 and 60 percent to the EU. Estonia exports 26 percent to Finland, its primary market; Singapore exports 14 percent to Malaysia, its primary market.

In the case of Singapore, something odd occurred: its exports to the United States were increasing by percentage value, and concerns were raised. [The Singaporeans] said, "We don't intend to reduce the absolute amount of exports to the United States, but we must increase exports to other countries." That is, they didn't put all their eggs in one basket. Diversity is very important and is characteristic of all these countries [I just mentioned].

ACS: The two examples you mention are interesting because Finland is the gateway to Estonia. In the case of Singapore, much of its workforce lives in Malaysia and commutes every day.

FCO: A strategic objective is to maintain that diversity of markets and not to put all your eggs in one basket—that is, not to export 70 or 80 percent of your production to a single market because if that single market should fail or experience a recession, you may end up importing that recession. Another important factor for Slovenia is that it was very careful when negotiating its external-credit commitments, and it honored the external debt it had inherited from the Yugoslav Federation. It immediately joined the World Trade Organization. It negotiated a network of trade treaties to export mostly machinery, one of its strengths, but also to import various goods. At the same time, it began negotiating its entry into the EU, which was finalized in May 2004.

ACS: What motivated it to enter the European market?

FCO: [Slovenia's] incorporation into the EU and the European market did not happen without debate. To be sure about what they were doing, the Slovenians first had a broad discussion in which they identified the advantages and disadvantages and then made the decision by referendum. The discussion seems to me enlightening because it was not a matter of choosing between black and white. Both options had advantages and disadvantages, as always. Among the advantages of joining the EU, they identified these.

One advantage that carried a great deal of weight was external security. Let's not forget that while Slovenia was debating EU membership, the former Yugoslavia was violently unstable. So Slovenia thought, "Well, for external security, we should be linked to the EU." So argued those who favored joining.

A second advantage was the EU's harmony and stability in relation to trade. EU membership would mean the right to participate in developing a stable market of some 500 million consumers—which was not small potatoes.

As to the disadvantages, [Slovenia] would not be permitted to maintain any bilateral treaties once [it was] incorporated into the EU. But that would not mean losing access to those markets, which [it] would generally be able to maintain through EU treaties. Another disadvantage was the disparity between the smaller and the larger countries within the EU. But the Slovenians thought about this, and the advantages outweighed the disadvantages. In the end, in 2003, they voted 86 percent in favor of EU membership. That matched the figure for the vote for independence one decade earlier. Clearly, Slovenians are adept at building consensus.

ACS: Curiously, in 2004, which was the year Slovenia officially joined the EU, a group of sovereign republics entered the EU, ranging from countries as small as Malta to the Baltic republics of Lithuania, Latvia, and Estonia. Poland, a much larger country, also joined that year. [The entrance of all these countries] changed the structure and social composition of the EU. It is significant that Slovenia was forward looking and chose to join that group of countries.

FCO: I don't mean to say that the Slovenians have no problems. One problem that some commentators have pointed out recently is that

Slovenia has succeeded so well in so little time that the risk now is that they may become conservative. Only time will tell. But, certainly, it has been an extraordinarily dynamic country.

ACS: Paco, regarding unemployment, inflation, the cost of living, education, and health, how does Slovenia compare to other EU countries that were part of the Communist bloc before the fall of the Soviet Union?

FCO: During the early 1990s, production contracted, and unemployment increased. There was contraction for the first two years, but Slovenia managed to connect rapidly to the world economy. In 1993, economic growth began, and it has not stopped. The average growth for those countries has fluctuated between 4 and 6 percent. Once the 1990s ended, unemployment decreased, and at the beginning of the twenty-first century it was 5.9 percent. There has recently been some contraction; unemployment has increased slightly but is still around 5 or 6 percent.

ACS: How high is it in Puerto Rico?

FCO: To use a comparable variable, I will cite World Bank figures for 2000 and 2002. During those two years, the official unemployment figure for Slovenia was 5.9 percent; for Puerto Rico, it was 12.3 percent.

To this, I must add that the rate of participation in the workforce is extraordinarily low in Puerto Rico. In other words, the number of workers who are part of the workforce, whether employed or unemployed, out of the possible total, is 46 percent. In the countries of the old Communist bloc, participation in the workforce is 60, 65, or even 70 percent; these rates are high. In Puerto Rico, we have a low rate, which reflects, first, the existence of some dominant kind of informal economy and, second, an extraordinary pattern of dependency.

ACS: What are the facts about education?

FCO: Slovenia is an extraordinarily well-educated country. The figure for Internet usage that I mentioned is a strong indicator of this. [The Slovenians] have a good university in the capital city of Ljubljana, a traditional university, one that goes back to before the Tito regime, so they have a tradition that has given them enormous advantages, which they have put to good use. We must not forget that [Slovenia is] in the heart of the European continent.

ACS: And what about health?

FCO: The health indicators are positive. I'll mention one that is always mentioned because it has a powerful impact: the infant mortality rate, which is expressed in terms of the number of deaths for every thousand births. In Slovenia, the figure cited by the World Bank for 2003 is four; in Puerto Rico, it is nine.

ACS: I suppose that the health system as a whole also dates back to the time of Tito. Is that so?

FCO: Yes.

ACS: Because health is one thing the socialist system has always made a priority.

FCO: Of course. Let's not forget that, unlike other countries of eastern Europe, where social benefits have deteriorated, in Slovenia they made it a policy to maintain those benefits, and they have achieved that.

ACS: Paco, we have talked about how Slovenia has succeeded despite having a population barely half of Puerto Rico's and about how Slovenians have been able to make the transition from membership in the Yugoslav Federation under a Communist regime to independent status with a market economy and now to being a part of the EU. How would you explain this small-country phenomenon? Slovenia is not alone in its success. There are also Singapore and the Baltic countries. How have these small countries been able to achieve such dramatic development?

FCO: That is an interesting question because forty or fifty years ago there was much skepticism with regard to small countries. They were considered to be less than optimal economic communities, but today that is no longer so. Examples include Iceland, Cyprus, Malta, and Singapore as well as medium-size countries with small populations, such as Israel. I think that the key variable is the population. With 2 million inhabitants, Slovenia has a great future ahead of it, and it is no longer thought of with skepticism, but rather positively, as moving toward a good future.

We highlighted the political pluralism of Slovenia, but we must also stress its economic pluralism. Slovenia is an industrial country. Its principal export products are machinery and equipment because [it has] a well-developed metals industry, but it is also a country with good financial and health services. There is relevant agricultural activity, so it is a country with a multisector economy. There is economic pluralism even in terms of its institutions. That is, [it has] depended mostly on Slovenians for management because of their worker self-management tradition, but that does not stop [the Slovenians] from incentivizing external-capital investment, especially when such external capital will allow them to conquer foreign markets. So external capital, such as foreign investment, links them to foreign markets, which allows them to diversify their markets.

But we must also mention that years ago for small countries such as Slovenia, the economies of scale were cited as an insurmountable obstacle. Economies of scale means that production volume must be high so that the unit costs of production will decline, and the operation will be economically viable. If you have a small market, then, many activities are not viable. But in the modern world, this [obstacle] has been overcome thanks to international treaties.

Note that once Slovenia left the Yugoslav Federation, its first step was to establish a foreign-affairs ministry, whose mission was basically economic—that is, to negotiate bilateral trade treaties. It later joined the EU, but followed the same open approach to trade abroad because otherwise it would be limited by its size. In fact, a machinery and equipment industry would not be viable for a market of 2 million inhabitants or even for a country of 10 million inhabitants; it is viable for a market of *hundreds* of millions of inhabitants. And the hundreds of millions of inhabitants or consumers are accessible through that network of treaties. [Slovenia] initially accessed those consumers through bilateral treaties; today it is through the EU. This seems to be vital: political pluralism paired with economic pluralism.

ACS: How did Slovenia handle privatization?

FCO: [It] handled it very well. Because [the Slovenians] had the precedent of worker self-management, the state already had experience in ceding entrepreneurial prerogatives to entrepreneurial units, so the state granted credits to management teams and worker collectives in stable enterprises. In terms of actual operations, workers did not see a dramatic rupture; they simply moved from practicing self-management in a state enterprise to practicing self-management in an enterprise in which they had ownership rights. That is why, especially during the first ten or twelve years [after independence], foreign investment began to increase, but not dramatically.

One indicator used for measuring the impact of foreign investment is the relationship between national income—that is, the income of Slovenians—and the total value of production. In Slovenia, the national income of all Slovenians is 92 percent of the total value of production. In Puerto Rico, it is 63 percent. Why is this? It's because in Puerto Rico we have a great deal of foreign investment, and, as a result, a big part of Puerto Ricans' income escapes abroad. In Slovenia, very little income leaves the country because most of the production involves Slovenian owners.

ACS: But that will gradually change, won't it? Because Slovenia is part of the EU and is receiving investment from other EU countries—for example, an Italian company may want to buy a private Slovenian corporation.

FCO: That may well happen. As an example, the Irish are worried about the rate I mentioned just now—that is, the relationship between national income and the total value of production, which in their case [was up until recently] 75 percent. Ireland's percentage is higher than Puerto Rico's—whose rate is the lowest in the world—but it is lower than Slovenia's. This has the Irish concerned, and so they are trying to promote national industries more intensely. Indeed, they have recently managed to increase the rate.

An interesting case, different from this one, is that of Singapore, a country that has always depended heavily on foreign investors. It has compensated for this [dependence] by becoming, in turn, an investor abroad. In the same way that foreign investors receive income from Singapore, Singapore receives income from its investments overseas. For example, when Singapore sold its telephone company, it invested most of the proceeds of the sale in the European telephony industry. That is interesting. So in the case of Singapore the national income is practically equal to the GNP, which makes it a very particular case.

ACS: In fact, it is the same thing that China is doing. It has much of its investment in the US investment market, bonds, and the US external debt.

FCO: Yes, and I believe it is a wise policy.

ACS: The Chinese invest in US debt instruments and securities, and they also invest in Latin America and the Middle East. They are investing capital in these countries and are becoming the owners of key assets. By the way, the number of Chinese who are buying businesses from Italians in a city as unique as Venice is impressive. The biggest new investors in Venice are now the Chinese.

FCO: Note the moral of the story: it is not bad to be an importer of capital, but it is better to be an importer *and* exporter of capital at the same time.

ACS: Paco, what are the main lessons we can learn from Slovenia to apply to Puerto Rico?

FCO: Slovenia teaches us a lesson that had already been developed theoretically by a renowned British economist named Geoffrey Hodgson, who distinguishes "utopia" from "evotopia." He uses the term *evotopia* to refer to achievements obtained as a consequence of the progressive evolution of societies, whereas a utopia is a sort of ideal order toward which we should leap. Now, societies don't leap; they evolve. So Slovenia is an example of that evotopia to which Hodgson refers, not of a utopia. Utopia is a leap toward the unattainable; evotopia is evolution toward what can be done. I believe it is vital to move in this way because otherwise we are dreaming of political and economical orders that are impossible to achieve. And for the sake of achieving them, countless mistakes are made. I believe that is the great lesson from Slovenia.

There is a second great lesson related to this same evolutionist theory: a number of transitions can occur in a society. Let us not forget that Slovenia evolved from a socialist country into one that is not. We cannot call it a capitalist country because of the enormous number of social benefits it provides, but it certainly has evolved from a country with a centralized-planning regime into a more decentralized country that has joined the world's market economy. It has evolved from being a member of a federation, from not being sovereign, into an independent republic. It has moved from one monetary order to another twice in recent years: from the Yugoslav dinar to the Slovenian tolar to the EU euro. Over the same time, it has evolved from having no foreign relations as a sovereign country to having foreign relations and a series of bilateral treaties linking it economically to the world [and] to joining the great treaty that is the EU.

I am certain there have been other evolutions at the microeconomic level that we don't know about. Slovenia has also evolved from a state-property structure to a very particular private-property structure, most of which preserves the legacy of worker self-management from the previous regime. So Slovenia has experienced countless transitions because human beings are not monochromatic, but rather are extraordinarily complex, as are societies.

ACS: How would you compare Slovenia's position in 1991, when it became a sovereign country, with Puerto Rico's position today? If Puerto Rico today were starting a process such as the one Slovenia launched in 1991, what advantages would Puerto Rico have compared to the ones Slovenia had?

FCO: The first thing that makes Slovenia different from Puerto Rico is that when Slovenia declared its independence, the Yugoslav army was menacing it, and there was much uncertainty throughout the country. In terms of education, Slovenia has always had a well-educated population, as Puerto Rico does. So there is some common ground, too. Slovenia lacked foreign-currency reserves. When the tolar was its currency, it did not have one dollar or one euro in foreign currency. It had to bring much export capacity to bear to accumulate foreign currency, which is extraordinary. It started without any, with zero, and just three or four years after becoming independent it managed to accumulate foreign-currency reserves of $4 or $5 billion—still modest, but significant. This was achieved in 1995 or 1996. To do so, it had to make an enormous effort to establish trade treaties because foreign currency—which is the same as hard currency—is accumulated by exporting.

Puerto Rico currently has foreign currency because it is in the dollar zone. And it has a homogeneous population; there is some variation, but it is relatively homogeneous. We have no big regional or national differences. Guayanilla is not populated by Mongolians, but by Puerto Ricans; Ponce is not populated by Catalans, but by Puerto Ricans. So in this aspect, too, we resemble Slovenia.

Puerto Rico also has the possibility of strong relations with an economic center, such as Slovenia has with the rest of Europe. In our case, it is with the United States to the north and even with South America to the south.

At this time, it would not be too difficult for Puerto Rico to maintain its strong links with the United States and to establish closer links with Latin America; both are big markets. In addition, we might strengthen our links with the EU, where Spain—with which we have cultural links—might serve us as a point of entry.

It is curious that Puerto Rico exports less to Latin American than to Singapore, which is in the Pacific. Here is yet another lesson that Slovenia teaches us: strive for diversity in exports and imports while maintaining close links with the center, which in Slovenia's case is the EU.

ACS: All of this recalls the saying "Necessity is the mother of invention." Slovenia faced a dilemma that forced [it] to find creative solutions. This has not happened in Puerto Rico, which, because of all the welfare funds it receives from the United States, is in a comfortable position without having to do anything. That is part of the problem we face.

FCO: True. I also believe that the Slovenians have been wise to develop a democratic, parliamentary form of government that focuses on fostering consensus. The capacity to forge consensus comes with democratic, parliamentary forms of government. In Puerto Rico, a bipartisan political system has been entrenched. First, the lack of a parliamentary system has resulted in very poor communication between the executive and legislative branches. Second, the political system is bipartisan, oriented toward one [party's] displacing the other, not toward negotiation across political sectors.

ACS: In today's program, we have discussed Slovenia, a country that achieved sovereignty in 1991 after leaving the Yugoslav Federation and that joined the EU in 2004. Slovenia, with only 2 million people, half of Puerto Rico's population, has achieved some of the most impressive economic growth in the world.

Suggested Reading on Slovenia

Cox, John K. *Slovenia—Evolving Loyalties*. London: Routledge, 2005.

Mrak, Mojmir, Matija Rojec, and Carlos Silva-Jáuregui, eds. *Slovenia: From Yugoslavia to the European Union*. Washington, DC: World Bank, 2004.

Ramet, Sabrina P., and Danica Fink-Hafner, eds. *Democratic Transition in Slovenia: Value Transformation, Education, and Media*. College Station: Texas A&M Univ. Press, 2006.

Ireland

An island with the same population as Puerto Rico. Before, the people emigrated. Now, they are returning to their country to benefit from its progress.

—ÁNGEL COLLADO-SCHWARZ

Ireland in 2010

Population:	4 million
Territory:	70,000 square miles
Population density:	65 per square mile
Gross domestic product (GDP):	$211.4 billion
Gross national income (GNI):	$183.7 billion
GNI per capita:	$41,000
Unemployment rate:	11.7 percent (2006–2009)
Internet users:	69.7 per 100 people

Source: World Bank, *World Development Indicators* (Washington, DC: World Bank, 2011).

Updated Comments

For more than two decades, Ireland's rate of economic growth was more than 6 percent per year. During most of that period, growth was based on the coupling of Irish human capital to export-oriented investments. There was then a turning point—the precise time is still ill defined—after which speculation in real estate became excessively important to the economy, leading eventually to a bubble. Construction took on an excessive role as a leading growth sector, and Irish banks funded the speculative bubble with loans from other European countries.

Ireland has been in the grip of recession in the years since the bubble burst, with real GDP declining by 3.0 percent, 7.0 percent, and 0.8 percent in 2008, 2009, and 2010, respectively. No growth is foreseen for 2011. Current forecasts are for modest growth of between 1.3 and 2.1 percent from 2012 to 2015. Meanwhile, the unemployment rate has been higher than 13 percent at times.

Until 2007, Ireland's public debt was low: 25 percent of GDP that year. After the bubble burst, the government decided to bail out private banks by turning private debts into state obligations. As a result, public debt rose to 95 percent of GDP in 2010. The Irish government struck an agreement in late 2010 with the European Union (EU) and the International Monetary Fund to implement an austerity program supported with $112 billion in loans to capitalize banks and forestall a government default.

Like other countries, large and small, Ireland had relaxed financial regulations to the point of jeopardizing the entire economy. But the fundamentals of the Irish system are still strong: a young and capable labor force and a resilient productive sector oriented toward exports. It would be foolish to downplay the difficulties faced by the Irish economy, but so would it be to underestimate its foundations.

Francisco Catalá-Oliveras
Juan Lara

Interview

Interview aired on La Voz del Centro, *Univision Radio Puerto Rico and New York, May 27, 2007.*

ÁNGEL COLLADO-SCHWARZ: The Republic of Ireland is part of the European Union, and its population is very similar in size to that of Puerto Rico—4 million people. Ireland was one of the poorest countries in Europe. During the nineteenth and twentieth centuries, there was a huge wave of Irish immigration to the United States. In recent years, the situation has changed dramatically: now Irish immigrants are returning to their homeland to benefit from the new opportunities there. Paco, give us some background on Ireland.

FRANCISCO CATALÁ-OLIVERAS: First of all, the Republic of Ireland was one of the first [colonized] countries to achieve sovereignty in the twentieth century. In 1921, after a long war, the Anglo-Irish Treaty was signed, establishing an Irish Free State, which was still, however, subordinate to Great Britain. In 1949, when it was a free state, a kind of autonomous state, it became the Republic of Ireland.

We must make one distinction for the benefit of our listeners: Northern Ireland is not the Republic of Ireland. The island of Ireland is made up of thirty-two counties. Six of them, in the north, have remained under the sovereignty of Great Britain. The Republic of Ireland is in the south. It is strongly Catholic, unlike Northern Ireland, which is mainly Protestant. Based on such differences, political and religious lines of division have been drawn between the two jursidictions.

What is interesting about Ireland is that it has endured an extremely difficult past. The Great Famine of the nineteenth century, which people still talk about today, resulted in great floods of migration. However, to talk about times closer to our days and to establish a parallel with Puerto Rico, let's bear in mind that in the 1950s, after the republic had been established, more than 400,000 Irish men and women emigrated. By the way, that figure is very similar to the flow of migration out of Puerto Rico in the same decade, which points to the inability, both here and there, to generate enough jobs and the means for residents to make a living—something that eventually changed dramatically in Ireland. The change was so extreme—a complete somersault—that today, in 2008, Ireland is one of the richest countries in the EU.

Per capita income in Ireland is now higher than in Great Britain, its former colonial power. It has also just recently risen higher than in France and Germany, and that is an extraordinary accomplishment. Only a couple of other countries—also very small, by the way, Luxembourg and Denmark—exceed [Ireland] by that measure.

ACS: The founder and first president of the Republic of Ireland, Eamon de Valera, was an inspiration for Pedro Albizu-Campos.[1] During the years that Albizu-Campos lived in Boston, while he was at Harvard University, he studied the thought of that important twentieth-century leader. There were many Irish immigrants in the Boston area, among them the Kennedy family.

FCO: De Valera and Albizu-Campos had two things in common: their nationalism and their Catholicism.

ACS: Returning to the case of Ireland, Paco, tell us about the formula [it] used. How did [it] achieve such a dramatic change, from being the poorest country in Europe to becoming the vanguard state [it is] today?

FCO: After becoming a state in the 1950s or beginning in 1949, Ireland entered a period during which it still looked at the former colonial power as a source of problems and solutions because the colonial legacy weighs heavily. One cannot lift it off one's shoulders so easily. Little by little, though, [Ireland's] focus shifted in three senses: toward itself, toward continental Europe, and toward the world. I think this [shift] was fundamental. By the beginning of the 1970s, Ireland had joined the European Community—today the EU—and was beginning to establish certain industrialization programs, but very slowly.

In the 1960s, 36 percent of the labor force was still in agriculture, working on small and inefficient farms, with cruel seasonal unemployment. Emigration still weighed heavily.

---

1. Pedro Albizu-Campos (1891–1965), educated at Harvard University and former officer in the US Army, was the principal leader of the Puerto Rico Nationalist Party starting in the 1930s and led the Puerto Rico Revolution of 1950. He spent most of his adult life in prison.

The picture began to change with a program called simply "Economic Development," which had two central features. One was the mechanization and consolidation of farming. The objective was for the Irish to become more competitive with respect to Europe's food market and to export food products to that market. This [objective] contrasts with [the approach taken in] Puerto Rico, where agrarian reforms were conducted not to transform parcels of land into production units, but to distribute those parcels, which led to the creation of many small farms. In contrast, Ireland set out to mechanize and consolidate agrarian enterprises to make them competitive and able to export food products.

Of course, the increase in farm production owing to mechanization led to a reduction in agricultural employment: higher production resulted in fewer jobs. So the government complemented this increased production with a second element: it attracted direct foreign investment that would generate new industrial jobs, as had been done in Operation Bootstrap in Puerto Rico during the 1960s. The Irish had always planned to attract foreign investment to strengthen their economy and to foster entrepreneurial capacity.

In 1980, Ireland had not yet flourished, at least as we know it today. But even by then Irish-owned manufacturing enterprises were providing two-thirds of the jobs. [Ireland] did not, though, stand out for [its] export activities; those entrepreneurs generated only about one-third of manufacturing exports.

In 1987—and we are not talking here about ancient history, but just twenty years ago—per capita income in Ireland was 69 percent of the European average, so it was below average for Europe. Today, twenty years later, it is 140 percent—that is, 40 percent above the average for Europe. In terms of per capita income, Ireland is one of the richest countries in Europe.

What did it do, then, between 1980 and 2007? It certainly did something because it did not rest on its hands after mechanizing agriculture—something it did well—and after attracting foreign capital. In 1982, Ireland carried out an inclusive, broad-based study of its situation and produced a document called the *Telesis Report*. That study evaluated Ireland's industrial policies from the 1950s to 1982 and found, first, that government incentives were very costly. The *Telesis* authors reported, in effect, "We are giving subsidies, we are giving tax exemptions, and companies come, but then they go. Once their tax exemptions expire, they leave." If this story sounds familiar, it is not mere coincidence. Ireland also faced a poorly skilled labor force, a lack of research-and-development expertise in manufacturing, and weak links between foreign and national companies.

The *Telesis Report* back then painted a picture of Puerto Rico today. The problems it identified in 1982 are the same ones we have been pointing out in Puerto Rico for a number of years. So how did the Irish address those problems? They began to take simple, achievable measures. To stimulate national enterprises, they did something that seems to me so incredibly simple that I wonder how we ourselves failed to think about it before. First, they told the national enterprises: "We are going to undertake joint marketing of your products so that you can also export jointly to external markets. We are going to provide warehouses in foreign countries, say, in Spain, if that is the market we are targeting, or in Germany or in the United States. You will send your products there, and from there they will be distributed. This will be done by the state. We will provide joint warehouses. You, the participating enterprises, will help us, and by providing the warehouses, we will help you promote exports to foreign markets because, after all, the markets in these countries are relatively small." As we said at the beginning, we are talking about some 4 million inhabitants. To me, this concept seems absolutely extraordinary.

We have said in previous radio programs that one of the problems these countries sometimes face—and it is a problem in Puerto Rico, too—is the difference between the gross national income or gross national product, which is the income received by the residents of the country, whether by proprietors or by salaried workers, and the total volume of production generated in the country, the GDP. When there is a notable gap between these two, it means that much of the income generated in the country is leaving the country because most of the owners of the enterprises in the country are foreign.

Well, in Ireland, they were concerned about that, and it is also a concern in Puerto Rico—one that we have referred to on several occasions in previous programs. Puerto Rico's GNI is currently 63 or 64 percent of

GDP. In Ireland in the 1980s, it was nearly 70 percent, and they considered that a problem.

After [Ireland] began emphasizing domestic capital—without neglecting foreign capital—and after it began exporting some of that domestic capital to develop warehouses, the portion of Irish total production that was GNI, which had been 70 percent, increased to 85 percent by 2005 or 2006. [The Irish] set their goals and achieved them. And the change that took place between 1982 and the beginning of this new century—by 2000, Ireland was already referred to as the "Celtic Tiger"—was really extraordinary.

ACS: How did they manage the political issues?

FCO: Ireland has a parliamentary system that is basically centrist. It seems that politically [it has] moved away from the extremes. But unlike Great Britain, let's say, which has moved to the right, with privatization and other conservative-leaning policies, Ireland has been a somewhat more corporativist state. For example, Ireland in 2004 faced certain fiscal restrictions (again, the parallel with Puerto Rico is purely coincidental), in light of which the state froze the salaries of public servants and met with labor unions. In Ireland, they have what are called "trisector committees"; when formulating public policy and the like, they form committees with representation from the private or entrepreneurial sector, the labor unions, and the government sector. Well, [the government and private sectors] met with the labor unions, and the unions agreed to a salary freeze, but in exchange they requested that the national budget give priority to three things: education, health, and social welfare. The government agreed to that and in fact followed through with it.

In the 2004 national budget, those three elements came to $32 billion. Let me repeat that: $32 billion. If we add up those three elements in the budget of Puerto Rico and include all federal funds, the total is not even half that amount. This is what we are talking about: a far-reaching educational system and superb health services, for which, evidently, Ireland required a broader tax base than it had. We can talk about that when you like.

ACS: Paco, how did [the government] manage to move public opinion to achieve approval of that $32 billion?

FCO: To start with, let us admit that national spirit in the Irish Republic is enormous. Also, Ireland has two things that I consider fundamental. The first is a very broad tax base. Having a broad tax base means that no sector feels that its tax burden is too great. Let me explain further. Ireland's tax base includes corporate and individual taxes; a value-added tax, which is basically a tax on consumption; property taxes; and, of course, a tax for social security, similar to the Social Security tax that employers and workers pay here. There, employers pay double what workers pay into the social-security fund.

Now, because the tax base is very broad and quite efficient, no sector feels that it is paying too much. That tax base makes it possible for 42 percent of the GNI to be paid in taxes. In Puerto Rico, [that figure] is 15 percent, but with a tax base that is not very broad, so that some sectors feel they are being overtaxed.

Another thing is that Ireland [has], besides a broad tax base, an extraordinary public-transportation system. In Puerto Rico, 5 percent of the workers in the metropolitan area use public transportation; in Dublin, the Irish capital, public-transport users are something more than 40 percent because [Ireland has] first-rate public transportation in addition to top-flight educational and health services. In other words, [it has] a broad tax base that has translated into some extraordinary public services. That is the key: the Irish use public services to achieve consensus with regard to budget priorities.

ACS: You mention transportation, but if we look at the public-health services—not just in Ireland, but throughout the EU—we find that they are very superior to private services. You go to a public hospital like the ones I have been to in Europe, and it's as if you are entering a private hospital in New York or in any other big American city.

FCO: That is certainly so.

ACS: So you pay taxes, but you also receive the benefits of the high taxes you pay.

FCO: That way it is relatively easy to achieve consensus, and, of course, Ireland's labor sector is highly aware of it. Their participation in those tri-sector committees strongly reflects the priorities of the Irish people.

ACS: So Ireland has become one of the most advanced countries in the EU in just twenty years. People previously laughed at the Irish and even made jokes at their expense. Nobody is laughing at them now. Their country has the same population as Puerto Rico, and it has become the star of Europe. Paco, tell us about the Irish labor force.

FCO: We should start by noting that Ireland today has nearly 2 million employed people . . . 2 *million*.

The population is 4 million. Compare that to Puerto Rico, where the number of people with jobs is between 1.1 and 1.2 million. This indicates several things. First, that the unemployment rate in Puerto Rico must be much higher than in Ireland, which is in fact true. In Ireland, the unemployment rate is now around 4 percent; in Puerto Rico, it is three times higher, around 12 percent. Second, it indicates that the [labor-]participation rate in Ireland—that is, the number of people in the labor market relative to the total population—is much higher than in Puerto Rico.

In Ireland, for example, out of the population sixteen and older who can work, 70 percent are in the labor market; in Puerto Rico, the figure is 47 percent. So Ireland has a very dynamic labor market, and in terms of work it has a much more active population than Puerto Rico's.

But there is another fascinating issue. Let's take the agricultural labor force. In Ireland, more than 100,000 people are employed in agriculture. Of course, this is about 3 or 4 percent of the total [number of workers] because we are talking about 2 million workers. In Puerto Rico, agricultural jobs are really marginal; certainly, there is more agricultural land in Ireland than in Puerto Rico. Ireland has a little more than 70,000 square kilometers, whereas Puerto Rico has 9,000. Another element of the Irish labor market that I find very interesting is that 188,000 people are employed in the health sector, mostly in the public sector, and another 123,000 in education.

Clearly, health and education are priorities for Ireland, and we must take into account that health and education are two very particular forms of service. On the one hand, they are goods that you consume because you consume education and you consume health services. On the other hand, they are productive goods because with a healthier and better-educated population you generate more productive activity. And apparently a great part of the boom that Ireland has experienced for many years, especially from 1980 to 2007, has been a result of the high priority that government has assigned to health and education.

If we consider public-sector employees—for example, in management and defense and in central-government positions—we can say that in Ireland there are around 100,000 employees. If you add to them the employees in health and education, the number exceeds 300,000, which is a figure similar to Puerto Rico's. But there is a difference: those 300,000 are in a job market that already has 2 million people employed; here the 300,000 are part of a job market that has no more than 1.2 million people employed. Proportionately, there are more public servants in Puerto Rico than in Ireland, though in absolute terms the figure is about the same, 300,000. That is why I believe that the discussion of whether our government is large or small is out of focus. It all depends on what our priorities are in the public sector and how its growth compares with that of the private sector.

We do have a problem. But it is not that our government is too big, it is that the private sector is too small.

ACS: As we mentioned in an earlier discussion, the Singaporean government is heavily involved in the economic sector, and government quality standards are first rate.

FCO: Certainly. That is also the case in Ireland. They have high-quality services in health and education and in other areas as well. Here [in Puerto Rico] we have quite correctly perceived our public services as deteriorating in quality, and that is a trend we need to turn around as soon as possible.

ACS: It is interesting that in education Puerto Rico is more like Europe than like the United States. For example, in the United States, as we all know, the best universities are private, and public institutions are where students and professors go who can't get into private schools. Puerto Rico is like Europe in that the best university is the public university, the University of Puerto Rico. As a general rule, the best professors and students want to be at the University of Puerto Rico.

FCO: That is an excellent observation. We can even say that the United States is the exception in this, when you examine the same issue in the European and Asiatic countries and in Puerto Rico.

ACS: NASA goes to the Mayagüez campus to recruit the best graduate students. For example, the director of the Mars Exploration Program is a Puerto Rican who graduated from the Mayagüez campus.

Now, [if we go] back to the subject of Ireland's labor force, how many people are in the service sector as opposed to the manufacturing sector?

FCO: In nonagricultural productive activities, there are about 300,000 employees. In construction, there are nearly 200,000. If you add the 300,000 in nonagricultural activities and the construction sector, we are talking about more than 500,000 employees. The rest, about 100,000, are in transportation and communications; the others in services are mainly in financial and public services, such as we mentioned earlier. So there is a real base for productive activity. We say *productive* activity, but remember that all activities are productive; unfortunately, we economists have the bad habit of calling nonservice activities productive, as if services were not productive, when in fact they are. But when we talk about manufacturing and construction activities, Ireland's base is much broader than Puerto Rico's in terms of jobs.

In Puerto Rico today, manufacturing employment is barely at 130,000. And it has been decreasing. It was at 160,000 several years ago, and its base is getting smaller. The employment base in Ireland as well as in Singapore is broader. In manufacturing, Ireland stands out mainly in electronics. Ireland is one of the top exporters of software in the world, surpassing the United States and not only in software, but also in hardware—that is, in computers. It is the principal supplier of computers to the EU. So in the electronics sector—which includes information-management software and the hardware related to it—Ireland is a world leader.

To this, add the traditional pharmaceutical industry—as in Puerto Rico, it has been a priority in Ireland's industrial development—which recently has also been incorporating biotechnology. But what has caught my attention the most is Ireland's leading role in the computer and software business.

ACS: We need to point out that no single industrial sector dominates in Ireland, as has happened in Puerto Rico, where pharmaceuticals are a huge percentage of manufacturing production.

FCO: No. In Ireland, there is much more diversification. In fact, one of the weaknesses of Puerto Rico's economy, which we have commented on previously, is its reliance on a handful of manufacturing sectors. Nearly 65 percent of our exports are chemical and pharmaceutical products. That is not the case in Ireland, where there is more manufacturing diversification.

ACS: Do we have any data on Puerto Rico's commercial relations with Ireland?

FCO: On this subject, the foreign-trade frameworks may be confusing. In terms of imports from foreign countries into Puerto Rico, Ireland is number one. I believe we import between $9 and $10 billion from there. When you hear that, you might well ask, "What is happening here?" Well, what is happening is that some pharmaceutical companies here import substances from Ireland that are essential to the manufacture of certain medicines. With a single decision by any of these pharmaceutical companies tomorrow, this [scenario] could change instantly. Our exports to Ireland are very modest.

ACS: Paco, Ireland is like Singapore in that it has achieved all of this development without natural resources. We have long been told that Puerto Rico cannot be sovereign because it has no natural resources. Discuss that factor with us.

FCO: Ireland's economic development has occurred under very unfavorable conditions. If one had been a pessimist at the time, one would have said, "Well, it is not going to develop." First, one would have said that because of the lack of natural resources. Second, when Ireland became totally independent back in 1949, it was just after the Second World War. Europe had been the center stage of that war; this [situation] was entirely different from the [one] in Puerto Rico, which is part of the New World, where there was no scenario directly related to the Second World War. Also, during that time most of the manufacturing activity was located in Northern Ireland, which was and is still part of the United Kingdom. Most of the manufacturing activity was there, not in what is today the Republic of Ireland.

Because the Republic of Ireland was predominantly agricultural, the objectives were to generate an agricultural surplus and to finance the local manufacturing sector as well as to attract direct foreign investment. In these things, everything was against them.

Third, the Irish were affected—I would say even psychologically affected—by Great Britain's colonial legacy. In the beginning, they sought solutions to their problems from the former colonial power. They were dazzled by Great Britain. They passed several years in a kind of lethargy, a product of the colonial legacy, before they finally realized that they had to change their view of themselves, of the entire European continent, and of the world, though without rejecting Great Britain.

Ireland's principal client today is the United States, to which [it] export[s] about 20 percent, followed by Great Britain with 18 percent, then Germany and France. When you add them all up, the EU receives 40 to 50 percent of Irish exports. But when we look at individual countries, the United States is number one.

This shows how Ireland began to transcend the narrowness of the colonial tradition it had inherited and how it overcame that narrowness. Once [the Irish] overcame that mentality, they thrust forward into their industrialization programs and established trading links with Europe and the rest of the world.

ACS: We must emphasize that when the United Kingdom granted Ireland its independence, it retained a region in the North of the island, which was the most prosperous region economically. In that region, whose main city is Belfast, most of the population is Protestant, whereas the rest of the island is Catholic. That is why the fight in Ireland between North and South calls to mind a religious struggle, though in fact it has been a political and class struggle. Throughout the Troubles, the wealthy were pro-English Protestants, the poor were nationalist Catholics.

In 1972, I was in the north of Ireland, in Belfast and Londonderry, reporting for the *San Juan Star,* and I published a photo essay. I was twenty years old and a college student. The time I spent in the north of Ireland was an extraordinary adventure. The United States was playing a deeply ambiguous role: prominent Americans were raising funds for the free-dom fighters (the Irish Republican Army) even though the United States was an ally of the United Kingdom. It was a bloody war for both sides.

Fortunately, the violence has ended, and the island will eventually become one nation. Now the roles have been reversed, and the most prosperous zone is the South, the Republic of Ireland, and not the North, which is part of the United Kingdom.

FCO: Your observation is right on target. Remember that when independence was achieved, most of the industries were in the North, which was the prosperous sector. Now things are switched around—the prosperous sector is in the South, in the Republic of Ireland.

It is interesting what has happened in Northern Ireland, where there are several problems. First, the labor-participation rate is low; second, there is heavy dependence on government transfers. They have all the difficulties that tend to arise in colonies that become dependent on the colonial power: dependency and lack of economic activity.

In Northern Ireland, the public sector is disproportionately larger than the private sector because there are few incentives for private enterprises to establish themselves there; companies today would rather establish themselves in the South of Ireland. So things have reversed: now it is Northern Ireland that is suffering the problems that come with being subordinate.

ACS: Paco, I would like you to give us some data comparing Puerto Rico with Ireland.

FCO: Well, we are talking about two islands. The Republic of Ireland has 4 million inhabitants, and Puerto Rico has roughly the same. As for GDP—that is, the volume of goods and services produced—it is far higher in Ireland than in Puerto Rico. Using 2004 figures, we are talking about $183 million in Ireland and nearly $80 million in Puerto Rico, so it is almost $100 million higher in Ireland—a very great difference indeed.

Regarding the GNI—which is the income received by workers and entrepreneurs residing in the country—it is also considerably higher in Ireland. Logically, if production is higher, income will also be higher, but as I told you earlier, it is the share of production income that makes Ireland's GNI higher than Puerto Rico's. Here in Puerto Rico, that share is around 64 percent. In Ireland, at the time I first made the comparison, it was 75 percent; today, current figures show it is more than 80 percent.

This means [the Irish] have succeeded in stimulating national capital, obviously without neglecting direct foreign investment. It also means they have succeeded in generating linkages between national capital and foreign capital. We must remember that one of the key policies in developing a country is to have foreign capital stimulate the development of national capital. How is that achieved? By linking the two—that is, one sells to the other, one provides services to the other, the local sector on one side and the foreign sector on the other.

ACS: That was the opportunity Puerto Rico missed when it had [US Internal Revenue Code] Section 936 capital here.

FCO: That's right. I believe that 936 will go down in history as a lost opportunity, and it has been irreparably lost. When these absolute production volumes are expressed per capita—that is, in terms of how much per inhabitant—it is obvious that the difference is huge.

In Puerto Rico in 2004, per capita GNI was $13,000. In Ireland that same year, it was $34,000. In Ireland, that figure is [now] drawing close to $40,000—which, by the way, as I said at the beginning of this program, places Ireland in the top ranks of the EU, above Great Britain, France, and Germany, which are world economic powers.

Unemployment in Ireland [now] is only 4 percent.[2] In fact, in some sectors [the Irish] face the problem of having positions open for which they cannot find employees. In Puerto Rico, unemployment is around 12 percent and is remaining stubbornly at that level. That is the official figure and doesn't reflect that the labor-participation rate is very low. If the participation rate were higher, our unemployment would be 15, 16, or 17 percent, or who knows how high? That is not the situation in Ireland, where the labor-participation rate is very high. So we must qualify the comparison, as you quite correctly say.

Ireland's principal market is, obviously, the EU. But defining the market as being made up of nation-states, we have the United States accounting for 19 or 20 percent of Ireland's exports. Puerto Rico's principal market

2. For data after 2007, when the interview was aired, see the table "World Bank Statistics" in part 3, "Comparative Tables."

is the United States, at 80 percent. This [difference] tells us that Ireland has diversified its market links with the rest of the world and that Puerto Rico has not—its export market of choice continues to be the United States, without any diversification, which places us in a position that is strategically weaker than Ireland's. We have said so on several radio shows. In all the successful countries we have examined, we have pointed out this fact: they have greatly diversified their external markets.

ACS: Part of all this has to do with political status. Ireland is part of the EU based on the fact that it is sovereign. That is, when it joined the EU, it was as an equal partner with the United Kingdom, Spain, France, Germany, and so on. In this regard, Puerto Rico is at a great disadvantage, given its colonial status.

FCO: I believe that is Puerto Rico's *great* disadvantage, and it is about time that we Puerto Ricans admit it frankly and honestly, whatever our political persuasion. That is our great disadvantage when we compare ourselves with those other countries. We puff ourselves up—to put it bluntly—and talk about how Puerto Rico's competitors are Ireland or Singapore and so on, but we do not state the differences clearly. To compete, we will need to work out what the differences are to see what it is we must do to get ourselves into a favorable position so that we can compete globally and in the international market.

ACS: An important element in developing the economy of a country is being able to set the immigration policy. A sovereign nation can import the skilled manpower it needs for its economy. Our current colonial status does not allow us to set such a policy. We can't even grant tourist visas. We depend on Washington's public policy and priorities.

FCO: That's the way it is. And when we compare ourselves to Ireland in terms of health indicators, education levels, technological expertise, the use of computers and the Internet, Ireland surpasses us. In its budgets for education, health, transportation—that is, in its budget for public services—Ireland surpasses us. If they surpass us in all these items, how can they not surpass us in economic growth? How can they not surpass us in attracting external capital? How can they not surpass us in stimulating national capital? Well, they surpass us in all these latter items because they surpass us in the former.

ACS: Paco, let's go back to the subject of the study conducted by Ireland to develop its new economic model.

FCO: Look, in every economic-planning process, in every national development project, there are two basic, two principal things that must be done. One is a diagnosis. How are we doing? What are our weak sectors? What are our strong ones? What sectors will be our priorities? What is the root of our unemployment problem? And it must be more than a quantitative analysis; it must also seek to understand the *causes.* Is there enough diversification in the economy? Are there enough links to the rest of the world? That diagnosis must be done item by item.

Then after the diagnosis, we must establish policy instruments—that is, we must identify the tools we need to face each of the problems diagnosed, each of which may require different tools. So once we have identified the problems, we need to identify the policy instruments, in the best sense of the term, to face each of the problems.

In principle, this [process] is simple, but several things are required. Most important, it requires great honesty and political courage because a diagnosis is a confession. Just like in church, you need a confession, you need contrition, and you need true purpose to mend your ways. The purpose of mending your ways must be linked to public policies.

What did Ireland do in the *Telesis Report* of the 1980s, which is the plan that put [the Irish] in the position they are in today, [twenty-five] years later? What did [it] do?

First, Ireland examined one by one its government incentives and their costs, whether these incentives were to promote infrastructure—such as tax subsidies—or were exemptions or credits. The Irish asked themselves, "What are the costs? Are those costs justified by the jobs, production, and exports they are generating?"

They did a thorough examination and found that those incentives were costing too much, so they needed to revise them. Not eliminate them, but *revise* them. When you say "revise," people here sometimes think you mean to eliminate, isn't that so? But no, they revised them, one by one. It's as if you took the Industrial Incentives Act here in Puerto Rico and revised it. Now, if what we have is social costs that are too high, accompanied by privatized benefits that do not match those social costs, then we have problems.

Second, what is the behavior of enterprises in our country, the national and foreign companies? What causes that behavior? To what markets are they exporting? How long do they stay here? What do they do when some incentives expire? Why do some leave and others stay? That is, the behavior of enterprises must be examined—in this case, of course, the behavior of private-sector enterprises.

The Irish found that there was a flood of "runaway" plants. By "runaway," they meant that many enterprises closed when their tax exemptions, analogous to ours, expired; some of them closed even without their exemptions expiring—they were leaving for other reasons. What, then, were those reasons?

[The Irish] found that foreign enterprises were leaving in part because they had no linkages to national capital. Because of that, it was less costly for them to leave. When they have established linkages and are receiving services from national enterprises, leaving is more expensive for them. So public policy must be designed to make it expensive for foreign enterprises to leave the country. There are always some that will leave. This [situation] is very dynamic, however—others will come. But those linkages must be established. Ireland set out deliberately to stimulate linkages between national capital and foreign capital.

The Irish also found that few national enterprises were engaged in export activities. This [situation] is analogous to that in Puerto Rico today, where most exporting is done by foreign capital. Some national enterprises export goods or provide services to the foreign sector, but they are the exception. That was the same problem Ireland faced in 1982.

So what could the Irish do about that? They arrived at something concrete. [The solution] was not about slogans—they did not simply call for support for local businesses—it was something concrete. As I mentioned earlier, they said, "Let's establish warehouses in foreign countries, in any market you wish, wherever you want to export to. Let's set up those warehouses to handle distribution to those foreign markets." This idea was simple in principle, very concrete, and designed to stimulate exports.

It was targeted at solving a very concrete problem that had been identified. There were small businesses that could not enter a foreign market on their own, but those businesses formed groups whose members were not competing among themselves because they represented different export sectors. So they joined the effort to do joint marketing and used the same warehouse in the foreign country, in the foreign market.

The *Telesis Report* also assigned a high priority to research and development and to the development of information technology. We are talking about the 1980s. Giving priority to those sectors enabled Ireland to become an information technology–exporting power, and it was done jointly with the development of educational centers specializing in science and technology.

You will recall that health and education are among the key public services in Ireland. Well, [the Irish] have given a great push to the field of education since 1982, to the development of science and technology education centers. I think the *Telesis* program explains the enormous development of Ireland.

To that we must add a kind of philosophy. No country is Icaria. No country is Shangri-La. No country is a utopia. But in Ireland they made improving the quality of life a top priority so that development denoted increased quality of life. Production indicators may increase, but if the quality of life does not improve, something is wrong.

For example, the increase in vacation time in Ireland was no coincidence, nor was the shortening of the work week. The work week in Ireland cannot exceed forty-eight hours, including overtime. So they have also focused on cultivating a good life, a life better characterized by being than by having.

I find these measures fascinating—increases in vacation time and reductions in the work week to forty-eight hours, including overtime—because in Puerto Rico this discussion is somewhat out of focus.

ACS: In today's program, we have discussed Ireland, a country with the same population as Puerto Rico, 4 million inhabitants, that just twenty-five years ago was one of the poorest countries in Europe. Based on a platform of sovereignty, Ireland joined the EU and became the star among the developed countries of Europe.

Suggested Reading on Ireland

Jones, Eric. *The European Miracle: Environments, Economies, and Geopolitics in the History of Europe and Asia.* Cambridge, UK: Cambridge Univ. Press, 2010.

O'Sullivan, Michael, and Rory Miller, eds. *What Did We Do Right? Global Perspectives on Ireland's Miracle.* Dublin: Blackhall, 2010.

Sweeney, Paul. *The Celtic Tiger: Ireland's Economic Miracle Explained.* Dublin: Oak Tree Press, 1998.

Israel

A small country in the desert that has managed to establish a high-tech economy and an agricultural program to supply all its food needs and also export farm products.

—ÁNGEL COLLADO-SCHWARZ

Israel in 2010

Population:	8 million
Territory:	22,000 square kilometers
Population density:	359 per square kilometer
Gross domestic product (GDP):	$217.3 billion
Gross national income (GNI):	$207.2 billion
GNI per capita:	$27,170
Unemployment rate:	7.6 percent (2006–2009)
Internet users:	65.4 per 100 people

Source: World Bank, *World Development Indicators* (Washington, DC: World Bank, 2011).

Updated Comments

Israel's economy grew better than 5 percent per year during 2004–7. After a 4 percent gain in real GDP in 2008, Israel felt the global recession in 2009, when growth slowed to virtually zero (0.6 percent). Unemployment peaked at 7.6 percent in 2009.

The global recession did not hit Israel as hard as it did other countries, and its effects were felt mostly as a drop in exports to the United States and the EU. The Israeli government countered the global lull with a fiscal-stimulus program and a fairly aggressive monetary policy. By 2010, real GDP was already growing at more than 4 percent. Such growth is projected to continue during 2011–15.

Francisco Catalá-Oliveras
Juan Lara

Interview

Interview aired on La Voz del Centro, *Univision Radio Puerto Rico and New York, June 24, 2007.*

ÁNGEL COLLADO-SCHWARZ: Israel is a country that has been involved in controversy ever since it was formed in 1948. Its creation provoked war with its neighboring countries. In spite of this complicated situation and the fact that it is largely a desert country, it has managed to establish a successful economic model, in manufacturing and high technology as well as in agriculture. Not only do [the Israelis] supply all their local food needs, but they also export agricultural products.

Paco, let's give our radio listeners some background on Israel.

FRANCISCO CATALÁ-OLIVERAS: Well, the whole area where Israel is located has been described as a place of conflict and a land of hope, which seems somewhat contradictory but I think pretty well describes Israel's circumstances.

In 1947, the partition of Palestine was brought about through Resolution 181 of the United Nations, under the leadership of the United States, and other nations. Immediately afterward, that same year, the State of Israel was founded, and in 1948 its status was formalized.

You will remember that we have described other nations here that came into existence through struggles for independence, some in one way, some in other ways. Slovenia took one path, Ireland another, and Singapore yet another. Well, this case is also very particular. At the time [the State of Israel was born], in Palestine there were nearly three hundred Israeli or Jewish communities, around half of which were collective-farming settlements called kibbutzim.

At the time, Israel's population was about 800,000. Today it is nearly 7 million, which tells us that from the time Israel was founded to this day, there has been a great flow of immigration.

If one were to describe Israel in broad strokes, one might say that it has been defined by three elements: immigration, the importation of capital, and the constant of war. Perhaps I should add a fourth element because [Israel] was very innovative. When no one was talking about free-trade agreements yet, Israel had one with the European Union (EU) [in 1974]—which back then was known as the European Community—and another with the United States [in 1984]. Before the United States signed its famous free-trade agreements with Canada and Mexico, it had one with Israel; and Israel had a second one besides, with the EU. So it was linked to two centers of economic activity. That was for starters.

JUAN LARA: Comparing Israel to Puerto Rico is a very interesting idea. Obviously, we must leave aside the enormous differences between the two with regard to Israel's political and military situation, which contrasts so sharply with ours. But observing its economic evolution and thinking about how its economic policies and strategies might serve as models for Puerto Rico are a fascinating exercise. The impression you get when you make this comparison is that in Israel they have managed to do what we intended to do here, but what we never managed to do, for a series of reasons. For example, when you look at the state of manufacturing in Israel, you find that it is part of the knowledge economy. Israel is not talking about getting there—it already *is* there—and the same is true with agriculture. I would like us to discuss each one of these sectors in detail.

In Israel, a country where more than half the land is arid or semiarid, agriculture is highly productive. Though agriculture is a small part of the economy, it has played a very important role in the country's development. In fact, Israel is self-sufficient in food—something that contrasts dramatically with our situation in Puerto Rico. In addition, they have achieved something that we in Puerto Rico talk a lot about wanting to do: they have forged links between Israeli industries founded with national capital and foreign industries that have operations in Israel. For decades, we have been saying that we want to do the same in Puerto Rico, but we have not achieved it yet. Also—and perhaps this contrast is the most interesting of all—in Israel they have managed to establish these linkages while attracting immigrants. In Puerto Rico, we have not achieved these linkages, and we have been sending our people out.

As everyone knows, Puerto Rico's industrialization experience has been characterized by sending Puerto Ricans abroad. Israel, on the contrary, has based its very existence on bringing the world's Jews home to itself. Obviously, it is impossible to bring them all to Israel—there are too many—but as you said at the beginning, Francisco, it is a nation whose population has grown dramatically because the State of Israel has had that as a purpose—to reverse the diaspora. In our case, we have been sending our population *away* from Puerto Rico.

So it is interesting that the Israelis have achieved what they have precisely to the same degree that we have not and that they have succeeded while attracting people instead of losing them. In our case, we saw the population as redundant. In their case, they saw population growth as vital.

ACS: Juan, regarding what you said about self-sufficiency, it is important to note that we are talking about a largely desert country. The land is not fertile, yet [the Israelis] have *made* it fertile.

Another interesting point is that though Israel is a capitalist country with a market economy, it has adopted socialistic measures in health and education. In other words, it has harmonized the two concepts.

JL: True. For example, Israel has universal health insurance, which is something we have talked about very tentatively in Puerto Rico because no one is confident that we can do it in the near future. But I would like to talk in more detail about some of these subjects because they are really fascinating.

Regarding agriculture, for example, it is impressive that more than half of Israel is arid or semiarid, yet [the Israelis] have developed an agricultural base that satisfies 93 percent of their food-consumption needs. This [development] has been based in part on irrigation technology, but above all on organization, creativity, discipline, and the will to change. They import the other 7 percent of their food simply because it is impossible for them to produce those products. For example, coffee and cocoa cannot be produced there, just as in Puerto Rico we cannot produce apples or pears. We will always need to import products like those.

But they can easily pay for the food products they import by exporting the foods they *do* produce. That is, they have a trade surplus, a high surplus, in foodstuffs. As we would say in economic terms, they export enough agricultural produce to more than cover the 7 percent they do not grow locally. So from the standpoint of the need for foodstuffs, Israel is self-sufficient.

Israel's agricultural exports total $1 billion. We in Puerto Rico would love to be able not just to produce enough food for our own needs, but to export $1 billion in food products. Israelis call themselves "Europe's greenhouse" because they provide the European market with fruits and vegetables during the winter when other countries cannot produce them. Europe grows its own in spring and summer and then relies on Israeli production in the winter, when [its] own agricultural production is halted.

So the Israelis have managed not only to achieve huge agricultural productivity, but also to establish important export markets in Europe, which has to do with what Francisco mentioned at the beginning. They were also innovators at the institutional level in that they were among the first to negotiate free-trade agreements, something that everyone is talking about now. But the first free-trade agreement of this kind was the one between Israel and the EU, not with the United States. The agreement with the Americans came afterward.

FCO: What impresses me, Ángel and Juan, thinking back to the previous program in which we discussed agriculture in Ireland and how it

consolidated and mechanized small, inefficient operations to form a prosperous agricultural industry, is that a desert country such as Israel has
established a prosperous agricultural industry. Economists often say that
the keystone topic in economics is the optimization of restrictions. Well,
it's all about overcoming restrictions, which contrasts with the agricul-
ture-averse culture we have in Puerto Rico.

For decades in Puerto Rico, we have cultivated—if I may use that
term—profound skepticism about any kind of farming project. I am not
suggesting that agriculture should become the backbone of Puerto Rico's
economy; that will never be so, nor should it be. But we can have a much
more prosperous agricultural sector than we do now. I maintain that more
than half a century ago, when [our government leaders] thought about
making agricultural reforms in Puerto Rico, they used the mechanism
of handing out nonproductive land—even very fragmented parcels of
land—and they did not develop a real agricultural production project, as
was done early in Israel's history as well as in Ireland.

ACS: It is important to stress that Israel is practically on a war footing.
[The Israelis] are in a hostile part of the world with respect to the Arabs,
yet in spite of that they have developed their agriculture and their high-
tech industries.

FCO: And if we are listing the issues that Israel has to address, we
ought to add the status of Jerusalem, the return of Palestinian refugees,
and the withdrawal of Jewish settlements on the West Bank. Even so, they
have managed to attract capital and population and to develop agriculture
and the economy as a whole. They have overcome extraordinary hurdles.

JL: Taking into account what Francisco has just said, about Ireland
and other countries, if we are to draw lessons for Puerto Rico from their
experiences, one of the obvious lessons relates to agriculture.

In Puerto Rico, we have given up on agriculture, even though the hurdles we face in that sector are probably more imaginary than real. Puerto
Rico *must* develop its agricultural potential, but there it lies, abandoned,
neglected. As Francisco said so well, this does not mean that Puerto Rico
should become an economy primarily or even in large measure based on
agriculture. Even with all we have said about Israel, agriculture represents just 2 percent of Israel's GDP. The point is that in Puerto Rico that

figure is less than 1 percent. So we are saying that Israel's agriculture is proportionately a little more than twice what ours is.

It would not be too ambitious a goal to bring agriculture up to 2 percent of Puerto Rico's GDP. This should not be beyond our reach because we know we have plenty of underutilized agricultural resources here. The farming population of Israel today is around 5 percent, which is small but is still proportionately more than in Puerto Rico. In other words, we are not saying that Israel has dedicated itself to agriculture; we are saying that Israel has developed agriculture and made the most of its potential [to grow food].

Of course, what you were saying a while ago—that Israel's security, its very survival, is under constant threat—is a powerful incentive to become self-sufficient in food. People who feel besieged by hostile forces try to achieve food security.

For Puerto Rico, however, I would not necessarily set food self-sufficiency as a goal. I would instead aim to have Puerto Rico satisfy its own consumption needs as much as possible; I would also want it to develop the capacity to export farm products to markets such as the United States and Europe, which we can definitely do. We already know it is being done.

In Puerto Rico, our production is almost boutique production. For example, our gourmet coffee sells very well in European and Asian markets, such as Japan, so we should be producing much more than enough for our own consumption in Puerto Rico.

ACS: We have not maximized our mango exports. Several years ago there were Israeli firms producing them on the south side of the island, no?

FCO: Yes, in Santa Isabel.

ACS: What happened?

FCO: In fact, you can still see the mango plantation when you drive down the highway. I don't know how active it is. Sometimes I have seen mangos in the supermarket, and I presume they're from there, but I honestly don't know. Still, that shows it is possible to structure that kind of project here.

JL: The simple fact is that we have plenty of good farmland that is being underutilized. For example, today the Lajas Valley is practically unfarmed. That is incredible. The best farmland in Puerto Rico is not being used. I am not saying we have failed to cultivate difficult land, marginal land. In the case of the Israelis, all their land is difficult and marginal. They do not have the quality of land that we do. But they have taken advantage of the production capacity and potential of their soil, which we might also do. The difference lies in organization, the will to do it, and culture. As Francisco pointed out a while ago, in Puerto Rico we have developed an antifarming culture, and we need to turn that around.

There was a time when people believed—mostly in the later years of the [Luis] Muñoz Marín era—that we had great obstacles to overcome in agriculture. Now, they don't even think *that;* now they think there is no value *at all* in agricultural production. There is an attitude of contempt for what might be produced by that sector, and people who hold that contempt are deeply mistaken.

FCO: You know, I think there is a mistaken view of what development is. We always say that development implies changing the relative structural weights of the different sectors of the economy, and that is true. For example, that is what has happened in developed countries: the relative weight of agriculture has diminished as manufacturing has been developed. Then later the relative weight of manufacturing diminishes as services are developed, which does not mean that when manufacturing and services are developed, we should dismantle agriculture. When you think about it, in Puerto Rico changing the relative sizes of economic sectors has been taken to mean "dismantling." Agricultural production was dismantled in Puerto Rico, and in our time we have seen the dismantling of manufacturing as well. I think that in this sense we are going in the wrong direction.

ACS: One product we haven't mentioned is the pineapples we grow in Puerto Rico, which are considered among the best in the world, superior to Hawaiian pineapples. Years ago we exported pineapples, but that industry has collapsed.

JL: Curiously enough, I was telling Francisco that several weeks ago I attended an event held by a religious group in which religious leaders from the United States visited Puerto Rico as part of an international program to fight hunger and so on. They asked me to talk about Puerto Rico to that group, most of whom were Americans. At the end of my remarks, one of them came up and asked me if we produced mangoes here. I said: "Why, of course, we have a mango tree in practically every yard." He asked me if they are exported, marketed. I said: "It has been done, but not right now, no." He said: "That is odd. It has to be possible to produce mangoes here, because I work on a mango-production farm in California, and there everything is more expensive than here. If we can produce mangoes and export them, it must also be possible for you to do so."

ACS: Moving on to the subject of manufacturing, Paco, describe for us the situation in Israel.

FCO: Israel has an educated and technologically skilled population. Besides machinery and equipment, [the Israelis] export software. They are active in the information industry, textiles, and chemical products. They are big exporters of cut diamonds—that is, they import rough diamonds, process them, and reexport them. It is quite an important part of their total exports. I would like Juan to expand on that.

JL: I believe we can carry on with something that Francisco said a little while ago—the idea that in our economic development we Puerto Ricans have created new sectors and dismantled the ones we already had. Francisco mentioned that in Puerto Rico not only has agriculture been dismantled, but recently manufacturing has as well. I think we should continue on that subject precisely because one of the important contrasts between Puerto Rico and Israel is that in Israel, unlike in Puerto Rico, manufacturing has been growing. The manufacturing sector, especially high technology, has been growing, and employment has increased. You know that in Puerto Rico for a period of easily fifteen years we have had a sustained reduction in manufacturing employment. It is part of what Francisco pointed out when he said that in our economy, manufacturing has gradually been dismantled.

However, for the past two decades—a period in which the United States and Europe have been talking about a decline in both manufacturing jobs and the contribution of manufacturing to the economy as a whole—Israel has had a different experience. It has had substantial manufacturing growth, concentrated in high technology. I was saying at the beginning that one of the things I notice most about the Israeli experience in contrast to ours is that here we have been talking for some ten years—and more insistently in recent years—about the knowledge economy, about the need to insert Puerto Rico into the knowledge economy. In the case of Israel, [it is] already *in* the knowledge economy. [It has] already achieved what we talk about all the time as an objective, what we still see as the future.

Why do I say this? There are some interesting elements in the case of Israel that contrast with ours. First, [the Israelis] already have a research-and-development (R&D) and science-and-technology platform that we neither have nor want to develop. That is, most of Israel's competitiveness as a high-tech industrial economy rests on its technological capacity and R&D capacity. That is the big step you need to take before you can say you are in what is called the "knowledge economy." They have taken it, and they keep on taking it.

Second, they have established strong linkages between industry supported by Israeli national capital and industry supported by foreign capital—something we have set out to do but have not yet achieved. In Puerto Rico, when we talk about developing "strategic innovation clusters" in the knowledge economy—the whole cliché—we are basically talking about creating industrial conglomerates characterized by two things: linkages between Puerto Rican industries and American industries in high-tech and intensified R&D activity so as to strengthen our capabilities in science and technology, so that we aren't merely bringing in knowledge from abroad. That is what we have been proposing.

That is what the Puerto Rico Industrial Development Company, the Department of Economic Development, the Government of Puerto Rico, the Manufacturers Association, the Chamber of Commerce, and everybody else in Puerto Rico says is the central element of our economic-development strategy. No one says we already have it. The more optimistic people may say we have a foundation to build on, but we don't. We have not done it. In Israel, it is already a reality.

ACS: Why do you think [the Israelis] have achieved it and we haven't?

JL: For many reasons. One of them is tradition. Israelis have a resource to build on that we don't. They have literally a thousand-year tradition of intellectual and scientific capacity that is not necessarily physically in Israel: it is in the big research centers and in the big universities in Europe and the United States. The Israelis have been able to tap that Jewish human capital, not necessarily Israeli, because [those Jewish human resources] may be German or Swedish, people from all parts of the world. [The Israelis] have managed to get these people to help them develop capabilities in Israel's universities and research centers.

Imagine if we were to have fifty [Puerto Rican] Nobel Prize winners distributed around the world's universities, and we were able to bring them here as guest professors and to establish research centers and to serve as mentors for our people. Israelis have been able to *do* that because they *have* that. We do not. That is part of their tradition. They also have the management capability and institutional agility that we have always lacked. For example, in R&D the Israelis have scientific research and technology-development agreements with all the European countries. When you see the list of research centers with which they have agreements for real—not rhetorical—collaboration in R&D , you notice that [the agreements] are with big centers in England, Germany, Switzerland, Italy, Spain, and so on, as well as with the United States, obviously. We don't have any agreements that I know of with any important R&D center in the United States, though in principle it should be easy for us to do that.

FCO: I notice that Israel, being in an economic-development condition superior to that of Puerto Rico, according to all the economic indicators and so on, has relatively larger agricultural and manufacturing sectors than Puerto Rico, and employment is growing.

In Puerto Rico, when employment in the manufacturing sector decreases, we rationalize it. We say, "Well, that is just because now we are developing the services sector, and it is natural for that [decrease] to occur." No, no, it is not natural for that to happen, as we were saying a moment ago. You cannot dismantle one sector to develop another.

So why does this happen? Juan has mentioned three factors. One is linkages between enterprises, especially between national capital and foreign capital. Ireland's 1982 *Telesis Report* referred both to that and to R&D, and now there is Israel, too. But along with that R&D activity, there are Israel's international links with the R&D centers all over the world. To this, I would add the diversification of foreign markets. When you look at the nations we have examined and will later examine to compare with

Puerto Rico, we immediately notice the diversification of foreign markets in those countries, especially when measured in terms of exports. Compare this [diversification] with the unilateralism of Puerto Rico's trade with regard to the United States.

JL: You just mentioned two things, Francisco, on which I would like to elaborate. The first is that in Puerto Rico we have been rationalizing the decline in manufacturing employment. One of the things we used to say in Puerto Rico and that we still say is that this decline in manufacturing employment is normal because it is what has been occurring in the United States and in Europe. Israelis say something quite different. They say, "We know that this is what is happening in the United States and Europe, but it is not what is happening in Israel." Let me point out that Israel's population is approximately twice ours. We are talking about somewhat more than 7 million, and employment in manufacturing in Israel is more than 400,000. In Puerto Rico, it is a little more than 100,000 and at risk of falling lower than that number. In other words, with [only] double our population, they have four times our manufacturing employment.

Manufacturing employment in Israel is thus proportionately at least twice what it is here on a per capita basis. Also, ours is decreasing, and theirs is growing. That is a very significant difference.

FCO: The same thing has happened in Singapore and in Ireland. It seems to me that this should be a matter of concern for those in charge of developing public policy in Puerto Rico.

JL: It also has to do with what you were saying before, which is the other point I wanted to highlight, about Israel being very agile in managing its international relations to promote foreign trade and in deliberately seeking diversification. The United States is of enormous importance to Israel, politically and militarily. The Jewish population in the eastern United States is one of Israel's most important assets in every sense. One would think that Israelis would be, well, obsessed with the United States, focused exclusively on the American economy, but that is not so.

Israel exports as much to the EU as it does to the United States. With imports, the same [is true]. In other words, in terms of trade Europe is as important to Israel as the United States is. That is definitely not the case with us, and we are focusing more and more on the US market. That [focus] is obviously affecting our success in developing a high-tech industrial sector with growth potential. The fact that our industrial sector has been contracting and that Israel's has been expanding is no coincidence. And [that contraction] is quite deliberate on our part. It is part of a strategy that was established very early on and that has been promoted ever since. We should not underestimate the enormous importance of Israel's free-trade agreement with the EU.

FCO: Which was signed in 1974.

JL: When no one was talking about free-trade agreements, the Israelis were negotiating one with the EU. Then ten years later they negotiated another one with the United States. I recall that when we began talking about the famous North American Free Trade Agreement (NAFTA), the United States already had a free-trade agreement with Canada, and what NAFTA intended was to incorporate Mexico into that earlier agreement. In everything written at that time, it was said that the conception of the free-trade agreement between the United States and Canada—an agreement that would later incorporate Mexico—had its origins in the free-trade agreement between the United States and Israel, and that agreement had been derived from Israel's free-trade agreement with the EU. So we would not be exaggerating if we said that the Israelis have been innovators, precursors, and pioneers in free-trade agreements, which today are customary throughout the world. This shows great imagination, ambition, and institutional-management capacity.

ACS: To this we must add their political situation. From your first moments in Israel, you realize you are in an unstable environment. You have a parliament with a very important Arab minority and Arab residents living in occupied territories. The Palestinians resemble Puerto Ricans because they belong to Israel but are not a part of Israel, much as Puerto Rico belongs to but is not part of the United States. Israel does not want to incorporate those territories. As a democratic country, it would have to grant Palestinians the vote and eventually control of the country. Despite this tense and complicated environment, [the Israelis] have managed to excel with their economic model in part because they have one thing we lack: the sovereignty to decide which strategies and treaties are most suitable for them.

FCO: Also, we must avoid a very popular explanation of Israel's development—one that in my opinion is faulty. People sometimes explain this development as a result of transfers of funds from outside the country—from the Jewish community abroad and from the US government. The latter transfers, to a very high degree, involve military assistance. Some people even refer back to the German reparations. Certainly, these transfers have been important, but transfers have been made to other countries, even to Puerto Rico, and there has not been such development. That is, transfers do not explain the development. As Juan was saying a moment ago, [the development] is explained instead by Israel's management of institutions; its management of trade, science, and technology policy; and its management of industrial policy and industrial linkages. This is what explains Israel's development. Transfers, if they were simply transfers, would explain dependency and nothing more.

JL: I completely agree because if the Israelis did not have the management capability and the motivation that comes largely from feeling threatened, transfers would have turned [Israel] into a mere refugee camp in the desert, without any economic, social, or political development. Their development has been a result mainly of this management capability.

FCO: Also, a huge part of those transfers is consumed, unfortunately, by their particular military situation.

ACS: They spend vast amounts on defense and intelligence and on taking in immigrants, who arrive penniless and for whom the state provides all.

Juan, if we were to compare Puerto Rico's course with Israel's, how would you sum it up?

JL: It is an interesting exercise. Israel was formally created in 1948, which was basically the same year that Puerto Rico's industrialization and modernization began. That is, Operation Bootstrap and the State of Israel began together, and they did so under very similar initial conditions. Obviously, we must take into account the huge differences in their political and military situations, but their economic conditions were very similar. Israel had almost no manufacturing industry. At the time, it depended almost entirely on agriculture. Obviously, its income and production levels were much lower than they are now; it did not have a modern infrastructure in terms of electricity, communications, and transportation. All of that needed to be created, and that [period] basically coincides with the period in which Puerto Rico was creating the same things. Puerto Rico was developing an industrial platform, a basic economic infrastructure, and transforming itself from an agrarian economy into a higher-income industrial economy.

So there were two parallel tracks, basically with the same objectives and the same course.

But, as we have seen, Israel's results have been much more fruitful than Puerto Rico's. In a sense, in Puerto Rico there was atrophy. There was certainly atrophy in agriculture, and there was also some atrophy in manufacturing, whereas in Israel both sectors have shown very successful development. And the Israelis have achieved what we in Puerto Rico have always identified as the missing element in our economic development: they have managed to develop a modern high-tech industry based on national capital, an industry with its own capabilities in science and technology and in R&D.

These two countries set off from very similar situations at almost the same time. If you examine the production structure in 1950, agriculture was ahead of manufacturing; it was almost the same scenario in both. Over time, those courses of development drew apart, and the situation in which we have ended up is very different from theirs.

In Puerto Rico, we talk a great deal about the "Puerto Rican economic miracle," a period when we had extraordinarily high economic growth, during the 1950s and 1960s. After that, we had a period of crisis, immediately after the first oil shock. Growth rates fell by almost 3 percent or something near that. Then we entered a phase of near stagnation during which economic growth was very, very slow. Israel had the same experience. There, during more or less the same period, the 1950s and 1960s, [the Israelis] registered extraordinarily high economic growth rates, of 8, 9, and 10 percent per year. They also talked about their "economic miracle." Then in the early 1960s came the oil shock and a decrease in economic dynamism. For some time, they experienced slow growth, but, unlike us, they recovered. Their growth took an upward turn, which we have not yet managed to achieve.

In recent years, Israel's economy has been growing at around 5 percent, which is very good. [Israel has] recovered [its] capacity for economic growth. Puerto Rico needs to do the same. Israel long ago managed a turnaround that we still have not been able to make.

FCO: The parallels are remarkable. We are talking about Israel and Puerto Rico, but if we were to consider Ireland, we would find the same thing: the Irish also recovered from a decline.

Where does the parallel break down? I think in two ways. First, both in Israel and in Ireland they assigned a high priority to developing national capital; in Puerto Rico, we did not. Second, I think that Puerto Rico froze up institutionally in the 1950s and acts as if the circumstances of the 1950s still prevail.

The 1950s were very different from today. Europe had been destroyed, Japan had been destroyed, and China might as well have been on Mars. Puerto Rico had privileged access to the United States, which was the only industrialized economy that remained intact after the Second World War. All of that changed. It changed for Israel, it changed for Ireland, and it changed for Puerto Rico, with one difference: Ireland and Israel have adjusted institutionally. Take the free-trade agreement that Israel signed with the EU in 1974. Around that same time, Ireland joined the European Community. Puerto Rico continues to act today as if the circumstances of the 1950s were still current. Israel, Ireland, and other countries have made appropriate institutional adjustments. That is what we are missing. And to make the pertinent adjustments, sovereignty is essential. It is an indispensable condition.

ACS: In our program about Singapore, I mentioned that at a meeting [I had] with the director of the University of Singapore's Economics Department, she said that they had copied the Puerto Rico model and industrialization program, but that they also continued to adapt it to the times, whereas Puerto Rico took the road to dependency.

JL: The second factor you just mentioned and Francisco also mentioned is in my opinion the most important. There was an institutional freeze in Puerto Rico. We are working with institutional fossils, and with those fossils we want to develop an up-to-date economy, which is not possible. We have also run out of imagination. There was a time when we did not even know which way to move—and I think in many ways we still do not. For example, in Puerto Rico when we talk about industrial incentives, there is little capacity to think beyond tax exemptions. What other things can be done? What other approaches can we adopt?

In Puerto Rico, most of the people involved in these kinds of decisions and in defining which road we will take still don't have the answers to these questions. This means we are still trapped mentally in a world that is at least three decades behind. We need to break with that mindset so that we can join today's world. Countries such as Ireland, Singapore, and Israel obviously never fell into the trap we did.

ACS: Paco, moving on to socioeconomic indicators, let us compare Israel to other countries and to Puerto Rico.

FCO: We always think about strictly economic indicators, such as per capita income, which in Israel is around $19,000, higher than in Puerto Rico. And we think about population: 7 million [in Israel]. By the way, Israel's population density is high. There are 320 persons per square kilometer. In Puerto Rico, it is even higher: 428. [So] we are not talking about an underpopulated country.

But we sometimes disregard health and education indicators that I think are very important. For example, Puerto Rico's infant mortality rate, which measures mortality for every thousand births, is double Israel's. That gives you an idea of the health services in that country. Also, there are almost three times as many Internet users in Israel. That gives you an idea of the use of technology there.

Then there is what economists call the "Gini Index," which measures equality or inequality of income. In Israel, this index is much lower than in Puerto Rico, which indicates that there is less inequality in income distribution. Israel is a quite equitable society in terms of wealth and income distribution. So we are not talking exclusively about quantitative indicators in assessing economic activity, but also about qualitative ones in the sense of economic justice and access to health and education. Development ultimately means an increase in the quality of life, not merely an increase in economic production. Israel is superior to us in these quality-of-life indicators despite its unique and difficult circumstances.

JL: Yes, when we analyze the education and health situation, we notice not only Israel's achievements, but also its methods. We mentioned earlier a curious thing about Israel: it is clearly a capitalist country politically and economically—and I would say even philosophically—but it is also a country that has always in its political and economic ethics placed extraordinary emphasis on promoting equality and participation, on ensuring that fundamental services are accessible to all segments of the population, on looking after the needy.

In part, this [emphasis] comes from its self-definition as a nation that was formed to take in immigrants, many of whom arrived destitute. It comes from the fact that Israel made it its project to absorb these people into a modern, dynamic society and to raise their quality of life quickly. That philosophical approach, which is so different from ours, has moved [Israel] to embrace a societal model that more resembles Sweden or Denmark than the United States: a model that focuses on promoting equality and ensuring access to services.

For example, Israel has an integrated health system controlled by four big organizations that provide services through a universal insurance system.

[The Israelis] also have an excellent educational system. Obviously, it is free and guaranteed up to the age of eighteen. It is very high in quality, which enables them to compete in R&D. In science and technology, Israeli universities compare favorably with very good universities in Europe and the United States, so in education [Israel] also [has] a different emphasis.

How have we dealt with poverty and social exclusion in Puerto Rico? We have tried to hide poverty instead of eliminating it. Israel's attitude toward poverty, evidently, is that it must be overcome. I think that is a basic difference.

FCO: This [distinction] reminds us of Ireland, where three priorities are evident in public expenditures: education, health and social welfare, and social security. None of these three priorities is linked to a policy of permanent dependency or welfare. Their purpose is precisely to *conquer* dependency and poverty, not to perpetuate them.

I think that in Puerto Rico we need to alter the structure of dependency totally and give real priority to the elements I have just mentioned.

ACS: The study conducted by the Center for the New Economy and the Brookings Institution notes that for a person in Puerto Rico it is a better deal to be dependent than to get a job.

FCO: Yes. That [conclusion] calls for a serious debate on the way the labor market operates.

JL: Now the basic, the fundamental thing is how important it has become for an economy to be able to create well-paid jobs for its people. When we settle for an economy that generates only half the jobs we need, we are automatically adopting an attitude that allows half the population to be outside the labor market, marginalized and dependent. We have never said so explicitly, but in a sense this [attitude] is an element of Puerto Rico's development model—one that has been assimilated and accepted by practically everyone.

ACS: On today's program, we have discussed Israel as an economic model for Puerto Rico. We have seen how so small a country, with a population almost twice ours, has achieved extraordinary growth even though it has had to face problems that Puerto Rico has never had: minority policies, an environment of war, and location in the desert. The Israelis have overcome these challenges based on a platform of sovereignty, using their imaginative and creative human capital to find solutions to their problems.

Suggested Reading on Israel

Nitzan, Jonathan, and Shimshon Bichler. *The Global Political Economy of Israel.* London: Pluto Press, 2002.

Rivlin, Paul. *The Israeli Economy from the Foundation of the State Through the 21st Century.* London: Cambridge Univ. Press, 2010.

Senor, Dan, and Saul Singer. *Start-Up Nation: The Story of Israel's Economic Miracle.* New York: Twelve, 2009.

New Zealand

Two islands, isolated from the rest of the world, with the same population as Puerto Rico, have successfully developed their agricultural, manufacturing, and service industries.

—ÁNGEL COLLADO-SCHWARZ

New Zealand in 2009

Population:	4 million
Territory:	268,000 square kilometers
Population density:	17 per square kilometer
Gross domestic product (GDP):	$126.7 billion
Gross national income (GNI):	$124.2 billion
GNI per capita:	$28,770
Unemployment rate:	6.1 percent (2006–2009)
Internet users:	83.0 per 100 people

Source: World Bank, *World Development Indicators* (Washington, DC: World Bank, 2011).

Updated Comments

Real GDP growth in New Zealand averaged about 3 percent per year during 2004–9. The contraction in the crisis years was relatively mild: –1.1 percent in 2008 and –0.6 percent in 2009. The unemployment rate has been between 6.2 percent and 6.5 percent. The government responded to the global recession with expansionary fiscal policies and cuts in interest rates. Recovery was already under way in 2010, when real GDP increased 1.7 percent. The forecast for 2011–15 is for annual average growth of between 2.4 percent and 2.9 percent.

The financial crisis evidently did not affect New Zealand as strongly as it did those economies that had been afflicted with a speculative bubble. Nonetheless, the government is concerned about weak external demand and is focusing on developing infrastructure and fostering productivity growth.

Francisco Catalá-Oliveras
Juan Lara

Interview

Interview aired on La Voz del Centro, *Univision Radio Puerto Rico and New York, July 22, 2007.*

ÁNGEL COLLADO-SCHWARZ: New Zealand is an island country east of Australia, off the path taken by most travelers. Interestingly, at the beginning of the twentieth century, one of Puerto Rico's most important patriots, Rosendo Matienzo-Cintrón, described New Zealand as the most advanced country of its time. In part, his statement had to do with the social changes that New Zealand was undergoing—in particular, with the fact that it was the first country to grant women the right to vote, in 1893. In social matters, it was in the vanguard.

Paco, I would like to begin the program with some background on New Zealand.

FRANCISCO CATALÁ-OLIVERAS: It is certainly a fascinating country. So much so that—allow me to say, as a footnote—it was the place
chosen to film the *Lord of the Rings* [series], which has done so much good
for the country's tourism. Now, I think we should stress that New Zealand
is somewhat different from the other countries we have been reviewing
in this program.

First, let's consider its size. It is pretty large compared to the other
countries we have discussed. Puerto Rico has roughly 9,000 square kilometers; Slovenia 20,000; Ireland, the largest country examined so far,
70,000; Israel 22,000; Singapore only 699; and Estonia, which we will consider in our next program, 45,000; whereas New Zealand has 268,000.

New Zealand is a series of islands—with two main ones, the North
Island and the South Island—and it is quite large. When you look at the
world map, it seems rather small, but that is a false perception: New Zealand looks small because it is right next to Australia, which is huge. But
make no mistake—New Zealand is four times larger than Ireland. Its
population density is very low, with only 15 [people] per square kilometer,
compared to Singapore, which has more than 6,000 per square kilometer,
and to Puerto Rico, at 428, and Israel, at 313.

Even so, its population is similar to that of the other countries concerning us here. It has around 4 million people, which is just about what
Puerto Rico has and more or less the same as Ireland and Singapore. We
are comparable in this regard.

Its history and political structure are also different. James Cook, an
English naval captain, was the first explorer to chart the coasts of Australia
and New Zealand. During the nineteenth century, innumerable wars were
fought in New Zealand because its original inhabitants, the Maori, immediately found themselves in conflict with the British colonists. All through
the nineteenth century, the battles came one after the other, until sometime
around 1870, when British colonial power was established indisputably.

Skipping forward somewhat in history, New Zealand gained its independence in 1947 and is currently a parliamentary democracy, whose
monarch [it] share[s] with the United Kingdom. Actually, today [it has] a
governor-general who represents the queen, though as we all know, the
queen is only nominally the head of state. The real power lies in the head

of the government, the prime minister, who as we speak is Helen Clark, who leads the Labour Party.

New Zealand has a multiparty system with two principal parties: National and Labour. The National Party is more conservative, and the Labour Party leans more to the left. There are also other minor parties.

The government is unicameral. In other words, the Parliament has a single chamber with 120 members. Representation is proportional. That is, the number of seats each party has in the Parliament is proportional to the number of votes it received in elections. It is interesting that six or seven seats are reserved for the Maori, who at this time are about 15 percent of New Zealand's total population, which is, as I said, around 4 million.

New Zealand has yet another peculiarity. The other countries we have discussed so far are mainly industrial, and their principal exports are manufactured or industrial products. Though New Zealand is an industrialized country, its main exports are primary goods such as agricultural products. In other words, New Zealand is an agricultural power. That distinguishes it from the other models we have considered.

Its common denominators with our other countries are, first, its population and, second, that it is active in many sectors, including tourism, agriculture, and manufacturing, though the latter is not its strongest export area.

ACS: It is also noteworthy, Paco, that isolation has been a great disadvantage for [New Zealanders]. Getting to New Zealand is rather complicated. The fact that [it is] in the shadow of Australia is something else [its people] have had to cope with and find a positive way to manage.

You mentioned that the prime minister is a woman. Interestingly, it is one of the few countries—or at least the only one I know of—where all the important government figures are women. The president of the Parliament is a woman. The prime minister is a woman; the chief justice is a woman; the queen of England, Elizabeth II, who is also the queen of New Zealand, is a woman; and the governor-general is a woman. They all are women.

FCO: They all are women, and the previous prime minister was also a woman.

ACS: Juan, would you care to comment on New Zealand's economy?

JUAN LARA: When we compare New Zealand's situation with Puerto Rico's, we notice a real difference in economic models, though that does not mean we cannot draw some useful lessons from New Zealand. As Francisco was saying a moment ago, it is worth noting that the importance of agriculture to New Zealand is considerable. It represents about 5 percent of its total economy.

Manufacturing is important but does not constitute even 30 percent of the economy; it is somewhere around 25 or 26 percent, according to recent data. Also, manufacturing in New Zealand is very closely related to the country's natural resources. That is unlike our manufacturing, which is high tech and is not based on Puerto Rico's own resources, technology, or knowledge, but rather on importing materials from other parts of the world to process and then export. In New Zealand, we are talking about an industrial platform based on the country's own natural resources: agriculture, agricultural processing, mining, and forestry. When we look at New Zealand's exports, we find that farm products prevail as well as manufactured products based on agriculture, mining, and forestry. So it is an enviable country, one that, instead of importing materials from other parts of the world, has managed to found its industrial development on its own natural resources.

We all remember that in school they used to tell us that Puerto Rico was a small country with few natural resources and that our history has been a constant attempt to find a way to become viable without having to depend on our natural resources because they are scarce. The history of New Zealand is very different; its people have made the most of their natural resources to construct something of their own.

ACS: What are their most important farm products?

JL: If we are speaking of exports, dairy products are important. New Zealanders have a large livestock industry, as one would expect of a country with so much land, not only because of the size, but also because of the temperate climate, which is very appropriate for the kind of large-scale livestock production that we also find, for example, in some parts of the United States and South America. So they have meat products based on the livestock industry and lumber based on their rich forests, though they use them not to export wood, but to export products made of wood. Besides manufactured wooden products, they also export fish. They have a fairly important fishing industry. Note that all of these products come from the primary sector. Their manufacturing is based on their primary products.

FCO: For many years, New Zealand was protected by British concessions and depended basically on exporting primary products to Europe. Since then, it has slowly transformed itself into a more industrialized economy, independent of those concessions. But what is most interesting is that it has never sought or promoted foreign capital for particular enclaves—that is, for industrial sectors isolated from the rest of the economy. This [approach] contrasts with [that of] other countries and even with Puerto Rico, which started from agriculture and then passed through an industrialization process that was not connected to the preexisting agriculture and consequently is divorced from it. We should also point out that in recent times New Zealand has emphasized food processing. Because [New Zealanders] have such an important agricultural sector, it was natural for them to industrialize that production, so they began processing foods for their own market and for export.

By the way, food processing has great potential for Puerto Rico. It might serve both to develop Puerto Rico's agriculture and to increase imports because that industry would import raw materials, process them for internal consumption, and export the rest. At the same time, it might stimulate production in Puerto Rico's agricultural sector. That is why I find exemplary the emphasis that New Zealand places on food processing.

ACS: Australia tells many jokes about New Zealand like the ones we have here about Dominicans and that the Dominicans have there about Haitians. Australians say that New Zealand has many more sheep than people, putting down the talents of New Zealanders. What is sure is that almost everywhere you go in New Zealand, there are sheep.

FCO: That is why it is also a big meat exporter in addition to a dairy-product exporter.

JL: Of course, being a country with a temperate climate, its wool production is essential for producing winter clothing and for export to England and to other European markets. Something important that we can see here, thinking now about drawing lessons for Puerto Rico—on which we might elaborate a little later—is that when we look at these countries that are small but successful, we see that they have in common the fact that they have managed to make transitions. They have not remained trapped in the same model or in a model that is never modified and does not evolve. I think what Francisco mentioned a while ago is very important: at the beginning, New Zealand was basically a huge production farm for England, to supply it with farm products, and the viability of its economy depended on the English market, which was also a market to which it had preferential access, privileged access as part of the colonial system of the British Empire, which allowed it at the time to avoid competing with so many other countries that were also exporting to that market.

But what I want to highlight is that [the New Zealanders] did not allow themselves to become trapped in that system permanently or to become dependent on that model. Instead, they transformed themselves into an economy that was able to stop depending on such concessions from the British Crown and on exporting primary farming products almost exclusively. And they also modified their international trade, which is very important.

England is not New Zealand's primary market now. It has not been for a long time. New Zealand has been cultivating and developing its primary markets. In this, we can see the evolution of the model, something that is absent in Puerto Rico's experience, which is undoubtedly one of the reasons why we are experiencing stagnation in our country, whereas other small countries with similar experiences have had more success and have achieved greater viability than we have.

ACS: Along that same line, Juan, [the New Zealanders] have not had just one successful industry in agricultural and dairy products; they have also developed an important service industry, particularly in the creative sector, tangent to what Paco began saying about *Lord of the Rings*. New Zealand has a very important film industry, which has won prizes in world festivals. In addition, [New Zealanders] have a very advanced and creative advertising industry, one that is very highly regarded internationally.

Another industry they have been developing is the wine industry. They produce extraordinary wines, particularly white wines, and they export them. So they have not been resting on their laurels but have continued to reinvent themselves and to identify new opportunities.

FCO: Note that the development of these industries, such as film and others, advertising services, and even the wine industry, has had the result that tourism, more or less since 2003, is now the principal source of foreign currency. The principal source of foreign currency is no longer the export of primary goods. For the past three or four years, it has been tourism. Certainly, the development of tourism in a country as distant as New Zealand must be linked to an extraordinary service framework, such as the one you just described.

ACS: Also, its tourism is not based on casinos or golf courses, but on the country's natural attributes. For example, in New Zealand you can go skiing *or* surfing. Because it is an archipelago, it can offer variety that other countries do not have.

Also, its conservation laws are very strict. Even though it has a great deal of land, it has very severe regulations.

FCO: In addition to tourism, which brings in foreign currency, and the production of primary goods, we should not underestimate manufacturing. New Zealand has an important sector that produces machinery, mainly transportation equipment. That is also very significant in [its] economy.

We have to point out that in its manufacturing, its agriculture, and its exports, there is something we have already underscored in reviewing other countries: diversification. When we talk about New Zealand's principal industries, besides mentioning food processing and primary goods, wood products, paper, and transportation equipment as important export items, we also need to mention services offered in finance, insurance, tourism, and advertising. There is much diversification of products as well as of export markets.

For example, New Zealand's principal market is—for obvious reasons—Australia, where 22 percent of its exports go. And the rest? To the United States, Japan, China, Great Britain, and other countries of the European Union (EU). So it is diversified. Interestingly, its primary market, the closest one, giant Australia, receives only 22 percent of its exports. Once again, this [fact] emphasizes the importance of diversification.

Another interesting element is that all of this economic activity is subject to relatively high taxes. Let me give you some examples. The average nominal tax rate for local resident companies is 33 percent; for nonresidents, it is higher, at 38 percent. Individual tax rates range between 20 and 40 percent. Taxation is progressive and depends on the level of income.

There is also a consumption tax of about 12 percent. So taxes are not low. In fact, New Zealand has had a budget surplus over the past few years; that is, government revenues have exceeded expenditures. Though there is interest in reducing taxes, especially among supporters of the National Party, the Labour Party—which is currently in power—is more inclined to implement social improvements, mainly in the labor field, and it has resisted reducing taxes for now. For foreign industries to establish themselves in New Zealand and for local industries to operate with a certain margin of profit, there obviously have to be other advantages.

What I want to point out is that business, which is of course not indifferent to tax rates, does not base its decisions exclusively on tax structures. Other criteria govern the conduct of business.

JL: I would like to comment on a couple of things that Francisco just said. We observe, for example, that [the New Zealanders] have managed to diversify their international trade and to move from a time in which they were focused on preferential access to the British market, with concessions, to a much more diversified market, focused mainly on Australia and Japan—that is, more on the Pacific than on the West. Francisco is saying that in spite of that [shift], trade with Australia, its principal trading partner, is [only] about 20 percent of its total trade. In other words, Australia has not appropriated New Zealand trade, as one might expect when you consider [the two countries'] sizes and geographical proximity, nor has New Zealand become a satellite of Australia.

So what one can read between the lines—maybe it is my imagination or perhaps my fantasy—is that there is a will not to become economically colonized. New Zealanders have a will to remain in control of their country's economy. They developed their model in such a way that they were never captured in a space where they might very well have been captured. They could easily have retained a model of protected farming production, dependent on the British Crown, or a model based on primary goods and industrial production, captured by the size of that huge neighboring country, Australia, but those things have not happened, which is quite interesting.

FCO: It is interesting and, again, an example for us. It contrasts with the strategy of economic and political dependency that has characterized Puerto Rico.

ACS: Paco, regarding the labor force, the Central Intelligence Agency (CIA) *World Factbook* Web page has data from all the counties of the world. Curiously, in 2006 New Zealand was reported there as a country with a labor force of 2,180,000, which is almost 50 percent of the total population.[1] How does that compare with Puerto Rico?

FCO: The labor-participation rate in New Zealand is much higher than [it is] in Puerto Rico. If in New Zealand it is 50 percent of the total population, in Puerto Rico we [barely] reach 30 percent because Puerto Rico has about 1,200,000 in its labor force out of a total 4 million inhabitants. [Barely] 30 percent. By the way, of all the countries we have been reviewing, the one with the lowest labor-participation rate is Puerto Rico. It is by far the lowest.

ACS: It is also interesting that when we break down the New Zealand labor force by occupation, again according to the CIA *World Factbook*, only 10 percent work in agriculture, 25 percent in industry, and 65 percent in services. This is 1995 data. Curiously, with agriculture being so very important to [its] economy, it does not require that a greater proportion of the labor force work in that sector.

FCO: This means [New Zealand has] high productivity, which is a trend that a country should experience as it achieves development—particularly in agriculture, where we have seen productivity increase and employment decline. Regarding New Zealand, let's not forget that one of the principal industries is the production of machinery. I suspect that [industry] is also linked to an increase in productivity.

JL: It is important to highlight labor because the labor-market statistics, employment and unemployment, in New Zealand contrast dramatically with those of Puerto Rico. As you correctly stated, we are talking about a population that is basically the same size as ours, some 4 million people.

---

1. For data after 2007, when this interview was aired, see the table "Central Intelligence Agency *World Factbook* Statistics" in part 3, "Comparative Tables."

Of that 4 million, [there is] a labor force of somewhat more than 2 million, whereas Puerto Rico's is a little more than 1 million. In other words, it is a country with basically our same population [but] twice the number of persons in the labor market than we have. That in itself explains many of the differences between New Zealand's standard of living and economic indices and ours.

It is no coincidence that the per capita income of New Zealand is about twice ours. If [its] active labor force is twice ours, with the same population, it is no coincidence that [it] also [has] double our per capita income. The fact that most of that labor force works in the service sector, followed by manufacturing, with a smaller proportion in agriculture, is also interesting. That is something worth emphasizing.

When we talk about the importance, necessity, and urgency of developing Puerto Rico's agricultural capacity, many people think that means returning to yesterday's agriculture. They think we are talking about a traditional view of the agricultural sector and that we are saying, "Come on, Puerto Ricans, let's leave the cities and go back to the land to become farmers like our great-great-grandfathers were." That is not what we are talking about.

Every country that has turned agriculture into an important sector in its economy and whose economy is relatively large and well developed has done so fundamentally based on productivity. And productivity entails development and expansion of agricultural production, but the proportion of the population engaged in agriculture declines. This [scenario] is characteristic of all the world's agricultural powers. In our case, we would be able to do it if we had 6 or 7 percent of the labor force in agriculture.

FCO: Ángel, [the New Zealand] case is similar to one we examined earlier, that of Ireland: 4 million inhabitants in Ireland, 4 million in New Zealand, 2 million people in Ireland's labor force, 2 million in New Zealand's, in contrast to a little more than 1 million people in Puerto Rico's labor force—a high labor-participation rate in Ireland and New Zealand and a scandalously low one in Puerto Rico.[2]

---

2. For data after 2007, see the table "World Bank Statistics" in part 3, "Comparative Tables."

JL: Also, [New Zealand has] a very low unemployment rate, nearly 4 percent, which means that practically all the 2 million people in the labor market are employed.

FCO: Once again this is a huge contrast with Puerto Rico, where we have a low participation rate and a high unemployment rate—nearly 12 percent in recent years.

ACS: Paco, do you have the comparative table of Puerto Rico and New Zealand statistics? What other significant figures does it show?

FCO: One that stands out—not an economic indicator, but related—is Internet use: [there are] 672 Internet users per 1,000 inhabitants in New Zealand, compared to 234 in Puerto Rico. [New Zealanders,] perhaps given their geographical isolation, have been more inclined to use new communication technologies. In fact, of all the countries we have examined, New Zealand's Internet-use rate is the highest—even higher than Singapore's, where it is very high.[3]

In terms of infant mortality—to quote a health indicator—when we compare the number of deaths per 1,000 inhabitants, there are five in New Zealand, which is one of the lowest infant mortality rates in the world, and nine in Puerto Rico. The figures I am using here are 2003 figures from the World Bank. Income distribution in New Zealand is among the most equitable we have seen, and this is significant. It is more equitable than in Puerto Rico. That is, New Zealand is more equitable economically than Puerto Rico.

JL: Another important element we must stress is the Gini Index, which we mentioned when we discussed Israel. This index is used to measure inequality in income distribution. In New Zealand, the Gini Index is low, 36 percent. That places New Zealand in a very good position in terms of equality of income distribution. It is interesting because we are talking about a country with many differences in population. We, with a homogeneous population, have a considerably higher inequality rate: nearly 50 percent.

FCO: That is correct. And even higher.

ACS: And what about per capita income, Paco?

3. For data after 2007, see the table "World Bank Statistics" in part 3, "Comparative Tables."

FCO: Per capita income in New Zealand is between $25,000 and $27,000. In Puerto Rico, it is about half that, as Juan said. [In New Zealand,] they have a relatively high per capita income. It is a country with high incomes, no question about that.[4]

JL: I would like to stress that point, which reminds me of a hypothetical point that is presented in a book from the Brookings Institution and the Center for the New Economy on restoring growth in Puerto Rico. It says that if Puerto Rico were to take its participation rate in the labor market and its unemployment rate to levels comparable to those of the United States, that alone would almost double its income per capita. And that is practically what we are seeing here [in New Zealand]. We have a country with our same population, [but] with double our labor-participation rate and double our per capita income.

ACS: Juan, you mentioned Puerto Rico's homogeneous population as compared to New Zealand's. I think this element is very important because when one examines New Zealand's ethnic composition, according to the CIA *World Factbook* only 60 percent is European. That means that 40 percent is not. In other words, [the New Zealanders] have a situation that in theory should be problematic, but for them it has not been so.

FCO: It has not been. The truth is that when the native population was near 15 percent, there were times of considerable disturbance. However, they have managed to deal with that and solve it, and it has not translated into economic disaster. As I said earlier, the native population has a right to a proportion of the total number of seats in Parliament.

ACS: [New Zealand has] also allowed foreign investment; [it has] been fairly open. For example, I know a fellow—one of the most important dairy farmers in Venezuela—who has invested in dairy farms in New Zealand and become a leader in the dairy industry, where he has used all the experience he acquired in Venezuela.

FCO: Of course, one might ask, "How do [the New Zealanders attract foreign business] if they have relatively high tax rates?" First, they have

4. For data after 2007, see the table "World Bank Statistics" in part 3, "Comparative Tables."

some very particular attractions, the natural resources they have available and so on. But, in addition, the structure of their government is clearly defined, and they also have technical expertise and the proper infrastructure, as I mentioned a moment ago regarding communications. And their businesses have established linkages between local capital and foreign capital.

ACS: We were talking about how Ireland is so fortunate to have such large amounts of land and a developed agricultural industry. Even if some people might simplify this [factor] and say, "That is why New Zealand has been successful," we need to stress that this, in fact, is not the reason for [its] success. [New Zealanders] have been successful because they have planned well and because they have made the best use of their human capital and natural resources in an orderly way.

For example, look at Argentina. Argentina is a bigger, richer country, and it has more natural resources than New Zealand, but we know all the problems [it has] faced throughout [its] history.

Paco, you were speaking of New Zealand's strategies and formulas for success.

FCO: Bear in mind that economic development is not based on one single variable or strategy. The promotion of industries, whether national or foreign, is not based on one incentive, but on a multiplicity of factors, and that was what I wanted to emphasize. In Puerto Rico, we tend to be somewhat monochromatic. Here we think about tax exemptions, and that's it. But there are other things. We mentioned technical expertise, a government with a clearly defined structure, the scope of trade policy and linkages—that is, linkages between different sectors of the economy, between agriculture and manufacturing, and between manufacturing and services. But we have also mentioned linkages between certain foreign-capital enterprises and local-capital enterprises, among which several kinds of linkages can be established—for example, some enterprises providing services to others, selling production inputs or promoting mixed capital enterprises.

To this we must also add a diversification policy—diversification not only in the production profile or exports, but also in sources of capital: sources of local capital, sources of foreign capital, sources oriented to different sectors of the economy, from the farming sector to the manufacturing sector and to the service sector.

In addition, obviously, New Zealand has an entrepreneurial type of government. I think that government, especially in small developing countries, should not be passive or merely a facilitator. It should be an entrepreneurial entity. It has been so in all these cases.

JL: It is interesting that in spite of its size, New Zealand is comparable to Puerto Rico in terms of its small, open economy. I mean, an economy that has 4 million inhabitants, basically our same population, cannot have a large internal market. So in that sense it is a small economy.

One thing that strikes me about New Zealand is that its GDP comes to billions of dollars. It exceeds Puerto Rico's GDP. We know that our GDP includes a big component that is the production of enterprises that are not from Puerto Rico. That is why, when we talk about our economy, we really prefer to use gross *national* product, which is a smaller figure, instead of using GDP.

When we compare New Zealand's GDP with ours, we find that [its] economy is easily 30 or 40 percent larger than ours. Even so, it is still a small economy in terms of total size and internal market. Hence, it is an economy that must depend on exports. In addition, the fact that [New Zealand's] internal market is small implies that attracting external capital into New Zealand cannot be based on the promise of that internal market. It is easier for a country with a large internal market to attract external capital. For example, it is attractive for any enterprise to enter Brazil or India simply because of the market size—just to be there, in such a large market—where [the enterprise] can develop a large business and have high yields.

Enterprises that set up in New Zealand are not looking for its internal market, just as enterprises that come to Puerto Rico are not looking for its internal market; they come looking for economic capacity that enables them to do other things in the world economy.

New Zealanders have managed to become successful exporters. Yet even though they have a small, open economy oriented to exports—and in that regard they are similar to us—in spite of that their development strategy is not one that promotes foreign investment. They are open to foreign investment, as you said a moment ago, but that was not always the case. In fact, there was a time when they had important restrictions on foreign investment. They have liberalized that, but their strategy, as opposed to ours, is not focused on promoting foreign investment. Another thing I notice is that foreign enterprises have a higher tax rate than domestic ones. So they tell people, "If you want to come here, you must be willing to pay more taxes than a New Zealander would pay."

FCO: I find that very interesting. To add to what Juan just said, remember that New Zealand's GDP for 2005, according to the World Bank, was $109 billion. Its GNI was $106 billion—that is, its GDP is quite comparable to its GNI. This means that payments for external factors are not as large as in Puerto Rico's economy, which has so much foreign investment. In Puerto Rico, the difference between the GNI and the GDP is approximately $30 billion because payments for foreign factors and external investment are considerable.

JL: Another way of saying it is that New Zealand's economy belongs almost entirely to New Zealanders.

FCO: That is fundamental. Again, though there is a difference between the tax rates applied to foreign enterprises and those on local enterprises, it is not very big. Both pay a lot of taxes.

In Puerto Rico, there is something peculiar: national capital enterprises have a very high nominal tax rate, and exempt enterprises have a very low rate, ranging between 2 and 7 percent, and perhaps even no taxes if they qualify. I think this is one of our problems, which we may need to address in the future in order to level the playing field.

ACS: We can see the results of the present policy: underdeveloped local industry owing to a lack of vision, incentives, and planning.

FCO: That is true. Ángel, I think that the culture of dependency has been significant in all of this, the culture of political dependency and economic dependency—that is, dependency in the form of welfare and dependency in the form of a single source of capital and the giving of everything to the source of that capital.

ACS: We say that New Zealand's tax rates are high, but the people are receiving the services for which they are paying. The quality of life in New Zealand is on par with that in the EU and higher than that in the rest of the Pacific countries. We mentioned that Venezuelan who entered the dairy industry in New Zealand. I know of another case, a person who was one of the most important creative minds in the world of advertising, a winner of important awards at the Cannes Festival, who retired from the advertising business and took up wine making [in New Zealand]. I also know of a top British executive who left London for New Zealand. New Zealand is doing something right when it is able to attract so much excellent human talent in spite of its distant location.

Educational levels [in New Zealand] are the same as in the EU. Both education and health services are free for all citizens. How do [the New Zealanders] manage [that]?

FCO: Well, Ángel, talking about high tax rates or the size of government—it is now the fashion to say that the government is too big—is a relative thing. The problem is not that the government is too big or too small in this or that place. The problem is what services that government provides. What is the quality of those services? How effective is the delivery of public services? Here we have a case that illustrates that.

New Zealand *does* have high tax rates. It has a budget that is large for the economy. For example, [its] public-expenditures budget is around $38 billion, much higher than Puerto Rico's consolidated budget.

This means that [New Zealand's] budget expenditure per capita is about $9,000. In Puerto Rico, it is $5,000 or $6,000. It is less in Puerto Rico in relative terms. In the case of New Zealand, however, that [difference] translates into top-quality public services, into excellent health services, which in turn translate into excellent health statistics, income, and income distribution as well as [into] economic-justice indicators that are superior to Puerto Rico's and comparable to those of Europe and even superior to those of the United States, which is an industrialized country with considerable inequality in income and wealth distribution.

So this [question of taxation] is not merely about comparing the size of governments. We must compare government services with government services: quality, effectiveness, and citizen satisfaction. That is the key.

ACS: Curiously, New Zealand has a group of islands called the "Cook Islands" that are independent but in a free association with New Zealand. New Zealand handles [the islands'] external affairs, but the Cook Islands handle their own local affairs. They have their own government in a free association with New Zealand—an association they can end at any time and declare themselves independent.

FCO: That's interesting. The Cook Islands are called the "Cook Islands Associated Autonomous State." They have about 20,000 inhabitants. And there is also Niue, the Free Autonomous State of Niue, with 2,500 inhabitants. Based on what you say, those two free, associated autonomous states, with 20,000 and 2,500 inhabitants, respectively, have more rights than Puerto Rico's 4 million people have with respect to the United States.

JL: When we look at the health and quality-of-life indicators for New Zealanders, it is evident that this country makes important investments in its people. That is, [it] invest[s] in the development of [its] human resources, which implies investment mainly in education and health. At the same time, [it has] developed a first-rate infrastructure—which is one purpose for which revenues collected by the government in the form of taxes should be used—to provide not only direct services to the people, but also infrastructural services for the people and the economy as a whole. In addition, we have what Francisco mentioned a while ago about Internet penetration and the excellence of [New Zealand's] telecommunications systems.

It is odd that in all we have seen about New Zealand, we have not heard the cliché of the knowledge economy, something everyone is talking about nowadays, and [New Zealand has] the conditions to develop in that direction. [It has] already made the required investment in [its] people and [its] infrastructure to be well positioned to take real advantage of the so-called knowledge economy, which in most countries, including Puerto Rico, is a mantra you hear every day. One does not see that obsessive emphasis on the subject in official New Zealand government documents, yet [New Zealanders] have already made the investment necessary to pursue that goal.

ACS: In today's program, we have discussed New Zealand as an economic model for Puerto Rico. As I mentioned at the beginning of the program, our illustrious patriot and thinker Rosendo Matienzo-Cintrón had already described it at the beginning of the twentieth century as the most advanced country in the world, in the vanguard in social and economic matters. Its formula is based on a strategic plan, with continuous reinvention and a mindset to maintain a high standard of living and a parliamentary democracy.

Suggested Reading on New Zealand

Birks, Stuart, and Srikanta Chatterjee, eds. *The New Zealand Economy: Issues and Policies*. Wellington, New Zealand: Dunmore Press, 1997.

Hawke, G. R. *The Making of New Zealand: An Economic History*. London: Cambridge Univ. Press, 1985.

Kelsey, Elizabeth Jane. *Reclaiming the Future: New Zealand and the Global Economy*. Toronto: Univ. of Toronto Press, 2000.

Estonia

A small country, with 1,300,000 inhabitants, a former colony of Denmark, Sweden, Prussia, Russia, Germany, and the Soviet Union, which attained sovereignty in 1991 and became one of the most prosperous and advanced countries in the world.

—ÁNGEL COLLADO-SCHWARZ

Estonia in 2010

Population:	1 million
Territory:	45,000 square kilometers
Population density:	32 per square kilometer
Gross domestic product (GDP):	$19.2 billion
Gross national income (GNI):	$19.4 billion
GNI per capita:	$14,460
Unemployment rate:	13.7 percent (2006–2009)
Internet users:	74.2 per 100 people

Source: World Bank, *World Development Indicators* (Washington, DC: World Bank, 2011).

Updated Comments

Estonia has the smallest and most vulnerable economy of the six interview countries. Starting from the lowest base in the group, it experienced the highest growth rate in the years before the global financial crisis in 2008. Real GDP growth was 7.2 percent in 2004, 9.2 percent in 2005, and 10.4 percent in 2006. Even in 2007, the economy grew at an impressive 6.3 percent. But the collapse of investment and consumption that followed the bursting of a real-estate bubble caused a sharp economic contraction. Real GDP dropped 3.6 percent in 2008 and 14.5 percent in 2009, pushing the unemployment rate up to 17.5 percent.

The Estonian government has been consistently conservative in its fiscal management. In 2007, the public debt was only 7.7 percent of GDP. However, this low debt did not shield the economy from the effects of the global financial crisis. A sharp focus on exports to European neighbours such as Finland and Sweden helped start a recovery in 2010, when real GDP posted a 3.1 percent gain. Sustained growth of between 3.5 percent and 3.8 percent per year is projected for 2011–15.

Estonia joined the Organization for Economic Cooperation and Development in 2010. In January 2011, it adopted the euro.

> Francisco Catalá-Oliveras
> Juan Lara

Interview

Interview aired on La Voz del Centro, *Univision Radio Puerto Rico and New York, August 26, 2007.*

ÁNGEL COLLADO-SCHWARZ: Paco, let's give our radio listeners some historical background on Estonia.

FRANCISCO CATALÁ-OLIVERAS: The first thing we have to do is give Estonia's geographical location because I am sure that many of our listeners do not know about Estonia. It is located between the Gulf of Finland and the Gulf of Riga on the Baltic Sea. It has borders on Russia to the east and on Latvia, another Baltic country, to the south. The remaining Baltic state, Lithuania, is farther south.

Estonia is the smallest of the Baltic republics; it has only 1.3 million inhabitants. In fact, of the countries we have reviewed, it is the one with the smallest population. Its history has been truly difficult, I would say even unfortunate. It is not exceptional in that regard because there are many countries that have had quite unfortunate histories.

So, Ángel, during the sixteenth and seventeenth centuries, Estonia was ruled by the Swedes. Then in the eighteenth century it was ceded to the Russian Empire. In the nineteenth century, it generated a fairly strong nationalist movement, which was eventually to lead the fight against the German invasion during the First World War.

In February 1918, Estonia declared its independence and defended itself against the Soviet Union's attempt to annex it. Finally, the Soviet Union acknowledged Estonia's independence in 1920, and Estonia managed to be independent for eighteen or twenty years, until 1940, when it was again annexed by the Soviet Union. This, by the way, was after the infamous German–Soviet Nonaggression Pact signed in 1939, which the Germans themselves broke when they later declared war on the Soviet Union.

During Soviet rule, under [Joseph] Stalin, there was much conflict. Many Estonians who resisted Stalinist policies ended up buried in faraway regions of the Soviet Union, as we all know. Afterward, during Leonid Brezhnev's rule at the beginning of the 1980s, clandestine opposition to the Soviet Union developed in Estonia.

Toward the end of the 1980s, a party known as the "Independence Party" was founded, and a popular front was established, composed, interestingly, of both nationalists and Communists. Both groups promoted separation from the Soviet Union.

All these factors, along with the destabilization experienced by the Soviet Union in 1990 and 1991, opened the opportunity for Estonia to declare its independence once again on August 20, 1991. That same year it joined the United Nations. The year 1991 marked the beginning of an interesting postsocialist or post-Soviet history in that small country—a modern history, if you will, but modern in the most immediate sense of the term, which I think has something to teach us.

ACS: We should point out that [the Estonians'] language is Estonian, and because they are the only people who speak this language, that is a problem for them. To this, we must add what you just said, that Estonia has been invaded by practically all its neighbors: Denmark, Sweden, Prussia, Russia, then Germany and the Soviet Union. In other words, [it] experienced situations in which it was practically impossible to survive. Tell us how [it] managed to hold on, in spite of everything, to become a model economy.

FCO: Estonia's recent history is characterized by two key factors relating to both [its] monetary policy and [its] fiscal and trade policy: openness and stability.

What do I mean when I say "openness"? I mean openness with regard to the rest of the world. For example, Estonia joined the European Union (EU) recently, on May 1, 2004. Prior to joining, Estonia was already very open to international trade. In fact, when it joined the EU, Estonia's customs duties were lower than the EU rates with respect to the rest of the world, so it was already an open economy before joining the EU, and its integration into the EU did not produce any traumatic change.

Also, that openness—a strategic variable in [the Estonians'] policies— is owing mainly to the fact that they acknowledge that their local market, their national market, is very small—a little more than 1 million people. This [factor] has led Estonia to formulate a strategy that is somewhat different from Slovenia's—another case we have discussed—one that has focused more on attracting direct foreign investment and on internationalizing its national enterprises.

Estonians realize that the internationalization of their national enterprises is inevitable in light of their modest market, so if they want to grow, they need to go beyond their own borders. That is why, for Estonians and their government, getting to know foreign markets is imperative. They do a great deal of intelligence work on foreign markets because it is based on that knowledge that they have managed to place themselves in a good competitive position in the international arena. Of course, understanding the markets also makes it possible to reduce risk and uncertainty. In addition, internationalization has made it possible for Estonia to access foreign sources of financing and new technologies, particularly in information management and telecommunications.

In addition to this, there is what [Estonians] call—and the literature refers to it in this way—their national "innovation system." They have built a strong foundation of interaction between national organizations (government, universities, research centers, enterprises) and the counterparts of these [organizations] in foreign countries to guide technological innovation. That interaction between internal and external elements has produced benefits.

Of course, initial conditions are always pertinent. I find it interesting, for example, that Estonia has an extraordinary tradition of libraries, which began in the monasteries of the thirteenth century. Estonia—keep in mind that it has a little more than one million people—has 560 [local] libraries and 20 central libraries. In addition, it has eighty vocational schools, each with its own library specialized in the school's vocational fields. So the tradition of information management goes back to the monasteries' libraries, and that is a very interesting quality of the culture.

So, on the one hand, there is this openness, one of the critical variables for Estonia's trading policy, and on the other, side by side with this variable, there is the attempt to achieve a stable macroeconomy. How have [the Estonians] managed to do it?

The first step was to change the monetary system. Remember that they were using the ruble, and it collapsed. There was a hyperinflation from 1989 to 1991. How could they get rid of the ruble in the middle of the Russian central-bank crisis? It was not going to be easy, but Estonia managed to become the first country in transition to leave the ruble zone and introduce a national currency, the kroon, and it did so in a very particular way, the main objective being to achieve stability.

The new currency was organized by adopting what is known as a "currency-board system." How does that work? The initial intention, I repeat, was to give the new currency credibility and stability. By the way, as a footnote, let me tell you that the International Monetary Fund (IMF) was not fond of national currencies because it associated them with vulnerability. Estonia had its work cut out for it to establish the credibility of its new currency in the eyes of the world.

The first thing [Estonia] did was to peg the new currency to a hard currency at a fixed exchange rate. It was initially pegged to the deutschmark and later to the euro. The fixed rate could not be altered by Estonia's National Bank without Parliament's authorization.

So the currency was pegged to a fixed exchange rate. Moreover, the number of krooni in circulation in Estonia could not be altered except in relation to fluctuations in their foreign-currency reserves, particularly in euros. Hence, though [the Estonians] still did not have euros, their currency, the kroon, was already closely tied to the euro. On the one hand, this guaranteed its stability; on the other, it gave the kroon such credibility that inflation fell to less than 5 percent. They still need to reduce that [rate] further. Right now it is around 4 percent. They want to reduce it to 2.5 percent in order to join the monetary union.

In fact, Estonia is not expected to enter the euro zone before 2008, and some speculate that it will occur after 2010.[1] In any case, [the Estonians] have their monetary system intimately linked to the euro, which gives it stability. They have also achieved stability in their fiscal policy. First, they have a balanced government budget, the only exception being when they have to finance reforms in the pension system, and that is a particular issue. Estonia's population is long lived and is, in fact, declining, and that is a problem they are dealing with. They have a good pension plan, and the only exception to the balanced budget they want to maintain is the need to pay for increases in pension costs. Right now, Estonia's central government has a budget surplus.

So Estonia has managed to combine a series of objectives that have led to employment and growth but that are based on strong monetary and fiscal stability. I believe that is the key strategy that Estonia has used. Some accuse it of having an extremely passive fiscal policy in maintaining a balanced budget, but it must be understood that [Estonia] needed to achieve stability after overcoming the ruble crisis and the demise of the Soviet Union. It has not been easy.

ACS: It is important to point out that not only was Estonia part of the Soviet Union, but it also had the Communist political and economic system that prevailed in the Soviet Union. How, then, did [it] achieve such

1. Estonia would eventually join the Euro Zone in 2009.

a remarkable transition, from a centralized system where there was no market economy to this openness, in a civilized way, without a revolution or gunfire?

FCO: That transition involved many variables. Remember that in the political arena there were already political parties, formed previously, some of them working clandestinely. During the transition, this [factor] helped them politically because they already had that tradition, even if it was developed secretly. In the economic arena, it was not merely a matter of transforming [Estonia] from a planning system to a market system. It meant implementing countless institutional changes that required modifications in law, in finance, in property structure, and in government. [The Estonians] were managing a framework of variables, in macroeconomic and trading policies and in entrepreneurial management, that we cannot simply call "laissez-faire capitalism." In other words, they did this not by moving from planning to laissez-faire capitalism; instead, they moved from planning to a complex framework of institutions, including market relations.

Economic development—and this is perhaps common ground for many economists—always depends on a certain capacity for adapting institutions, which assumes that there is a national system of political economy and economic policy that accommodates change and innovation, one that is capable of organizing internal and external forces. Estonians achieved [such a system]. What is noteworthy about Estonia's transition is how different it was from Slovenia's. These paths to transition were different, both appropriate or all appropriate. Everything depends on the initial conditions.

The example of Slovenia is different from that of Estonia for several reasons. Slovenia was a part not of the Soviet Union, but of the less-centralized Yugoslavian system. Estonia was indeed part of the Soviet Union. [Its] initial conditions were different. Therefore, in 1990 Slovenia had an internal framework superior to that of Estonia. At that time, it had more entrepreneurial capacity, and for the kind of privatization process it undertook, it depended more on internal than external capital, which, by the way, contravened the advice of the IMF; the IMF expected privatization to be achieved by attracting foreign capital. Estonia used foreign capital more intensely than Slovenia because its starting conditions were different.

There is a lesson in the fact that both countries departed from the IMF in their policies: in Slovenia, because its privatization policy did not follow the IMF's advice; in Estonia, because its monetary policy introduced a national currency and so did not follow the IMF's advice. Later on, both the fund and other powers, other external institutions, had to admit the virtues of the two transitions.

ACS: As I understand it, Estonia's economic growth is 10 percent, greater than that of China, which is impressive.

FCO: [Its] economic growth has been huge. These are the data published by the Bank of Estonia for real gross national product (GNP) growth: for 2005, it was 10.5 percent, and for 2006, 11.8 percent. This was after growth of 7 and 8 percent in previous years.

For 2007 and 2008, [it is] anticipate[d] that growth will diminish a little, which is to be expected because figures such as 10 and 11 percent are off the charts. For both years, economic growth of around 8 percent [is projected]. Such growth is indeed impressive, analogous—as you have rightly pointed out—to China's remarkable growth.

ACS: Another interesting element is that Estonia's international credit rating is dramatically different from Puerto Rico's. For example, Moody's rates it A-1, Standard & Poor's A, and Fitch AA. The *Wall Street Journal's* Index of Economic Freedom ranked Estonia fourth with regard to ease of doing business. Only Hong Kong, Singapore, and Luxembourg enjoy greater confidence than Estonia.

FCO: It is evident that [the Estonians] have achieved this [economic growth] thanks to the macroeconomic stability policy that I commented on before, which has guaranteed, on one hand, a very responsible monetary policy and, on the other, a fiscal policy that has ensured a balanced government budget—indeed, better than balanced, a budget *surplus*. Their external debt management has been prudent, and the debt does not weigh heavily at this time. When you compare it to their GDP and the government budget, you find that they have kept their external debt manageable. I believe that their stability and openness have enabled them to achieve the level of confidence they enjoy internationally.

ACS: Paco, what is the employment situation in Estonia?

FCO: Unemployment was high until a few years ago. When I say "a few years," I am talking about three, four, or five years ago. In fact, four years ago it was 10 percent, and now it is around 5 percent.[2] So [Estonia's leaders] are anticipating that manpower will become scarce. Why? We have already mentioned the economic growth, in part supported by the extraordinary expansion of internal demand inside Estonia. The construction, commercial, and industrial sectors are showing robust growth.

Growth in private consumption is projected to be 15 percent for 2007–8. That is enormous, and it is associated with three main factors: employment growth in all sectors, income growth, and greater availability of credit. Bear in mind that with the transition [Estonia] experienced a sort of revolution in the financial system. Also, given the generation of more demand, pension increases have become important. Remember, as I told you, [Estonia has] a relatively long-lived population. On the one hand, the dynamism in internal demand generates great economic growth; and, on the other, as demand increases, it causes a certain imbalance in the current account—that is, between exports and imports. Estonia is importing more than it is exporting. Though its exports have increased, its imports have increased even more. This [difference] has translated into an imbalance in the current account, which is compensated for in part by remittances from abroad, both from investments made by emigrants prior to this recent boom and from workers generating income abroad.

The unemployment rate in Estonia has been decreasing, coinciding—and this is very interesting—with the record of a huge increase in real salaries. Real salaries in Estonia have been increasing at a rate of approximately 8 percent per year, which dramatizes the enormous dynamism of that economy. That is, [Estonians] have managed to reduce unemployment, and at the same time they have increased real salaries, and this

---

2. For data after 2007, when this interview was aired, see the table "World Bank Statistics" in part 3, "Comparative Tables."

[trend] will probably continue because they anticipate, as I said, a shortage of manpower.

In 2005, Estonia's GNI per capita was $9,100 according to the World Bank. It was still relatively modest, but it was already within middle-class levels, if I may put it that way. When the World Bank presents its data based on purchasing-power parity, which is a technical mechanism it uses to make international comparisons, Estonia is reported to have a per capita GNI of $15,420.[3] This [number] speaks well of [its] economy.

Estonia's income distribution is also excellent. In fact, its Gini Index is 33 percent, a very low figure. The lower the index, the less inequality there is in income distribution. It is a very, very good rate.

ACS: Paco, an interesting detail about Estonia is that it assigns a high priority to the educational system and to ensuring that new generations have all the knowledge necessary to further the country's progress. However, what seems especially interesting about [Estonia] is that [its leaders'] strategy for having an educated country goes hand in hand with job opportunities. That is, while developing a knowledge economy and an investment infrastructure, they bring about employment opportunities in parallel, so unemployment has been decreasing, just as you mentioned. I think that is Puerto Rico's big problem: a well-educated generation without the opportunity to progress. We have a top-quality higher-education system, but when our students graduate, they have to leave Puerto Rico because their level of education is too high for the job opportunities available here.

FCO: Yes. Unfortunately, in Puerto Rico we have a kind of gap—if I may use that term—between the dynamics of education and the dynamics of job generation, between, let's say, the educational system, both elementary and superior, and the economic structure. This gap translates into unemployment on the one hand and emigration on the other. In Estonia, they evidently have been linking the dynamics of education to the dynamics of the economy in a harmonious way.

3. For data after 2007, see the table "World Bank Statistics" in part 3, "Comparative Tables."

For example, the structure of service exports in Estonia is really note-worthy. In 1990, Estonia basically did not export *any* services. By 2005, according to the World Bank, [its] service exports amounted to $3 billion, mainly in transportation, insurance, financial services, and services related to the communications and information industry. This [shift] is really illuminating.

Let me repeat, as an indicator that Puerto Rico is lagging behind, a figure we have quoted in previous programs: in 2005,[4] Puerto Rico had 221 Internet users for each thousand inhabitants. The same year Estonia had 513, more than twice the number of users in Puerto Rico. Such intensive use of information and communications technology shows two things: a high educational level and a high level of openness to the rest of the world.

ACS: Thirty-three percent of the households in Estonia have a computer, which is an impressive figure. They have more than seven hundred public places that offer free access to the Internet over high-speed wireless connections. Seventy-two percent of Internet users do their banking transactions online.

FCO: Here I have another figure to complement those: 75 percent of Estonia's schools have access to the Internet.

ACS: Also, Estonia's government is probably one of the most technologically oriented governments there is. In 2000, the cabinet decided to call its meetings without using paper, which it replaced with an electronic-document and information-management system. You can even pay your taxes online. Practically all your transactions with the government can be done using your computer. That is impressive.

FCO: At the same time, [Estonia has] a large agricultural sector, which also seems important. That is a characteristic we have pointed out in analyzing other small countries, and it is illuminating.

ACS: Another relevant point is that [it has] a very simple tax system, based on a fixed rate of 23 percent on personal and corporate income. There are no exceptions; everybody pays 23 percent, and that's that.

---

4. For up-to-date data, see the table "World Bank Statistics" in part 3, "Comparative Tables."

FCO: Yes, very simple. Of course, with [Estonia's] incorporation into the EU, it took on income from the consumption tax. But [the] income tax is certainly a very simple, broad-based system.

ACS: In an e-government system, all income tax returns are filed over the Internet using a personal computer. [Estonians] avoid all kinds of unnecessary paperwork.

FCO: Imagine the savings that entails. They are saving paper, time, and effort.

ACS: Going back to [its] technology- and information-based economy, Estonia is attracting foreign investors seeking investment opportunities. Several companies that are very successful in Europe have their headquarters there, in Tallinn, the capital city, because innovative offerings are available to them. In Estonia, many young people are in important positions—that is, they have been given many opportunities. Though the population is aging, as you said, there are great opportunities for young people.

FCO: There was recently an incident, unfortunate in my opinion, that dramatizes Estonia's technological development. You must have read about it in the press. I am referring to the famous incident about the statue of the Unknown Soldier; the statue was in a plaza in Tallinn, and they moved it to a cemetery. They didn't tear it down; they simply moved it.

This caused some concern in Russia and among the Russian minority living in Estonia, which is considerable—25 to 30 percent of the population. Russia responded by starting what amounted to a cyberwar with Estonia, trying to cut off [its] access to the Internet. This [incident] dramatized the importance of information management and the international links that the country has as a function of such management. Estonia's dynamic economy functions in great measure in the context of the communications industry.

ACS: Regarding that incident, when I was in Tallinn, I visited a museum that is dedicated to the Russian invasion of Estonia. [It] depict[s] historical events such as the signing of the German–Soviet treaty, in which Ministers [Joachim von] Ribbentrop and [Vyacheslav] Molotov agreed to the annexation of the Baltic countries by the Soviet Union in exchange for allowing the Nazi invasion of Poland. Estonians resented that invasion very much because the Russians were very abusive. They carried off some Estonians to concentration camps in Siberia, and Estonians resented it terribly. In Estonia, there is a minority Russian population, which you mentioned. Let's not forget that the Russian strategy was to populate its republics with Russian citizens so that [the republics] would assimilate. With the fall of the Soviet Union, those Russians remained in the new republics in very tense circumstances, isolated from the local community.

FCO: Assimilation has evidently always been one of the governing principles for colonizing empires. By the way, Ángel, I was reading something about the history of the Roman Empire and how it had a policy of Latinizing all its provinces. This should serve as a lesson to all empires because in time Latin became a dead language.

ACS: Let's go back to Estonia's statistics. An item that seems significant is that eight out of ten Estonians have a cell phone. Gas stations in Tallinn are equipped with Wi-Fi connections that allow drivers to access the Internet while filling up their gas tanks. It is quite interesting. In Puerto Rico, we are way behind in terms of these Wi-Fi zones. But the other day, to my surprise, in the town square of Añasco, in western Puerto Rico, where I went to present my book *Voces de la cultura I,* I found that there is free wireless access.

FCO: Now that you have mentioned cell phone subscribers, I have a figure here from the World Bank. In Estonia, there are about 108.8 cell phone subscriptions for each 100 inhabitants. That is, there are more subscriptions than inhabitants. In Puerto Rico, there are a little more than 60 subscriptions per 100 inhabitants. The intensity of communications in that country is really extraordinary.

ACS: Estonia has a parliamentary government with a single chamber. As we know, most democracies of the world are parliamentary systems.

FCO: That is another example we ought to follow.

ACS: Paco, in terms of infrastructure investment, what data do we have on Estonia?

FCO: [Estonia has] made a good investment in telecommunications infrastructure, but also in roads and transportation. We must not forget—and this is linked both to the infrastructure and to the economic profile—that [it has] a well-developed, traditional lumber industry, which is now modernized. In fact, wood products have often made up around 15 to 20 percent of [its] exports. This [number] fluctuates; sometimes it is more, sometimes less.

So [Estonians], together with their modern, cutting-edge economy, also have modern agriculture. In the case of lumber, we're talking about products already in the manufacturing sector. But they also have a traditional agricultural sector generating primary food products. They produce potatoes, vegetables, meats, and dairy products. They have a good fishing industry. In fact, nearly 8 percent of Estonia's exports are food products. So they have a diversified and dynamic food industry, and their forests supply a significant lumber industry.

ACS: Talk to us about Estonia's labor force.

FCO: First of all, [it has] a capable labor force. One labor-intensive activity where the workforce is strong is agriculture. Some 11 percent of all workers are in agriculture. As I said earlier, [Estonia has] a good food-production sector and extraordinary resources in forestry, which supports a wood-products industry that supplies furniture, paper, and other products. Employment in manufacturing is around 20 percent. Most employment in Estonia—and this should not come as a surprise, based on what we have said already—is in the service sector, which represents 69 percent of all jobs. So it is also a big exporter of services.

Now, with [respect to] 11 percent of the jobs, agriculture contributes 4, 5, or 6 percent—it varies—of the GNP. For 20 percent of the jobs, manufacturing contributes 29 or 30 percent of the GNP. For 69 percent of the jobs, services contribute nearly 67 percent of the GNP.

Employees in manufacturing are making mostly wood products because they have significant forest resources. Also notable are products related to information and telecommunications. [Estonia] also [has] an apparel industry and make[s] chemical products.

The service sector, in turn, is headed by transportation, insurance, finance, and all the services related to information technology and telecommunications. Certainly, if I were to highlight one sector in both manufacturing and services that in recent years has left a mark on Estonia, it would have to be telecom and information management.

ACS: Paco, it's important to point out that Estonia's total labor force is 673,000. That is a 2006 figure[5] from the Central Intelligence Agency *World Factbook,* and that is more or less 50 percent of its population. Here we see a parallel with Ireland, where 2 million people are in the labor force out of a total of 4 million.

FCO: There is a parallel with Ireland, with Singapore, and with many of the relatively small, successful countries we have reviewed. It is in contrast to Puerto Rico's situation, where out of 4 million people our labor force is around 1,200,000. That would be about 30 percent. If Puerto Rico had half its population active in the labor force, as Estonia does, it would have 2 million workers. Certainly, Puerto Rico's rate of participation in the labor market is very low, which illustrates several problems: first, the economy is incapable of generating enough jobs; and, second, there is an extraordinary level of dependency here. Curiously, Puerto Rico's high unemployment rate coincides with a low labor-participation rate. In all the countries we have discussed, we have seen quite the opposite—decreasing unemployment rates with high participation rates. Estonia is only one example of this [trend].

ACS: Why do you think that is?

FCO: I believe there are several related problems here. In Puerto Rico, we are linked to a wealthy economy that sets the standards, the parameters. Let me give you an example of such parameters. "This population will apply for food stamps. These are the qualifying standards and parameters." According to those parameters, in the poorest state in the United States, Mississippi, between 10 and 20 percent of the population would qualify. When that same parameter is applied to Puerto Rico, 50 percent of the population qualifies. There is nothing wrong with people's receiving assistance from the state when they have no work and need to satisfy their basic needs. That is only human. But turning the effort to qualify for dependency into a public policy—that is, to make *that* our objective, not Puerto Rico's development—undermines the country's culture of work. It also gradually causes political vision to disintegrate.

---

5. For up-to-date data, see the table "Central Intelligence Agency *World Factbook* Statistics" in part 3, "Comparative Tables."

When we think about resident commissioners, we think about them attaining more funds for Puerto Rico's dependency. We do not think about a commissioner linking us to different markets to export products from Puerto Rico. Seldom do we think in terms of economic dynamism and empowerment for Puerto Rico. So this [system] gradually wears away our political vision. I think that these variables, which are intangible, have been turning Puerto Rico's economy into something porous, frail. Public management in terms of trade and development is minimal, and dependency prevails, as can be seen even in the headlines of our newspapers. This is no way to develop a country.

ACS: All of this has an effect on people's initiative. It generates a psychological factor that I think we need to stress. That factor is motivation—especially of young people, for whom Estonia is a place of opportunity, a place with a future. That motivation is lost when you have a society and economy based on welfare.

FCO: That is correct. And I think there is yet another element that has to do with the worldview. In Estonia, Slovenia, Singapore, and many other countries we have not mentioned here, when they talk about the rest of the world, they mean exactly that—the rest of the world. In Puerto Rico, when we talk about the rest of the world, we are referring to the United States, a country with only 6 percent of the world's population. It is an incredibly important country that we must take into account, but the world is much, much wider. When we think about markets, we need to think about *many* markets. When we think about sources of investment and sources of capital, we need to think about *many* sources of capital. When we think about capital promotion abroad, we also need to think about *many* markets. I believe that this narrow way of seeing things has diminished Puerto Rico as a country.

ACS: Paco, let's talk about Estonia's trade. As we know, Estonia is separated from Finland by the Baltic Sea. There is constant marine traffic between the two countries, more than with other neighboring countries, the other Baltic republics. In fact, there is even a ferry going back and forth constantly between Helsinki and Tallinn. How would you describe Estonia's trade dependency on Finland?

FCO: First of all, Estonia's export profile is quite diverse. It exports machinery, wood products such as paper, textiles, food, furniture, chemical products, and—as I said earlier—certain services. Among them, services related to the information technology industry stand out. As we have already said, Finland, one of its immediate neighbors, just across the sea, is its primary trading partner. Estonia's exports to Finland compose about 26 percent of its total exports. Note that—as is the case with all the other countries we have examined—though Finland is its primary market, that does not mean it exports 50, 60, or 70 percent to that single market. Exports [there] are always around 20, 25, or 30 percent, never more.

A second important export destination is Sweden. There is also Latvia, and then in fourth, fifth, and sixth places are Russia, Germany, and Lithuania. I assume that trade with Russia will decrease in the coming years. Trade with the remaining partners of the EU will gradually increase, for obvious reasons. Remember that Estonia has been part of the EU only since 2004.

It is interesting that Estonia in its trade policy has declared that one of its objectives is not to depend for its foreign trade on its immediate neighbors, such as Finland. Of course, it always considers Finland an important partner, the most important, but its objective is to expand its exports beyond its immediate boundaries, beyond its immediate neighbors, to other European partners and even to countries that are not EU members.

Remember that one of Estonia's distinctive characteristics, even before entering the EU, was its openness in trade, which I consider a key element. To this openness, we can add its macroeconomic stability as a function of its monetary and fiscal policies. And to that openness and stability we can add a third element that is also found in other countries we have examined: diversification, both in its export and import markets and in its internal economic profile.

We mentioned a while ago that Estonia has a large agricultural industry and diversified manufacturing and service industries, [even] with a population of only 1,300,000.[6] So we are talking about a fairly modest scale. In spite of that [small scale], however, diversity is central to its economy, which is yet another distinctive trait.

---

6. For data after 2007, see the table "World Bank Statistics" in part 3, "Comparative Tables."

I would say that in all the small countries we have reviewed, diversi-fication has played a central strategic role. This [fact] contradicts the old truism that a market of modest size has to be specialized. Not that [these small countries] do not have areas of specialization—we have already highlighted Estonia's specialization in information technology and tele-com—but there must be diversity because the markets of such countries are not defined exclusively by national borders. With today's openness in trade, the market for such countries is, as we said earlier, the world. Of course, in that world [Estonia] attend[s] to [its] most probable lines of access.

ACS: I think that what you just said is very important: having a bal-anced economy and labor force, not putting all your eggs in one basket, which in my opinion is one of the biggest problems facing Puerto Rico.

A healthy economy must have the active participation of the agricul-tural sector. Every country in the world has important agricultural activ-ity. In Puerto Rico, as we said earlier, it is only a marginal activity.

The *kind* of industry is of utmost importance. Here we have all our eggs in one basket, which is the pharmaceutical industry, whereas all these other countries we have studied, such as Ireland and Singapore, have diversified their participation in different sectors of the economy.

FCO: Yes, here we have confused structural change with absolute change. It is natural that as a country develops, its production profile and level of employment will gradually change; the weight of the service sec-tor gradually increases, and that of manufacturing and agriculture gradu-ally decreases. But this change is *relative*.

In the case of Puerto Rico, there has been a change in *absolute* weight. That is, agriculture has not decreased relative to other sectors; it has con-tracted in absolute terms. I think this is one of Puerto Rico's big mistakes. Yet, as you say, we should not put all our eggs in one basket. Here we are very proud of having a big pharmaceutical sector. That is fine, but it also contributes to our poor diversification because right now most of our manufacturing is pharmaceuticals. Seventy percent of our exports consist of pharmaceuticals. If that sector is affected, we do not have sufficient diversification to cushion us, so the lack of diversification in our economy and our markets should be a concern.

ACS: You mentioned dependency on welfare, which I consider very important in terms of how much it harms Puerto Rico. Though Estonians are not highly dependent on welfare, the government does provide people's basic needs, including [through] a high-quality education system and a very good public-health system—a *universal* health system, which every developed country has with the exception of the United States.

FCO: You mentioned that Estonia's tax system is simple and that taxes are relatively low; the highest marginal rates are *very* low. But [it] do[es] have relatively high social security taxes, to guarantee pensions and social security. This security is not welfare. You earn it with your work because [you] certainly need to have some guarantees for the so-called golden years.

In Estonia, besides developing first-rate schools, they have made an effort to improve health services. I will quote [a] figure just to show the contrast with Puerto Rico: for every 1,000 inhabitants, Estonia has almost 7.0 hospital beds; in Puerto Rico, we have 3.3 hospital beds for each 1,000 inhabitants. That gives you an idea.

ACS: In today's program, we have presented Estonia as an economic model for Puerto Rico. We have seen how a country with a population of barely 1.3 million and that has been been colonized by different countries for almost all its history has in just fifteen years—during which it achieved sovereignty—become a member of the EU, generated a growth rate as high as China's, and achieved a very low unemployment rate and a labor-participation rate of almost 50 percent.

Suggested Reading on Estonia

Grover, Alexander. *The New Estonian Golden Age: How Estonia Will Rise to Be One of Europe's Five Richest Nations.* Charleston, SC: CreateSpace, 2009.

Hannula, Helena, Slavo Radosevic, and Nick Von Tunzelmann, eds. *Estonia, the New EU Economy: Building a Baltic Miracle?* Surrey, UK: Ashgate, 2006.

Haavisto, Tarmo, ed. *The Transition to a Market Economy: Transformation and Reform in the Baltic States.* Cheltenham, UK: Edward Elgar, 1997.

PART 3

Comparative Tables

World Bank Statistics, 2010

	Puerto Rico	Singapore	Slovenia	Ireland	Israel	New Zealand	Estonia
Population (millions)	4	5	2	4	8	4	1
Surface area (in thousands of square kilometers)[a]	9	1	20	70	22	268	45
Density (population per square kilometer)	449	7,252	102	65	359	17	32
Gross domestic product (GDP) (in billions)	$96.3[c]	$208.8	$46.9	$211.4	$217.3	$126.7[d]	$19.2
Gross national income (GNI) (in billions)[b]	$63.3[c]	$203.4	$49.0	$183.7	$207.2	$124.2[d]	$19.4
GNI per capita[b]	$15,203[c]	$40,070	$23,860	$41,000	$27,170	$28,770[d]	$14,460
Unemployment rate (2006–2009)	13.4%	5.9%	5.9%	11.7%	7.6%	6.1%	13.7%
Internet users (per 100 people)	42.7	70.1	69.2	69.7	65.4	83.0	74.2

[a]Land only.
[b]Atlas method.
[c]Preliminary figures.
[d]2009.

Sources: For the 2010 statistics, World Bank, *World Development Indicators* (Washington, DC: World Bank, 2011). For preliminary figures, Puerto Rico Planning Board, *Economic Report to the Governor 2010* (San Juan: Puerto Rico Planning Board, 2010).

Central Intelligence Agency *World Factbook* Statistics, 2010

	Puerto Rico	Singapore	Slovenia	Ireland	Israel	New Zealand	Estonia
Area (in square kilometers)[a]	13,790	697	20,273	70,273	20,770	267,710	45,228
Population[b]	3,989,133	4,740,737	2,000,092	4,670,976	7,473,052	4,290,347	1,282,963
Labor force (in millions)	1.5[c]	3.075	0.930	2.15	3.08	2.32	0.668
Labor force as a percentage of population	37.5%[d]	64.4%	46.5%	45.7%	41.1%	54.0%	51.4%
Unemployment rate	12.0%[e]	2.1%	10.6%	13.7%	6.4%	6.5%	17.5%
Gross domestic product (GDP) (in billions)	$93.52	$222.7	$47.85	$204.3	$213.1	$140.4	$19.78
GDP real growth	−5.8%	14.5%	1.2%	−1.0%	4.6%	1.5%	3.1%
GDP per capita	$16,300	$62,100	$28,200	$37,300	$29,800	$27,700	$19,100
GDP composition:							
Agriculture	1.0%	0%	2.4%	2.0%	2.4%	4.6%	2.5%
Industry	45%	27.2%	31%	29%	32.6%	24%	28.7%
Services	54%[f]	72.8%	66.6%	70%[g]	65%	71.4%	68.8%
Year of sovereignty	NA	1965	1991	1921	1948	1907	1991

[a]Land and water.

[b]July 2011 estimate.

[c]2007. The Economist Intelligence Unit (EIU) gives 1.105 million for 2009.

[d]2007. Based on figures from the EIU for 2009, the number should be 28%.

[e]2002. The EIU gives 16.2% for 2009.

[f]2005 estimate.

[g]2009 estimate.

Source: U.S. Central Intelligence Agency (CIA), *The World Factbook* (Washington, DC: Directorate of Intelligence, 2010), available at https://www.cia .gov/library/publications/download/download-2010/index.html or http://www.cia.gov/library/publications/the-world-factbook/index.html, accessed July 22, 2011; and Economist Intelligence Unit reports for various countries and years, acquired and now owned by the Fundación Voz del Centro.

Growth of Real Gross Domestic Product (GDP, %), Five-Year Forecast: Economist Intelligence Unit, December 2011 (Ireland November 2011)

	2007[a]	2008[a]	2009[a]	2010[a]	2011[a]	2012[b]	2013[b]	2014[b]	2015[b]	2016[b]
Puerto Rico	-1.2	-2.8	-4.0	-3.8	-1.7	0.5	1.4	NA	NA	NA
Singapore	8.8	1.5	-0.8	14.5	5.1	4.0	4.6	4.8	5.1	5.3
Slovenia	6.9	3.7	-8.1	1.2	1.2	0.5	1.5	2.0	2.4	2.5
Ireland	5.2	-3.0	-7.0	-0.4	1.2	-0.2	0.7	2.0	2.4	2.6
Israel	5.4	4.2	0.8	4.7	4.5	2.7	3.6	4.4	4.8	5.3
New Zealand	3.6	-0.9	0.0	2.3	1.5	3.0	3.3	3.2	3.1	3.0
Estonia	6.9	-5.1	-13.9	3.1	7.3	2.2	3.4	3.4	3.5	3.7

[a]Actual figure.
[b]Economist Intelligence Unit forecast.
Source: Data compiled from The Economist Intellence Unit Limited. © The Economist Intellence Unit Limited, London 2011.

PART 4

Newspaper Columns
by Dr. Ángel Collado-Schwarz

Note: All columns were published in *El Nuevo Día,* Puerto Rico's leading newspaper. Reprinted here with permission.

Federal Laws Mean Hardships for Puerto Rican Consumers

January 26, 2006

Puerto Rican consumers have begun the twenty-first century struggling with increases in the cost of living—increases in power and water rates, in the price of gasoline, in tolls and bus fares, and in postage stamps, along with a possible regressive tax on consumption and so on. These increases are the result of international circumstances, such as the rise in oil prices, poor public administration by the political parties in recent years, and the political status we have had since 1898.

One of the most disastrous effects of Puerto Rico's political status on Puerto Rican consumers is the high cost of shipping by sea. In a study conducted for the [Puerto Rican] House of Representatives, economist José Antonio Herrero estimated that Puerto Rico is overpaying nearly $500 million per year in transportation of goods between Puerto Rico and the United States (at constant prices for 2000). Because Puerto Rico is an island, all merchandise enters and leaves the island by sea.

US maritime cabotage laws limit shipping traffic between US ports, including its territories and possessions, to ships built and registered in the United States. This legislation has applied to Puerto Rico since 1900, when Congress approved the Foraker Act, which provided that cabotage between Puerto Rico and the United States would be "regulated pursuant to the provisions of laws applicable to said maritime trade between any two coastal districts in the United States." When the Jones Act was passed in 1917, the cabotage laws remained in force, and their effects continue to this day.

Cabotage laws force us to use the US Merchant Marine exclusively, which is the most expensive and inefficient commercial shipping service in the world (it has not built a single ship for years). This imposition is an aberration in current times, when free trade and globalization prevail.

Puerto Rican consumers are unnecessarily paying more for products acquired in Puerto Rico. It is estimated that if cabotage laws did not apply in Puerto Rico, the costs of transporting the merchandise and raw materials we import would be reduced by as much as 40 percent. In addition, it would mean a reduction of almost $150 million per year in the transportation costs of our exports, which would improve the competitive position of our products in international trade. The results would have a multiplier effect in Puerto Rico's economy.

In 1931, the Brookings Institution, in a study titled *Porto Rico and Its Problems,* stated that "American coastwise shipping laws are a handicap to Porto Rican trade. . . . It increases the cost of Porto Rican goods. . . . The requirement that American ships shall be used tends to offset somewhat the advantage which the tariff gives to Porto Rico in selling in American markets. . . . If Porto Rico were free to use foreign shipping whenever it found an advantage in so doing, it is quite probable that it would be able to build up a larger trade with foreign countries than it now has."

The fact that Puerto Rico generates one-fourth of the total income of the obsolete US Merchant Marine is indeed ironic.

Puerto Rican consumers subsidize the colonial power. The Brookings Institution, in its 1931 report, said that "it is distinctly unfortunate that so large a share of the cost of carrying out such a policy is placed upon the shoulders of Porto Rican consumers, whose purchasing power is far below the American standard."

Cabotage laws are not equally applicable in all US territories. For example, the Northern Mariana Islands and Samoa are exempt from them, and in 1936 the US Virgin Islands were also exempted.

Puerto Rico does not have to change its political status to get exempted from the cabotage laws. In 1994, Representative David Noriega (Puerto Rican Independence Party) proposed a resolution in the Puerto Rico House of Representatives requesting that the US Congress exclude Puerto Rico from the application of these laws. The resolution was cosponsored by Representatives Aníbal Acevedo-Vilá (Popular Democratic Party) and Antonio Silva-Delgado (New Progressive Party), and it passed unanimously in 1995–96. The Senate also passed it later in a unanimous vote. It is significant that the resolution was supported by a legislature controlled by the New Progressive Party, with Roberto Rexach-Benítez and Zaida Hernández leading the Senate and the House of Representatives, respectively. Even though the resolution had the support of trading organizations and bankers, sadly it did not progress in the US Congress owing to the opposition of some U.S. unions, owners of the ships and the Democratic Party.

The Port of the Americas is one of the most remarkable development opportunities for Puerto Rico. However, as long as the cabotage laws apply to Puerto Rico, its development will be dramatically limited, and it will be in no position to compete with other transshipment ports that can maximize the opportunities provided by free trade. The transshipment port may very well end up being a stillborn project owing to the application of these laws.

The situation has gotten worse with the extension of the North American Free Trade Agreement to the Central American Free Trade Agreement. Now, Latin American countries have the same access to the US market as Puerto Rico does, but without the limitation of having to use the most expensive and inefficient system of commercial shipping in the world.

At a time when in Puerto Rico the central government and the legislature are looking to provide relief to consumers, and Congress is controlled by the Republican Party, a promoter of free trade, it is appropriate to reevaluate the targeting of lobbying resources to exempt Puerto Rico from these unfair cabotage laws. The exemption would provide relief to consumers and maximize the transshipment port's economic potential.

China and Latin America

February 23, 2006

Chinese civilization, which is thousands of years old, has been the most successful in the history of the universe. Its most extraordinary icon is the Great Wall, constructed more than two thousand years ago. It is the biggest construction project ever undertaken. Construction took dozens of years, and it is the only structure on the planet that can be seen from the moon. The wall was to protect China's civilization from barbarians. By the thirteenth century, the Chinese people already had printed books (one thousand years before Gutenberg's "invention") and gunpowder and had developed centralized systems of government.

Today in the economic field China continues its ascending path. The [Chinese] State Statistics Office announced several weeks ago that the Chinese economy grew 9.9 percent in 2005. China has surpassed France and the United Kingdom and is now the fourth most important economic power in the world, after the United States, Japan, and Germany. The Chinese economy has experienced an average growth of 9.6 percent since 1979.

At the end of 1994, the president of China, Hu Jintao, visited Brazil, Argentina, Chile, and Cuba, launching a big political and commercial offensive by China in Latin America. Latin America, with 500 million inhabitants, is the second most important foreign investment target for China.

On his visit to Latin America, Hu made investment promises of $100 billion in the region as a whole.

Hu's tour resulted in concrete investments of $7.7 billion in Brazil and in letters of intent for projects in Argentina in the amount of $17.9 billion. The Asian giant, with the largest population on the planet, is interested in

Latin America, which is rich in the raw materials China needs to sustain its dramatic growth. China is seeking oil, gas, coal, steel, cement, rubber latex, copper, iron, aluminum, platinum, and nickel as well as soybeans and other foods. The region's trade with China jumped from less than $10 billion in 1993 to more than $50 billion in 2004.

The Chinese petroleum company Sinopec has signed an agreement with the Brazilian government of Luiz Inácio Lula da Silva for the construction of a gas pipe that will connect the South of Brazil with the North. Hu and Lula have signed cooperative agreements in the aerospace field with the objective of launching a satellite jointly in 2006. China has become Brazil's second most important trading partner.

In Argentina, [Néstor] Kirchner's government announced new Chinese investments in the amount of $20 billion in infrastructure, energy, and telecommunications development as well as in satellite technology and computer science projects.

Hu's visit to Santiago, Chile, formally initiated negotiations for a free-trade agreement with China. The mining concerns Coldeco in Chile and Minmetals in China have signed a long-term agreement for the Chilean company to supply China with copper shipments in the amount of $1.8 billion. China has displaced the United States as Chile's principal copper buyer.

Last year during the inauguration of the Mexico–China Business Forum, Mexican president Vicente Fox remarked that "Mexico and China are two clear examples of the advantages of opening the economy to trade and investment." In 2003, China became the second-largest provider of goods to Mexico, after the United States.

Venezuela, which owns the principal oil reserves outside the Middle East, is the main attraction for China, which has become the second-largest importer of oil in the world. Last year China signed nineteen agreements with Venezuela, where it is already operating oil wells and purchasing 120,000 barrels of oil per month. China has extended Venezuela a line of credit of $700 million for housing construction. In the last of his three visits to China, President Hugo Chávez unveiled a statue of Simón Bolívar in Beijing. Trade between Venezuela and China is worth nearly $3 billion, an increase of more than 100 percent.

China is investing in projects in Ecuador, Peru, and Colombia. The recently elected president of Bolivia, Evo Morales, visited Beijing in January 2006 and managed to negotiate an investment agreement to develop the energy sector of his country through conversion of Bolivian natural gas to diesel, thus minimizing damage to the environment.

I do not mean to say that diesel is cleaner than natural gas, but it is cleaner than burning crude oil or gasoline as fuel. So [the Chinese] are choosing diesel over oil, and they can use their natural gas to make diesel.

During the past few years, China has also penetrated the Caribbean. This is a move that the United States would never have allowed during the Cold War. Toward the end of 2004, Chinese president Hu Jintao visited Cuba, where two agreements were signed on biotechnology, education, telecommunications, and Cuba's external debt. China is the third most important trade partner of Cuba, following Venezuela and Spain. In 2005, Granada made its relations with China official and received millions of dollars in funding for infrastructure projects. Dominica also made its relations with China official, and it has the promise of investment amounting to $112 million over the next six years. The Bahamas and Guyana are also aggressively formalizing agreements with China. Last year China's vice president visited Jamaica to inaugurate the China–Caribbean Economic and Trade Cooperation Forum, the first official state-sponsored congress [for the region]. The eleven participating countries signed a multilateral economic and trade cooperation plan. In 2004, trade between China and the Caribbean reached $2 billion, a 42.5 percent increase over the previous year.

While the United States remains distracted by the Iraq War, China is penetrating and conquering Latin America and the Caribbean without firing a single shot. Yet while the [region] refocuses on the emerging Asiatic power, Puerto Rico must remain on the sidelines, a mere spectator, because its current status does not allow it to sign bilateral agreements, to take advantage of trade opportunities, or even to use the most efficient and economic transportation services, as do our neighboring countries, including tiny Dominica and Grenada.

The Visits of Five Presidents, a Pope, and a King

March 30, 2006

In the five hundred years that have passed since its colonization, Puerto Rico has had official visits from seven figures of the highest international rank. All of these visits took place after the US invasion in 1898.

The first visit was on November 21, 1906, when President Theodore Roosevelt stopped over in Puerto Rico on his way back [to the United States] from a trip to the Panama Canal to inspect the installations being built there. The trip broke with American tradition: for the first time, a US president had traveled outside the continental United States. Roosevelt disembarked in Ponce and was greeted by his friend Governor Beckham Winthrop and by Mayor Simón Moret. Traveling along the Central Road, making stops in Aibonito, Cayey, and Caguas, the delegation arrived in Río Piedras, where the president delivered a speech vowing to obtain US citizenship for Puerto Ricans (a promise that he could not keep owing to opposition in the colonial power). A reception was given in his honor at La Fortaleza, the governor's official residence, and the next day he left on an express train for Arecibo, then on to Utuado, Adjuntas, and Ponce, where he embarked to continue his trip back to the United States. While in Puerto Rico, Roosevelt had the opportunity to see firsthand the three main industries of the country: tobacco, sugar, and coffee.

The second visit took place three decades later, on July 6, 1934. President Franklin D. Roosevelt arrived in the heavy battle cruiser USS *Houston* and docked in Mayagüez, where he was greeted by the disastrous governor Blanton Winship, who had been appointed by Roosevelt himself and who would be responsible for the Ponce Massacre of 1937. Roosevelt visited Ponce afterward and then passed through Juana Díaz, Cayey, and Caguas on his way to San Juan. There was a reception for him at La Fortaleza, which various Puerto Rican political figures also attended, including the two main political leaders, both annexationists: Senate president Rafael Martínez-Nadal and House of Representatives president Miguel Ángel García-Méndez. Also present was Resident Commissioner Santiago Iglesias-Pantín, himself an annexationist and the author of at least one bill in Congress calling for statehood for Puerto Rico.

Both [Teddy and Franklin] Roosevelt had previously been undersecretaries of the navy. They had a great interest in the role of Puerto Rico as a military bastion and as the gateway to the Panama Canal.

After the Second World War, President Harry S. Truman visited Puerto Rico on February 21, 1948, with his chief of staff, admiral and former governor of Puerto Rico William D. Leahy. They were received by US secretary of the interior Julius A. Krug, Governor Jesus T. Piñero, and other local dignitaries. Truman visited the forts in Old San Juan, the Fanguito slum, a factory, and a hospital in Bayamón. Then he had lunch at the Jagueyes Hotel in Aguas Buenas with Senate president Luis Muñoz Marín, House of Representatives president Francisco Susoni, Chief Justice Martín Travieso, Resident Commissioner Antonio Fernós-Isern, and other local dignitaries and members of the military. There was a reception at La Fortaleza afterward, and President Truman spent the night on a navy battleship. This visit was the prelude to a meeting chaired by Leahy in which the [US] Armed Forces gave back to Puerto Rico the land they had occupied during the [Second World] War.

On February 22, 1960, President Dwight D. Eisenhower visited Puerto Rico. This fourth presidential visit was scheduled as a technical stopover at Ramey Air Force Base in Aguadilla so that the president could rest before continuing his journey to South America. Governor [Luis] Muñoz Marín's lobbying efforts ultimately obliged Eisenhower to land at the airport in Isla Verde for a thirty-minute photo opportunity, after which the president would take off and land at his Puerto Rican destination, Ramey Air Force Base. Days later, on his return from South America, Eisenhower landed at Ramey, played golf, and flew by helicopter to Dorado Beach to have lunch with his friend Dr. Henry W. Wriston and with members of [Wriston's] organization, the American Assembly.

The fifth and last presidential visit was on December 15, 1961, by President John F. Kennedy, who visited Puerto Rico en route to Venezuela and Colombia. He was received by Governor Luis Muñoz Marín, who was serving his last term as governor. President Kennedy referred to Puerto Rico as "an island which has an entirely different tradition and history, which is made up of people of an entirely different cultural origin than on the mainland of the United States." The president spent the night at La Fortaleza. Given the Cuban Revolution of 1959, the Cold War escalated dramatically in the Caribbean, making Cuba and Puerto Rico vital pieces on the geopolitical chessboard.

On October 12, 1984, Pope John Paul II visited Puerto Rico for a few hours and was greeted by US secretary of state George Shultz (representing President Ronald Reagan), Governor Carlos Romero-Barceló, and an audience of about half a million Puerto Ricans. As the pope finished the mass, which was celebrated in the parking lot of the Plaza las Américas, he exclaimed, "Long live Puerto Rico!"

On May 24, 1987, King Juan Carlos I of Spain was greeted by Governor Rafael Hernández-Colón. The king spent two nights at La Fortaleza. In his message to the people, the king warned Latin American countries, including Puerto Rico, against succumbing to assimilation attempts that were contrary to their own history and identity.

Why has no US president visited Puerto Rico officially since JFK's visit in 1961? Despite the fact that annexationists have governed Puerto Rico for twenty of the past thirty-seven years, they have not been able to secure a visit by a US president, not even when for sixteen of those twenty years the annexationist governor belonged to the same political party as the president (Republicans: Ferré-Nixon; Democrats: Romero-Carter, Rosselló-Clinton). And why is it the pope, one of the principal international diplomatic figures, and the king of Spain, a leader in the Hispanic world, are the ones to visit Puerto Rico and not US presidents? Is the metropolis sending us a message, or is it just coincidence? In everyday life, Puerto Ricans are getting a clear message when their "friends and neighbors" in the United States have not wanted to visit them for forty-five years!

The Bride Refuses to Marry

July 28, 2006

Statehood, which [José Celso] Barbosa referred to as the "regional home-land" and others have called "*jíbaro* statehood," does not exist. The United States is very different today from what the Founding Fathers of the first democracy conceived as a federation of autonomous states: it is now a centralized, federated country. Statehood is not an option for Puerto Rico because the United States does not want it, and the US messages on the subject have been consistent for more than one hundred years. But no one is so blind as one who chooses not to see.

Our colonial power has sent us these ten significant signs over the past century:

1. On January 21, 1899, President William McKinley met with our elected delegation, composed of [Eugenio María de] Hostos, Manuel Zeno-Gandía, and Julio Henna. The Puerto Ricans came out of the meeting dispirited after realizing that neither statehood nor independence was what the new colonial power had in mind.
2. In 1922, the chief justice of the US Supreme Court, William Howard Taft, confirmed that Puerto Rico is a unincorporated territory and declared that we belong to but are not a part of the United States. Taft knew the territorial situation very well because he had been the governor of the Philippines and later of Cuba, secretary of war, and president.
3. In 1932, the United States, which had arbitrarily changed our name to "Porto Rico" after signing the Treaty of Paris, returned

our name—"Puerto Rico"—to us, having given up hope of Americanizing our Hispanic country.

4. In 1934, the powerful resident commissioner Santiago Iglesias-Pantín introduced pro-statehood bills in several sessions, but they could not even get through committee. That was the decade when the pro annexation political parties controlled Puerto Rico.

5. In 1946, President [Harry S.] Truman vetoed a plebiscite bill passed by the Puerto Rico legislature. Truman announced that the United States was not willing to put the results of a plebiscite into effect.

6. In 1961, we had the last official visit from a president. Since then, we have had three annexationist governors of the same political party as the president of the United States, yet no president has visited us officially in almost half a century. Isn't it logical to think that if the United States is interested in making Puerto Rico a state, a president would have come to visit us?

7. In 1976, President Gerald Ford openly supported statehood for Puerto Rico, but nothing happened.

8. Between 1990 and 1991, President George Bush, the Popular Democratic Party, the New Progressive Party, and the Puerto Rico Independence Party endorsed a plebiscite bill, which then died in a Senate committee. On that occasion, there was consensus, but they did not act because they were not willing to commit to granting statehood to Puerto Rico.

9. In 2001, President George W. Bush referred to Puerto Rico as "our friends and neighbors, and they don't want us there."

10. In 2005, one of the principal thinkers and professors of Harvard, Samuel P. Huntington, raised a cry of alarm against Hispanic immigration and compared us with Native Americans: "Indian tribes were recognized in US law as dependent, but separate nations, and they are, along with Puerto Ricans, the only ethnic groups to which lands have been assigned exclusively."

To these signs we must add events as significant as the departure of the [US] Armed Forces from Puerto Rico, the four reports produced by the permanent government, and the elimination of tax incentives that were in place.

These and other signs say it all: the bride refuses to marry. And [Americans] have been telling us so for one hundred years. It is unworthy of us to continue fantasizing with an impossible dream, waiting for the bride to change her mind some day.

They do not want Puerto Rico to be a part of the United States. That is their right, and we have to respect it. It is not a matter of being pro-American or anti-American; it is a reality check. To continue discussing the advantages and disadvantages of statehood for Puerto Rico is a sterile exercise. Americans do not respect people who do not stand up for themselves. They respect people who respect themselves.

Statehood is available for those Puerto Ricans who wish to relocate to the United States.

Puerto Rico itself has only two real options: territorial status or sovereignty.

Ireland Is Stealing Our Cookies

May 31, 2007

Fifty years ago Puerto Rico was a model for Ireland. Now the roles have switched: Ireland is the star of the European Union, with a per capita income higher than that of Germany, France, or its own former colonial power, the United Kingdom. [Although Ireland's situation has deteriorated in recent years, it is in a stronger position than Puerto Rico, and the pharmaceutical companies continue to move to Ireland.] Ireland has the same population as Puerto Rico, and its history, like ours, is marked by the immigration of people seeking better opportunities. The big difference is that Puerto Ricans emigrating now are skilled and educated workers, whereas the Irish are returning to their country to benefit from its opportunities. The main manufacturing industry in Puerto Rico, the pharmaceutical industry, is gradually leaving Puerto Rico for Ireland. This has happened right under the noses of our two principal political parties. And what is even worse, our last annexationist (i.e., pro-statehood) government irresponsibly made it possible to eliminate Section 936 of the US Internal Revenue Code, which provided incentives for the pharmaceutical industry, but without devising an alternative plan.

A successful American entrepreneur who used to manage a pharmaceutical plant with operations in Puerto Rico recently said to me that his company had set up an operation in Ireland years earlier and had begun to produce their newer products there. Today, they no longer have operations here, but only in Ireland. He remarked that practically all the pharmaceutical companies established in Puerto Rico have operations in Ireland, where they produce most of their newer products.

Though it is a fact that Puerto Rico's pharmaceutical industry is currently larger than Ireland's, it is equally true that the future of the industry is in Ireland, not in Puerto Rico. One of the primary reasons for this is that Ireland has international treaties with forty-four countries by which it offers these companies a double tax exemption—in Ireland and in the country of origin. The countries that have these treaties with Ireland include the United States, Australia, China, Canada, France, Germany, Japan, Estonia, India, Israel, Mexico, New Zealand, Slovenia, and Spain. The fact that Puerto Rico, as a territory of the United States, cannot enter into international treaties by itself places it at a disadvantage with respect to sovereign countries such as Ireland.

One of Ireland's positive qualities is that it has a broad, fair, and efficient tax base, and no single sector feels that it carries the greatest tax burden. Moreover, the people receive high-quality services. Ireland, as is the case in other developed countries except for the United States, provides its citizens with universal health service, which is free and effective.

Two million of the four million inhabitants of Ireland are employed; in Puerto Rico, with the same population as Ireland, we have a little more than one million people employed. This means that the number of persons in the labor market is much higher in Ireland than in Puerto Rico. The unemployment rate in Ireland is 4 percent, whereas in Puerto Rico it is 12 percent.

Ireland has not put all its eggs in one basket. It is one of the top software exporters in the world, surpassing the United States, and it is the main supplier of hardware, or computers, to the European Union. Along with these achievements, Ireland has 100,000 jobs in agriculture, whereas in Puerto Rico agricultural employment is marginal.

According to the Economist Intelligence Unit (2005), Ireland is the best country in the world to live because of its low unemployment rate, the political freedom, the public health and education systems, and the safety and quality of life. Following Ireland are Switzerland, Norway, Luxembourg, Sweden, Australia, Iceland, Italy, Denmark, and Spain.

Puerto Rico's deterioration can be attributed to its two principal political parties, which have created an economy based on dependency and have failed to change its colonial status. It is a shameful position for a country when its extraordinary human capital has to emigrate to look for job opportunities abroad. Puerto Rico's colonial power, for its part, tries to solve the problem by increasing fund transfers. That is like trying to solve the problem of a son who does not want to work or study by sending him money. Does that solve the problem in the long term?

While we continue to avoid discussion of the problem—which would require confronting our colonial status and accepting that it is impossible for Puerto Rico to become a state—sovereign countries such as Ireland are "stealing our cookies."

Puerto Rico: An Archipelago Without Fresh Seafood?

July 26, 2007

One of the biggest surprises for visitors to the archipelago that is Puerto Rico is the lack of a healthy and well-developed fishing industry, such as exists on every other island or country with a coastline. The main restaurants in San Juan import seafood or offer fresh conch or deepwater red snapper as delicacies when they can find them. Otherwise, we have to take visitors to colorful restaurants in the coastal areas, where "fresh" seafood is sometimes offered, though knowledgeable folks realize it is frozen.

There are historical reasons why the fishing industry has not been as important as it was at one time for the Taíno Indians. For the countries that invaded Puerto Rico—Spain and the United States—its role was as a military bastion. The powerful military structures built by the two empires are evidence of that (El Morro Castle, San Cristobal Fort, Roosevelt Roads, Ramey [Air Force] Base, and so on).

During the hegemony of the US Navy over Puerto Rico, marine conservation was an enemy of weapons practice in the Puerto Rican archipelago. Under Operation Bootstrap, the priority was industrial development and the establishment of petrochemical operations—both also enemies of marine conservation—on the coasts of Puerto Rico. Teodoro Moscoso himself, in the last years of his life, spoke to me about the huge mistake of not giving the development of our food sources the priority they deserved.

In 1988, there were 1,731 commercial fishermen selling their fish in fifty fishing villages. By 2006, that figure had declined to 1,163 commercial fishermen, a reduction of 33 percent. At the same time, it is estimated that nearly 200,000 recreational fishermen navigate in the waters off Puerto Rico.

In 1979, some 7,400,000 pounds of fresh fish were hauled ashore. In 2006, the catch was some 1,339,000 pounds, a reduction of 82 percent. Of the seafood consumed in Puerto Rico, 90 percent is imported. Only 10 percent is local, and because there is no developed fishing industry, the price of the local product is higher than that for imported seafood, and its distribution is limited mainly to the fishing villages.

Though there have been projects such as the Luis Peña Canal Marine Reserve in Culebra, they are isolated efforts and are not part of a master plan under the government's guidance. Marine conservation, with an orderly plan for the cultivation of fish, is one important step that would promote development of a healthy fishing industry. Such a plan should be accompanied by an educational plan aimed at commercial and recreational fishermen, the citizenry, and the rising generations who will eventually be the ones to enjoy our marine resources—or pay the consequences of their destruction.

Another important issue is the conservation of our coral reefs, which provide great diversity and many habitats. As Dr. Álida Ortiz-Sotomayor, the country's authority on marine biology, would say, "It is like a huge supermarket." Of the seafood we consume, some 90 percent come from the coral reefs.

Fortunately, there is an environmentally friendly, high-technology aquaculture project (Snapperfarm, Inc.) that cultivates cobia in Culebra. [The company recently moved its operations to Panama owing to lack of support from the federal and local government.] It was reviewed recently in National Geographic as a world-class model for the future of aquaculture. This private initiative is an indicator of the industry's enormous potential, and experts say it is the future of the industry. The government should get involved in innovative projects such as the Culebran Cobia Project and promote investment and the training of personnel. The Hawaiian government is already immersed in developing an aquaculture industry, which is cultivating fish from other areas.

Marine conservation and the development of fishing constitute an important industry in Singapore, New Zealand, Greece, Bora Bora, the

Canary Islands, and the coasts of Australia, France, and Spain. Countries such as Israel have managed to become food self-sufficient by harvesting fruits and vegetables in an arid desert. But Puerto Rico is not able to make full use of the resource that surrounds it.

None of Puerto Rico's administrations has seen the potential of the fishing industry as a source of food and economic development. Can that be because it is much easier to get increases in federal transfers for food or unemployment benefits?

The Bahamas, Small Yet Sovereign

October 25, 2007

Throughout our history, we have been told that to be sovereign means to be like the poor states of the Caribbean. We have avoided discussion of remarkable examples from all over the world of countries of a scale similar to that of Puerto Rico that have achieved economic and social development after abandoning their colonial status for sovereignty. Our very own Caribbean area provides us with one model, in this case a country with a much smaller population than Puerto Rico has.

The Bahamas are an archipelago of seven hundred islands some fifty miles off the coast of Florida to the north of Cuba. They were discovered by Christopher Columbus on his first voyage in 1492 and were part of the Spanish Empire until 1647, when English colonists began to settle there and eventually turned the Bahamas into an English colony in 1783. In 1973, the inhabitants of the Bahamas voted for independence, attained sovereignty, and joined the British Commonwealth. Since their independence, the Bahamas have shown impressive development, particularly in tourism, international banking services, and investment management.

The Bahamas have a population of 305,655 (Puerto Rico has 3,944,259) and a per capita income of $21,600 (Puerto Rico's is $19,300). Its real growth (gross domestic product) is 4 percent (Puerto Rico's is 0.5 percent). The labor force of the Bahamas is 58 percent of the total population (Puerto Rico's is 33 percent). The Bahamas describe themselves as an "investment paradise." In their advertisements, they quote ten reasons for investing in the Bahamas: (1) a stable and peaceful democracy; (2) proximity to the principal financial centers in North America and Latin America; (3) skilled professionals; (4) ideal weather for recreation and rest; (5) a safe investment environment; (6) tax exemption on capital gains, inheritance, corporate and personal income, and dividends and interest; (7) proactive incentives for investments; (8) essential public services and modern infrastructure; (9) a legal system based on English common law, with judicial independence; and (10) a sound economy guided by a prudent fiscal policy.

In 2005, they received an award from *The Banker Magazine* (published since 1926) for having the best international financial center in the Western world (Singapore received the award for Asia): they enjoy a favorable fiscal environment, political stability, and an efficient legal structure and regulatory system. Another point highlighted by the magazine is that the Bahamas keep up a close dialogue between the public and private sectors. The latter [characteristic] has played a key role in cultivating an environment that favors continued economic growth.

Though the Bahamas are a sovereign country, airline flights enter the United States as domestic flights because immigration and customs are handled in the Bahamas before passengers board the planes.

Puerto Rico is in a much more advantageous position than the Bahamas. In a world where the principal development resource is human capital, Puerto Rico excels in all fields. Relative to the Bahamas, Puerto Rico is better developed in high-tech manufacturing, and our higher-education system has no parallel in the region. This being the case, why are Puerto Rico's growth and per capita income rates lower than those of the Bahamas? And why does our future appear less prosperous than theirs?

Being a sovereign country, the Bahamas can develop an economic model and establish whatever trade treaties suit them the best. Whereas the Bahamas can exploit opportunities in the high-tech, globalized world, Puerto Rico, with its extraordinary human capital, has to settle for colonial status, dependence on the will of an indifferent Congress. As a consequence, our economic model, our quality of life, and the very fiber of our society are gradually declining. Puerto Rico's pathetic situation is forcing our educated population to immigrate to other countries.

Given all this, we should not be surprised that the little Bahamas, in our own Caribbean region, have surpassed Puerto Rico in economic terms. The boom in the Bahamas began in 1973 when they achieved sovereignty. That, they concluded, was their only option: as in the case of Puerto Rico, the colonial power never did have annexation in mind.

The Spirit of Bangalore

November 29, 2007

Bangalore is the Silicon Valley of India—that is, the high-technology and information technology services center of India. It is the creator of the controversial outsourcing or transfer of information technology, accounting, and customer services of multinational firms. India is on its way to becoming the office of the world.

US employees are being substituted by skilled Indian employees, who work for a fraction of the cost. It is estimated that by 2015 the United States will have lost 3.4 million white-collar jobs, which will have been displaced to India.

With 1.2 billion inhabitants, India is the largest nation in the world that practices universal suffrage. Although it has a rich civilization more than 5,000 years old and the oldest of the principal religions, India also has the largest population of young people in the world, with 50 percent of its population under the age of twenty-five, and by 2015 it will have 550 million adolescents. India has managed to reinvent itself: in 2006, its 9 percent increase in gross domestic product made its economy second in growth after China.

In 1952, Puerto Rico was a model for India. On April 30, 1952, the US ambassador to India, Chester Bowles, through a telegram to the secretary of state, Dean Acheson, invited the governor of Puerto Rico, Luis Muñoz Marín, to visit India because its government was confronting problems similar to those in Puerto Rico. They asked Muñoz Marín to deliver several lectures at universities, contribute to some development programs in India, and inspire confidence in them about what they could achieve.

Fifty-five years later the roles of India and Puerto Rico have switched. Our skilled talent, educated in Puerto Rico, has been fleeing the island, looking for better opportunities, whereas in 2003 some 15,000 to 20,000 Indians left Silicon Valley to return to India. Of all the engineers in Silicon Valley, 30 percent are of Indian origin.

While Puerto Rico consistently loses jobs under the administrations of the Popular Democratic Party and the New Progressive Party, India has transformed itself into one of the principal research-and-development centers in the world. IBM, Intel, Cisco, Hewlett-Packard, and Microsoft have invested billions of dollars in India. IBM has created 43,000 jobs there, and its chairman has announced plans to increase that figure to 100,000 within the next three years. General Electric established its John F. Welch Technology Center in Bangalore.

India takes on each problem as an opportunity. It believes in a knowledge economy in which each mind is a potential asset. It understands that this [economy] requires a joint effort among private enterprise, government, and nonprofit organizations.

In India, education is the fuel for economic and social development. [It] graduate[s] 350,000 engineers each year; the United States graduates 70,000. In recent years, the number of working visas granted by the United States to Indians was 41 percent of the total number of visas granted to workers from all over the world.

India's reinvention has been dramatic. In 1947, its prime minister, a prominent Marxist, Jawaharla Nehru, founded a state with a closed economy, without downplaying his political preference for democratic principles. Today, India has evolved into a vigorous open-market economy, one that is taking full advantage of globalization. Though India faces great challenges in eradicating its extreme poverty, if it retains the positivistic spirit generated in Bangalore, it will become the second most important economic power in the world, after China, over the next several decades. China and India together are home to one-third of the entire human population.

India is the state with the most languages and religions in the world. Although 80 percent are Hindus, they have a Muslim president, a Sikh prime minister, and an Italian as the president of its principal political party. The tie that binds the union together is the desire to become a global power.

In 1952, Puerto Rico was a model for India. Half a century later Puerto Rico languishes without a future, with an archaic colonial status, and with an economic model that has outlived its usefulness. While countries such as India are reinventing themselves, Puerto Rico incarnates the antithesis of the spirit of Bangalore: it continues to lose jobs and to educate young people who leave to work in other countries. It shamefully depends on federal welfare; some of its people continue to dream of the day that [its] colonial power will agree to incorporate [it], and they are in a state of denial regarding the constant messages the United States sends about the impossibility of annexation.

The Neglect of Solar Energy

January 31, 2008

The sun is an electricity-generating plant of gigantic dimensions that costs nothing. It is estimated that this year the sun will shed on the earth around 4,000 times more energy than we will consume. The sun is a clean, renewable, and inexhaustible source of energy.

Puerto Rico has the good fortune of being on a latitude that receives solar energy throughout the year and that has short nights. However, not only do we not use this resource, but, according to a study conducted by the US Office of Energy, Puerto Rico is the country that spends the most energy per square kilometer in the whole world, and its energy expenditure is the third highest per inhabitant.

Germany is in the vanguard in the use of modern technologies to produce renewable sources of energy. Since 2004, it has been the world's top producer of energy using solar cells, surpassing Japan. Worldwide sales of solar panels grew at an annual rate of 20 percent in the 1990s. In the European Union, the average annual growth is 30 percent, and Germany has more than 80 percent of the equipment installed. Eighty-five percent of Germans see solar energy as the ideal source to replace traditional energy sources, such as crude oil, nuclear power, and carbon.

In Spain, solar-power generation has already exceeded the goals set by the government for 2010. Its objective is to revise its projections so as to surpass Germany in this achievement.

In 2013, Seville will be the province producing the most solar energy in the world. Some $2.5 billion will be invested to supply some 300,000 households, while reducing gas emissions.

The Spanish president, José Luis Rodríguez-Zapatero, has stated that "the fight against climatic change is an absolute priority for any responsible government in contemporary times, and we cannot afford to waste a single minute." He added that climate change is the "most serious challenge threatening life on earth, and it calls for a new contract between man and nature."

The Kyoto Agreement proposes that all governments change their energy policies to give high priority to increasing the supply of clean, renewable energy sources (such as solar and wind energy) without carbon dioxide emissions. Though 174 countries have ratified the agreement, the United States has refused to join the rest of the world's countries, even though in 1990 it was responsible for 36.1 percent of the greenhouse-gas emissions produced by industrialized countries.

In an initiative separate from the rest of the country, the State of California passed legislation to invest $3.2 billion in small-scale solar-energy systems, with the objective of installing one million solar roofs within a decade, capable of producing 3,000 megawatts of solar energy.

There are several powerful reasons to begin building a country based on solar energy: to help in the conservation of the planet, to eliminate or reduce expenditures on electricity by its citizens, companies, and government; to generate income for individual citizens by collecting free energy and eventually sell the unused energy to the energy company (at least at the same price at which the energy company buys it); to eliminate dependency on oil, which is often imported from countries with totalitarian or fundamentalist governments; and to create jobs that can generate a new economic sector—an industry to provide the necessary equipment, parts, and services.

In the twentieth century, countries with crude-oil resources were the fortunate ones. As the twenty-first century advances and the use of new renewable energy sources is developed, there will be few oil importers, and the countries with good climates that know how to maximize renewable energy sources will benefit the most.

In addition to its geographical location, Puerto Rico has extraordinary human capital, as was evidenced by a team of professors and students from the Mayagüez campus of the University of Puerto Rico who

managed in 1990 to develop a solar-car prototype that performed wor-
thily in a competition in Australia. There, our team surpassed that of MIT
while competing against automotive industry companies with million-
dollar budgets.

All we need is political leaders with vision, determination, and com-
mitment to build an energy self-sufficient country, one that can serve as a
model to other countries of the world.

An Agricultural Country Without Agriculture

June 26, 2008

In the 1940s, the last foreign governor of Puerto Rico, Rexford G. Tugwell, exclaimed in amazement: "Imagine, food is imported. They have lost the art of the tropics. No one under that sun, with good soils and 40 inches of rain, should suffer hunger." With respect to its land and sea, Puerto Rico enjoys perfect conditions to achieve self-sufficiency in food production.

Many years ago agriculture played a leading role in our society and economy. In 1935, Interior Secretary Harold Ickes held the United States responsible for destroying our agriculture: "Puerto Rico . . . has been the victim of the laissez-faire economy which has developed the rapid growth of great absentee owned sugar corporations, which have absorbed much land formerly belonging to small independent growers, who in consequence have been reduced to virtual economic serfdom. While the inclusion of Puerto Rico within our tariff walls has been highly beneficial to the stockholders of those corporations, the benefits have not been passed down to the mass of Puerto Ricans. These on the contrary have seen the lands on which they formerly raised subsistence crops given over to sugar production while they have been gradually driven to import all their food staples, paying for them the high prices brought about by the tariff. There is today more widespread misery and destitution and far more unemployment in Puerto Rico than at any previous time in its history."

Years later the situation worsened with Operation Bootstrap, which continued to debilitate agriculture. Priority was given to the industrialization program based on foreign investments. The goal was immediate results even if they were only temporary. Teodoro Moscoso himself commented to me during the last years of his life on what a big mistake it had been to abandon agriculture.

It is sad that today the only farm product grown in our fields that exceeds the production of ornamental plants is plantains. Ornamental plant sales are four times higher than mango sales.

It is even sadder that mangoes harvested in Puerto Rico have been displaced by bananas from Costa Rica and pineapples from the Dominican Republic in the cargo ships that transport such products to Europe. It was recently reported in the press that ships arrive here without space for our container cars packed with mangoes. This industry produces seven hundred jobs and generates $18 million each year. But federal cabotage laws, by making us use US maritime transport, considered the most expensive and inefficient in the world, not only work against export of our agricultural production but also increase the costs of the food products we import.

The quality of our agricultural products is unsurpassed. Three examples of products that have gained international recognition are our pineapples, which experts consider better than those of Hawaii; our coffee, which is served as a delicacy in fine-dining restaurants in Europe; and our mangoes, which are very well received in Europe. Experiments such as rice growing, which was attempted in the 1970s, were abandoned because the government of that time was unable to create incentives for local entrepreneurs.

We should look at Israel as our principal model for the development of agriculture. [It has] managed to farm the desert. Israel satisfies all the food requirements of its citizens and in addition exports its agricultural products to Europe. However, its economy is not limited to agriculture; agriculture complements its modern, high-technology industry. In Israel, agriculture constitutes 2 percent of the gross national product; in Puerto Rico, it is less than one percent. Israel has twice the population of Puerto Rico but four times the number of employees working in manufacturing.

Israel, like other former colonies, has attained these economic successes based on a platform of sovereignty. In Puerto Rico, current circumstances allow for improvements in agriculture, but our political status restricts the development and potential of our agriculture. Federal cabotage laws constrain such development, and so does our lack of power to negotiate international treaties.

The other important element is the workforce, which is very small because it is much more comfortable to live off federal welfare than to work. What makes the situation ironic is that we do not even have the power to import the labor we need to cultivate our fields.

Violence, Mental Health, and Status

February 26, 2009

The headlines were recently all about a young American tourist, Sarah Kuszak, who was kidnapped and raped and had her throat slit. Kuszak, who was six months pregnant, was intercepted while jogging through the lovely countryside around Ceiba. The gruesome incident cast an image of a Puerto Rico in decline, a violent and dangerous place—an image that cannot easily be neutralized by means of local and federal police operations, street signs written and police cars identified in English, or investment in promoting tourism.

To this horrendous crime add the discovery of a dismembered body on the bank of the Caguitas River and a man's beating his own brother with a pipe over a land-boundary dispute in San Lorenzo. Equally alarming was the man in Trujillo Alto with a history of domestic violence who as he surrendered to the police shouted, "I killed my wife, I killed her."

These are some of the hundred-plus murders that have occurred in the first sixty days of this year.

Such killings are not isolated: they are part of recurring violent scenarios, which include domestic violence, the abuse and rape of children, suicides among the elderly, and even abuse of dogs. The state of Puerto Ricans' mental health is at the root of many of Puerto Rico's problems with violence.

Though violence has been present throughout our history, the state of our mental health has contributed to a high incidence of drug addiction, which desensitizes and depersonalizes human beings and leads to an increase in violence—something that had not occurred previously.

193

The solution to these problems is not to increase the number of police. These violent incidents underscore the prevailing social and psychological problems facing today's Puerto Rico, which the majority of local politicians ignore or even deny. A recent case that dramatizes this denial is the announcement by the Family and Children Administration that it was canceling the psychological services received by 1,500 abused children.

To this add recent remarks by the World Health Organization, an agency of the United Nations, highlighting how the economic crisis affecting the world has contributed to depression, increased stress, and other mental disorders.

An important aspect of this problem is that the model used for our mental-health programs is that of the United States. The *Washington Post* reviewed a study that found the United States to be the country with the highest rate of mental illness in the world. One-quarter of the population meets the criteria of having suffered some kind of mental illness, and one-quarter of these people have had a serious disorder that has significantly disrupted their ability to function.

The study was conducted in 2005, before the economic crisis, and was commissioned by the National Institute of Mental Health. It emphasized that the country must recognize the ubiquity of chronic mental illnesses in the population. It also indicated that despite the availability of effective treatments for many mental illnesses, including depression and anxiety, close to one-third of the people in need of help rely exclusively on nonprofessional resources such as online help groups and spiritual counselors.

Some of the factors that worsen the problem include inadequate health insurance, the persistent stigma surrounding mental illness, and failure to heed warning signs.

The deplorable state of mental health in the United States is related to the high incidence of crime, rampant drug addiction, a growing prison population, the lack of universal health care, the lack of controls on gun sales, the exaltation of violence in films and on television, and the imposition of the death penalty.

One of the advantages of attaining sovereignty for Puerto Rico is that it would allow us to study and implement the programs of sovereign countries that have achieved levels of mental health adequate for a better quality of life.

A sovereign Puerto Rico would be able to participate in the United Nations and the World Health Organization and take part in their studies and programs. Those two organizations define mental health as a state of well-being in which individuals can realize their potential, manage the normal stresses of life, work productively and fruitfully, and contribute to their community.

Sovereign Gardens

March 27, 2009

Rexford G. Tugwell, the last foreign governor of Puerto Rico, was amazed in the 1940s by the fact that Puerto Ricans, having the perfect climate and soils to be self-sufficient with regard to food, imported their food. Six decades later the situation has deteriorated to the point that we must import coffee to supply the local demand even though we produce some of the best coffee in the world. We consume some 32.5 million pounds of coffee a year, but this year's harvest was no more than 15 million pounds.

The main problem facing large-scale agricultural production in Puerto Rico is the scarcity of workers willing to work the fields. But who would swap a federal welfare check for a day's work? And how can we import workers in need of jobs from other places when we do not control immigration in Puerto Rico? Lack of sovereignty is the main obstacle to achieving food self-sufficiency.

Yet despite our helplessness, which is the result of a lack of power and the economic crisis, there are ways to improve the situation. Albert Einstein said, "Crises are the greatest blessing that can come to people and to countries because crises bring progress. . . . It is in crises that initiative, discoveries, and great strategies are born."

During the Second World War, before food rationing, the US government promoted the planting of what were called "Victory Gardens." The objective was for citizens to consume the fruit and vegetables they themselves produced. In 1943, some 20 million Victory Gardens were planted in backyards, on roofs, and in empty lots. The crops harvested that year amounted to one-third of the total consumption of vegetables that year.

A movement that has arisen in recent years in the United States—the Kitchen Garden Project—called on President Barack Obama to launch a project similar to the Victory Gardens. Margaret Lloyd, a researcher working with these kitchen gardens at the University of California, stresses that though the United States is food self-sufficient, there are good reasons for this movement: the economic crisis, the concern of people interested in consuming safe and healthy products, and global warming.

The processes of planting, fertilizing, processing, packaging, and transporting the foods we eat take a great deal of energy and contribute to global warming. Gardens mitigate global warming by reducing the pollution that food production contributes to the warming process. The miles traveled by food products from the farm to the table are reduced to the distance from the garden to the table.

This Kitchen Garden Project has had remarkable results in the United States, not only in terms of growing produce, but also in terms of making children aware of the importance of a healthy diet and creating a spirit of community.

In Europe, the production of high-quality crops at home has become a high priority in local communities and even for Michelin-starred restaurants.

In Catalonia, gardens have become commonplace. Ignasi Juliá of the Hort Urbá enterprise (www.horturba.com) says that "little by little, people do become interested, tired of paying too much money for flavorless tomatoes at the supermarket." Hort Urbá provides information on how to set up a kitchen garden. With just a terrace, a balcony, or a backyard with good sunlight and a water faucet, you can produce lettuce, tomatoes, green peppers, eggplants, onions, garlic, cabbage, spinach, and more.

In other parts of the world, such as Vietnam, whose economic development has been remarkable, urban vegetable gardens are very common; the result is a country without misery and without homeless people.

Most Puerto Ricans receive federal assistance to buy food. In 2008, some $1.47 billion was paid out in nutritional assistance, and most of it went for consumption of imported products.

Puerto Rico's current situation should encourage citizens to cultivate some food products. Many spices used for cooking can be grown in a bowl near a window. Kitchen gardens or urban vegetable gardens are a necessity in Puerto Rico not only because of the global economic crisis, but also as a rallying cry on the part of those who believe in ecological farming, sustainable development, and protection of the environment.

Our kitchen gardens ought to be called "sovereign gardens" because they are living examples of the sovereignty process, which extends one the power to resolve one's own problems without interference from external forces.

Alaskan Statehood

June 25, 2009

In 1867, the United States acquired the Territory of Alaska from Russia. In 1912, Alaska took the first step toward being a state of the union by becoming an incorporated territory. (Puerto Rico is an unincorporated territory.)

In the conquest of the West, Alaska was the last frontier. It was populated and colonized by white Americans, fortune hunters. It was they who had political and economic control, and they displaced Alaska's scarce native population.

Such groups of settlers were the ones who began the pursuit of statehood through lobbying and plebiscites.

The main factor in attaining statehood is not local support for statehood, but rather the contribution that the new state can make to the nation and the reasons for that contribution's being advantageous for the United States.

During the 1950s, 80 percent of Alaskan residents were white, and 20 percent were natives. Up until 1945, there were signs in public establishments that prohibited entry to the native Alaskans.

In his book *The Battle for Alaska Statehood*, Ernest Gruening, a former governor and senator, explains Alaska's military importance for the US Armed Forces and the aggressive lobbying for statehood by the air force and the navy.

Lieutenant General Nathan F. Twining, commander in chief of the Alaska Command, testified before Congress that "statehood for Alaska would help the military . . . and be a great asset to military development."

In Puerto Rico, in contrast to Alaska, the closure of Fort Brooke, Isla Grande Naval Base, Ramey Air Force Base, Roosevelt Roads Naval Base, and the practice ranges on Culebra, Vieques, and so forth underscores the decreasing military importance that Puerto Rico ultimately has for the United States.

President Harry S. Truman actively favored statehood for Alaska, but President Dwight D. Eisenhower did not. Congress ignored the claims of the residents of Alaska.

Given local frustration, Alaska's political leadership decided to implement the "Tennessee Plan," part of which entailed electing two white senators and one white representative and sending them to Washington, DC, in 1956. But, according to Gruening, who was one of the senators sent to Congress, "We were not admitted to the floor of the Senate, as has been done in the case of Tennessee."

During the Second World War, the Japanese attacked Hawaii at Pearl Harbor and occupied some of the western islands of Alaska for more than a year. These events highlighted the desirability of Hawaii and Alaska for forces hostile to the United States.

The Cold War arose initially in Europe, but the Korean War and the triumph of Mao Zedong in China in the 1950s elevated the conflict to a global level. The few hours that separate Hawaii and Alaska from the Soviet Union and China suddenly increased the value of these incorporated territories in the eyes of the United States.

This new scenario led to Eisenhower's endorsing statehood for Alaska. The Senate approved HR 7999 on June 30, 1958, granting statehood to Alaska once assurances had been given that the new Alaskan and Hawaiian senators would not alter the balance of power between Democrats and Republicans in the Senate.

The vote was sixty-four in favor and twenty against, with twelve abstentions. Not voting for the bill were legendary senators such as Sam Ervin, J. William Fulbright, Herman Talmadge, Strom Thurmond, John Stennis, Prescott Bush (the father of George H. W. Bush), Albert Gore Sr., and Lyndon B. Johnson.

The 48,000 Alaskan voters ratified annexation by a majority vote of five to one. Extrapolating from the case of Alaska to that of Puerto Rico, what does Puerto Rico have to contribute to the United States? What economic contribution can it make now that local annexationists have destroyed the use of Section 936 [of the US Internal Revenue Code], which had the potential to create a strong economy, and have consolidated the welfare state with the addition of food stamps (both effective short-term electoral strategies)?

The United States has been consistent: statehood is available to Puerto Ricans but not to the unincorporated territory of Puerto Rico. The almost 4 million Puerto Ricans who have relocated to the United States have achieved statehood.

The incorporated territory of Alaska served as a strategic military asset to the Americans during the Cold War. What possible contribution might Puerto Rico make to the United States to convince Congress to grant it statehood?

The Most Exclusive Club in the World

August 27, 2009

The US Senate is the most exclusive club in the world. The vice president of the United States presides over this powerful legislative body, which is composed of two senators from each state.

In the beginning, senators were appointed by state legislatures, not elected by popular vote. The Founding Fathers did not want the Senate to be a populist body.

It was not until 1913 that senators came to be elected by direct popular vote for six-year terms, staggered so that the members of the Senate would not change all at once in an election. They are the "princes" of American democracy, an elite group.

For this reason, only senators have the power to approve treaties and to confirm appointments to the cabinet as well as of generals, admirals, ambassadors, and all public prosecutors and federal judges, including justices of the Supreme Court. It is they who pass judgment on the president in the case of an impeachment.

The Senate is not a good example of representative democracy, for each senator's vote has the same weight as that of any other senator. In other words, the two senators from Wyoming, who represent a population of 533,000, have the same voting power as the two senators from California, who represent 37 million people.

The House of Representatives is a better example of representative democracy because the number of members who represent a state is proportional to the state's population. But that body's powers are much more limited. The fact that all representatives must be elected every two years underscores their limited power.

It is in the House of Representatives that representatives of unincorporated territories such as Puerto Rico, Guam, the Virgin Islands, American Samoa, and the Marianas have a voice. In the Senate, these territories have no presence at all.

The entry of a state into the world's most exclusive club is by invitation only, but with the aggravating circumstance that each new member dilutes the current members' power. The desire to belong to the club is not a factor in being invited; what counts is whether new entrants serve the club members' interest.

The invitation is achieved by turning an incorporated territory into a state.

There must be compelling reasons for the club's members to accept the dilution of their power by new member states. In the beginning, expansionist strategy consisted of acquiring territories from the Atlantic to the Pacific and in Mexico north of the Río Grande. These incorporated territories were subsequently invited to join as states, and their senators were incorporated into the exclusive club. The new senators contributed the territories desired by the rest of the club's members.

The incorporated territories of Alaska and Hawaii, with their limited populations and location outside the continental United States, were not [originally] welcomed into the exclusive club that is the Senate. Not until the Cold War spread from Europe into Asia in the aftermath of the Korean War did the Senate accept statehood for Alaska, in 1959, after becoming aware of the danger of its close proximity to the easternmost part of the Soviet Union.

The fact that oil had been discovered in Alaska and that Texas-based firms had established operations there prompted powerful Texans such as Senate majority leader Lyndon B. Johnson and Speaker of the House of Representatives Sam Rayburn to withdraw their opposition to statehood for Alaska.

Hawaii's senators were admitted into the exclusive club along with Alaska's senators to maintain the balance of power between Republicans and Democrats in the Senate.

Who in his right mind could think that the members of the most exclusive club in the world would benefit by diluting their power to incorporate two senators from the unincorporated territory of Puerto Rico?

Sovereignty for Development

September 24, 2009

Puerto Rico's economic model froze in the 1950s. Corporations operating under Section 936 [of the US Internal Revenue Code] gave it some oxygen and managed to keep it going until the 1990s. Public debt and food stamps have kept the people from taking to the streets in massive protests.

During the past three years, the economy of Puerto Rico has contracted by 10 percent, and the official unemployment rate has risen to 16 percent. The labor-participation rate (the number of people who are able to work and who are employed or actively seeking a job) is 42 percent. In other words, more than 50 percent of Puerto Ricans are not even in the labor market.

Puerto Rico has lost its ability to attract new jobs; the government and the private sector are increasing layoffs; the construction industry is paralyzed for lack of financing; real-estate values are falling; 90 percent of the value of the Puerto Rico Stock Index has vanished; the government has increased taxes; energy costs are rising; social services are deteriorating; drug trafficking and rampant criminality are undermining quality of life; and the state of mental health continues to worsen.

Just as with the $1 billion sent by the [George W.] Bush administration some years back, the funds assigned by the Obama administration will not solve our economic and social crisis.

This "unincorporated territory that belongs to but is not a part of the United States" is not equipped to handle its own problems. The colonial power and the resident commissioner hope to solve Puerto Rico's problems by increasing dependency. That is much like a father giving money to his drug addict son instead of providing him with a cure for his disease.

The economy of the twenty-first century is different from the one we had when the industrialization program was established in Puerto Rico, sponsored by the federal government, the US Navy, and the local government. The world has changed, and Puerto Rico is resisting the change.

The world's economy has gone global. This world is now one of interactive networks with treaties among sovereign countries, a world in which Puerto Rico cannot take part. Moreover, our colonial power—which imposes its own laws on us and stipulates our transportation and immigration policies—has lost its economic hegemony and is impotent to halt the rise of China in the world economy and the dramatic growth of the European Union and India.

One example of the new international economic order is the US company Applied Materials of Silicon Valley, which has reinvented itself to manufacture solar panels. In the past two years, it has established fourteen new manufacturing plants: in Germany (five), in China (four), and the rest in Spain, India, Italy, Taiwan, and Abu Dabi—but none in the United States, much less in Puerto Rico.

All of these countries have aggressive policies for the use of renewable energy. Germany generates almost half the solar energy produced in the world and is becoming the world center for research, engineering, manufacturing, and installation of solar-energy systems.

A sovereign Puerto Rico, with a better climate than Germany, would be able to establish international agreements with that country to develop solar energy and grant visas to professors and professionals to create a world research center at the University of Puerto Rico at Mayagüez. It would also be able to regulate and promote the development of the industry following the best models in the world; and it would be able to use the most efficient and economical maritime transportation services. These are only a few of the many projects and ideas that might be developed.

The powers that would be inherent in a sovereign Puerto Rico are fundamental for its development. The other choice we have is to continue to languish, waiting for manna from Washington while our quality of life deteriorates.

A Quarter-Century Lost

December 30, 2009

In 1985, having experienced eight years of the Carlos Romero-Barceló administration, the Puerto Rico Planning Board circulated an *informe social*, a report on Puerto Rican society, which discussed the quality-of-life issue that was a concern twenty-four years ago, because "economic development, modern advances, growing technology and the problems related to them, have been shattering the peace, stability, and harmonious coexistence that were patrimony of previous generations."

The study reported that "the First Annual Conference on Quality of Life held in Puerto Rico identified a series of factors associated with the quality-of-life crisis that Puerto Ricans were experiencing":

1. A mass-education system in which most educators agreed that they provided only a little knowledge, without actually educating the individual.
2. Marked tendencies toward achieving quick results and toward uncontrolled ambition, turning a society that once was able to share and be generous with others into one that was egotistical and individualistic.
3. A level of unemployment never seen before.
4. A level of rampant criminality and vandalism that frightened citizens and made them prisoners in their own homes, behind their so-called "ornamental" ironwork.
5. A physical environment contaminated with noise and chemical compounds, with large-scale extermination of species and the

end of flora and fauna that once were sources of beauty for the
island.

6. Verbal aggression in the discussion of different public issues.
7. The constant bombardment of political issues.
8. Television programs that added nothing to the upbringing of our
   children and instead took away traditional values, destroying any
   model of what decent persons are.

The study concludes that if Puerto Rico's situation is not solved, "it
will increasingly contribute to the creation of insecure, fearful and anx-
ious citizens who are alienated from their families, their communities,
and mainly from themselves. These are the individuals who would be
key actors in broken marriages, juvenile delinquency, government dependency, mental institutions, and in the lack of tolerance to be seen in political discussions, educational institutions, the workplace, in the streets, in
public places, in the intimacy of homes, and wherever there is any kind of
human interaction."

A quarter-century has elapsed [since this report was issued], and no
one can say that the situation has been corrected; what is more, the consensus is that it has become worse.

Since the publication of that study, we have experienced eight years
of the Rafael Hernández-Colón administration, eight years of Pedro Ros-
selló, four years of Sila Calderón, four years of Aníbal Acevedo-Vilá, and
one year of Luis Fortuño.

None of the Popular Democratic Party or New Progressive Party governments has managed to rescue us from the crisis we have been living
through for twenty-four years. On the contrary, they have brought our
society to the breaking point and our economy to the point of bankruptcy.

Our recent governors have been of different ideologies, professions,
backgrounds, ages, regions, social classes, and genders. The fact that none
of them has been able to solve our crisis leads us to conclude that the problem is not in the governors, but in the structure of government—that is, in
Puerto Rico's political status.

While the world has changed in these twenty-four years, becoming a
global economy tending to favor the sovereignty of nations, Puerto Rico

remains in a colonial status, and its dependency on the colonial power has increased. China is replacing the United States as the principal economic power in Latin America, but Puerto Rico remains at the margin of global opportunity.

To solve Puerto Rico's problems, we must go to the root of the matter. We must develop a plan for a country that is sovereign, with the inherent powers needed to solve our problems. The alternative is to continue to languish as an obsolete colony, without quality of life, no matter who the governor in office may be.

The Bankers Club and Puerto Rico

January 27, 2010

The closing of the Bankers Club, the legendary icon of Puerto Rico's financial world, founded in 1939, illustrates the changes that Puerto Rico is undergoing. It was a death foretold from the moment that the club failed to continue to run its historic venue in Old San Juan on top of the first Puerto Rican "skyscraper," facing majestic San Juan Bay.

Important business negotiations were closed and historic meetings and social events held in that exclusive private club. But the Bankers Club could not survive the changes of the twenty-first century. Its situation was similar to what Puerto Rico's political, economic, and social model is currently facing.

Half a century ago the main corporations in Puerto Rico were headed by American executives whose social venues were the Swiss Chalet, La Rotisserie, Dorado Beach, and the Bankers Club. With the closure of the Bankers Club, an era has come to an end.

In the 1950s and 1960s, Chase Manhattan Bank and the First National City Bank of New York participated in the principal transactions in Puerto Rico, and they were represented by prominent American lawyers such as McConnell, Kelly, Griggs, Fiddler, Brown, Newson, and Goldman.

That was a Puerto Rico dominated by the presence of Americans on the island, a presence dramatized on Sundays by hundreds of uniformed US Navy personnel walking the streets of the city and swarming into Tony Tursy's night spots along the wharves in the evenings. There were army, naval, and air force bases scattered all over Puerto Rico, Culebra, and Vieques.

The military importance of the island evaporated formally with the end of the Cold War, the development of weapons technology, and the shift of the geopolitical center of the world to the Middle East and Asia.

Puerto Rico's banking sector is currently dominated by local, Spanish (Santander, BBVA), and Canadian (Scotiabank) banks. The main brokerage firms are Swiss (UBS), Spanish (Santander Securities), and local firms. Mexicans dominate the communications sector (PRTC, Claro) and the cement industry (Cemex). The French and the British dominate the advertising industry (Y&R, JWT, Grey, Euro RSCG, Saatchi & Saatchi, Leo Burnett) and have a strong presence in the cement (San Juan Cement) and polling (Hispania) industries.

Europeans also have a local presence in the pharmaceutical industry (Glaxo, Astra Zeneca, Roche, Sanofi-Aventis).

Japanese cars replaced American cars in Puerto Rico long before they managed to do so in the United States. The Spanish have a strong presence in the telecommunications (TLD) and insurance (MAPFRE) sectors.

As European and Latin American corporations have replaced American companies in the manufacturing and service industries, American investors have been replacing local firms in the retail market. This move capitalizes on the change from a productive economy to a consumer economy.

Megastores such as Wal-Mart, Sam's, Costco, Walgreen's, Marshall's, and Borders have replaced González Padín, Farmacias Moscoso, Amigo, Velasco, and García Comercial, among others. These megastores provide excellent products, manufactured mostly in China, at affordable prices for the Puerto Rican consumer.

Puerto Rico's economic model froze in the 1950s. Corporations operating under Section 936 [of the US Internal Revenue Code] gave it some oxygen and managed to carry it through to the 1990s. Today, Puerto Rico—with an unemployment rate at 16 percent and rising and with more than 50 percent of its people outside the job market—depends on public debt and federal transfers, which produce an economy based on consumption rather than production. That is why our professionals, who have graduated from our excellent centers of higher education, now find that they have to leave Puerto Rico.

The closing of the Bankers Club, founded in 1939, should serve as a warning to the oldest political organization in Puerto Rico, the Popular Democratic Party, founded in 1938, which refuses to accept that we are in the twenty-first century and that the world has changed.

Drug Trafficking and the Feds

February 5, 2010

Daily news headlines confirm that drug trafficking is the main cause of the high crime rate in Puerto Rico.

Drugs are not cultivated in Puerto Rico. They enter and leave our country through our borders. Who controls our borders? Who controls our coastlines? Who controls immigration in Puerto Rico?

The Foraker Act of 1900, the Jones Act of 1917, and Public Law 600 of 1950 confirm that the US federal government has complete control over our customs, immigration, and coastlines—the main areas used by drug traffickers to move their products.

Once drugs have entered Puerto Rico, the revolving door administration currently in office has to manage the drug problem.

Although it is true that neither the Popular Democratic Party nor the New Progressive Party administration has been capable of producing a master plan for fighting crime, it is the federal government that is directly responsible for drug trafficking because that is the government that allows drugs to enter Puerto Rico.

Drug users are people who are sick and need help, just like people who suffer from cancer or heart disease. Every time a shipment of drugs is seized, criminality rises. To the degree that supply decreases, drug prices increase, and the sick addict is forced to engage in criminal acts to "cure" his sickness.

If we do not medicate drug users following models like those used in Great Britain and the Netherlands, we will not be able to solve the problem. Politicians are afraid of taking this stance because the opposition

213

takes advantage of the opportunity to accuse them of being "weak in confronting the crime wave."

Judging by the rise in the murder rate in Puerto Rico—most murders are related to drug trafficking—the feds are not doing their job. If they have not been able to do it on an issue area in which they have sole responsibility, what makes us think they can solve our internal security problems? And still less when they are totally unaware of the root of the problem of drug addiction, which arises from a flawed health and prevention system?

Federalizing the local Department of Justice, for which to date no secretary has been appointed, is not the solution that Puerto Rico needs.

One of the missions of the US Coast Guard, according to its Web site, is to "protect America's maritime borders from all intrusions by halting the flow of illegal drugs, aliens, and contraband."

On January 17, 2006, the US government issued the following statement: "US Customs and Border Protection [CBP] consolidated air and marine assets, programs and personnel into the Office of CBP Air and Marine [OAM] to create the world's largest aviation and maritime law enforcement organization. . . . OAM uses its sophisticated fleets to detect, sort, intercept, track and apprehend criminals."

The mission of the Drug Enforcement Administration is to enforce its laws and regulations on controlled substances in the United States and its territories.

Puerto Rican politicians need to get out of denial and accept the facts of the situation: addicts are people who are sick and need medication. Puerto Ricans who are officials in [the government of] the colonial power have the responsibility to call upon the federal government to assume its obligations efficiently in its territory and to protect its residents against drug traffickers through customs, immigration, and border control, areas over which it and it alone has control.

While Puerto Rico remains in its current colonial status, the colonial power must assume its responsibilities.

Sovereign countries control their own immigration, customs, and coastlines, and they fight drug trafficking. There are 187 sovereign member countries in INTERPOL, the largest international police organization, founded in 1923. They also coordinate strategies against drug trafficking with the United Nations Office on Drugs and Crime.

A Federal Plebiscite—so Close Yet so Far

February 25, 2010

On January 17, 1989, Governor Rafael Hernández-Colón (Popular Democratic Party), Baltasar Corrada-del-Río, afterward replaced in the initiative by Carlos Romero-Barceló (New Progressive Party), and Rubén Berríos (Puerto Rican Independence Party) cosigned and sent a letter and joint declaration to the colonial power requesting that a plebiscite be held on Puerto Rico's political status.

On February 9, in his first address to Congress, President George H. W. Bush endorsed statehood for Puerto Rico and urged Congress to take the necessary steps to enable Puerto Ricans to decide their status by plebiscite.

Senator Bennett Johnston (D-LA), the chairman of the Committee on Natural Resources, which has jurisdiction over all matters regarding territories such as Puerto Rico, assumed the leadership of the process.

The committee found that should independence prevail, the Puerto Ricans who wanted to do so would retain their US citizenship: "Nothing shall affect the citizenship of any person born prior to the date of the ratification."

It also determined that under independence all acquired benefits (Social Security, veterans' and pension benefits) would continue in perpetuity because they had been contributed by the citizens and employers without regard to the place of residence of the citizen. The committee also decided that under independence all federal programs would continue operating until the end of the fiscal year, at which time they would become grants, payable every year for the following nine years.

[The committee] also confirmed the spirit of an agreement between sovereign nations "to affect a smooth and fair transition for the new Republic of Puerto Rico with a minimum of economic disruption, and to promote the development of a viable economy in the new Republic of Puerto Rico."

After months of public hearings, the House of Representatives unanimously approved a version of the bill that eliminated its self-executing character. The Senate committee voted on the bill, also having eliminated the self-execution condition because there was no consensus for committing to granting statehood to Puerto Rico, in case that should be the winning formula in the plebiscite.

Just hours before the vote took place, President Bush called on the committee to approve a plebiscite.

Though this effort was supported by all the political leaders of Puerto Rico and by the US president and had received a unanimous vote in the House of Representatives, Senate Bill 244, introduced by Senators Johnston (D–LA) and Malcolm Wallop (R–WY), died [in committee] on February 27, 1991, when it failed to break a tie of ten to ten.

Seven Republican senators and three Democrats voted against the bill. Some of the senators who voted for the bill said they had done so as a courtesy to Johnston, but that they would not necessarily vote for the bill on the Senate floor.

The most important objection was the opposition to statehood, [an opposition] for which the *New York Times* gave three primary reasons: the high cost of the federal assistance that the new state would require; the new delegation in Congress, which would be mostly Democratic and larger than the delegations of almost half of the states; and revival of the proposal for statehood for Washington, DC.

In 1991, both Puerto Rico and the United States were in a much better economic situation than at present. Puerto Rico had the [US Internal Revenue Code Section] 936 companies, and the United States did not have a deficit in the trillions of dollars.

Since then, the Senate has not discussed the matter of Puerto Rico's status, not even in 1998, when the House of Representatives passed the Young bill [with a vote of] 209 to 208. [HR 856 was introduced by Representative Don Young (R–AL), calling for a status plebiscite in Puerto Rico.]

The results of the local plebiscites of 1967, 1993, and 1998—two of them won by a formula that called for more powers for the commonwealth—have been ignored by Congress.

It is unfortunate that we continue in a vortex of confusion, evaluating status alternatives that are unacceptable to the colonial power. In 1991, it was made clear that statehood is not an option, and, after we lost our valuable strategic military position, a commonwealth with more powers is not an option either. We need to go through a reality check and stop fantasizing about impossible dreams.

The Territorial Clause Versus Sovereignty

March 25, 2010

The US Constitution adopted in 1787 specifies in Article 4, Section 3, that "the Congress shall have Power to dispose of and make all needful Rules and Regulations respecting the Territory or other Property belonging to the United States."

In the case of Puerto Rico, not only does the territorial clause apply, but so does the Treaty of Paris of 1898, in which Spain ceded Puerto Rico to the United States, specifying in Article IX that "the civil rights and political status of the native inhabitants of the territories hereby ceded to the United States shall be determined by the Congress."

Senator Joseph Foraker, author of the Foraker Act of 1900 (still partially in force) commented in his memoirs, published in 1917, that Article IX had been incorporated at the request of the US members of the commission because otherwise the Senate would not have approved the Treaty of Paris.

Foraker pointed out that in the case of the treaties for the purchase of Louisiana, Florida, New Mexico, and so on, there was a clause providing that these territories would become states of the union. The act annexing Hawaii states that it was expressly provided that the islands would become part of the United States. Foraker confirms that the Senate would never have approved that specification in the case of Puerto Rico. He also confirms that

Porto Rico belongs to the United States, but it is not the United States, nor a part of the United States. It will be observed that the Constitution, by

219

the language of this provision, draws a distinction between the United States and territory belonging to the United States. . . . Congress can sell or give away—dispose of—territory that simply belongs as property to the United States, but no one has ever pretended that the Congress has power to sell or part with any portion of the United States. Congress must govern the United States according to the Constitution, which is the organic law of the Union, but it can govern a Territory that simply belongs to the United States as it may think best, restrained only by the positive prohibitions of the Constitution and the general spirit of our institutions, which is above all written law.

Years after Foraker's comments, in the Insular Cases the US Supreme Court confirmed what this senator had said: that unincorporated territories belong to but are not part of the United States. Under the Territorial Clause, Congress has the power to determine which parts of the US Constitution apply in the territories.

During the visits from Congress in 1950 to approve a constitutional government law for Puerto Rico, the representatives of Puerto Rico confirmed that Congress would maintain plenary powers over Puerto Rico. In response to a question from Congressman [William] Lemke, Governor [Luis] Muñoz Marín said: "If the people of Puerto Rico were to go mad, Congress can always find a way to legislate again." Resident commissioner [Antonio] Fernós-Isern stated that the new law "would not change the status of the island of Puerto Rico with respect to the United States. . . . It would not alter the sovereignty powers acquired by the United States over Puerto Rico under the terms of the Treaty of Paris."

No matter what we call our current status ("Commonwealth of Puerto Rico" or "Free Associated State," for example), Puerto Rico is an unincorporated territory under the plenary powers of Congress. Once we place ourselves outside the clause, we will stop being a territory or colony and will achieve sovereignty, with two possible political options: free association or independence. Attaining sovereignty will insert us into the twenty-first century: a globalized world with 192 sovereign nations that chose pragmatism.

The Experts and the Territorial Clause
March 29, 2010

The interpretation of the Territorial Clause that matters is not that of the residents of the territory, whose perspectives are colonized, but that of the members of the colonial power who run the show.

The principal professors of law in Puerto Rico agree that the decision of the US Supreme Court in the Insular Cases of 1922, which defined Puerto Rico as an unincorporated territory belonging to but not part of the United States, is in effect and has not been revoked.

If Puerto Rico is not a territory under the Territorial Clause, why are all Puerto Rico matters handled by the Senate Committee on Energy and Natural Resources and the House of Representatives Committee on Natural Resources, whose responsibilities include the territories?

If Puerto Rico has a pact with the United States and is no longer a territory, why are its matters not handled directly by the US Department of State or the White House? Why, when discussing the inclusion of Puerto Rico in [Barack] Obama's health reform, did they refer to the inclusion of the territories (Puerto Rico, the US Virgin Islands, Guam, Samoa, and the Marianas)?

On October 8, 2009, the House of Representatives Committee on Natural Resources, which is responsible for territories such as Puerto Rico, issued a report stating that the US Supreme Court had defined Puerto Rico as an unincorporated territory. Nowhere does the report mention that Puerto Rico has a pact or any kind of relation in the nature of a pact with the United States.

What is more, the report highlights that the Territorial Clause of the Constitution grants Congress plenary powers over the territories. It says that in exercising its power, Congress can treat Puerto Rico differently from the fifty states, the District of Columbia, and the rest of the territories—that is to say, as it chooses.

The report of the House of Representatives, controlled by the Democratic Party, was issued just a few months ago.

In December 2007, the White House published the *Report by the President's Task Force on Puerto Rico's Status.* Now it was the executive branch speaking, which was controlled by the Republican Party at that time. The report reaffirmed that Puerto Rico is a territory under the Territorial Clause and that the Congress has plenary power over it.

The White House document says, "Thus, while the Commonwealth of Puerto Rico enjoys significant political autonomy, it is important to recognize that, as long as Puerto Rico remains a territory, its system is subject to revision by Congress."

According to the report, there are two types of property under the sovereignty of the United States: the states of the union and the territories. It also comments that the Supreme Court has determined that all lands that are not included in a state of the union must be managed by Congress (*First National Bank v. Yankton County,* 101 U.S. 129 [1879]).

Experts in the colonial power, in the White House and the Congress, are clear about the territorial character of Puerto Rico. Only the "experts" in the territory itself remain tangled in their colonial mindset.

It is a shame that these "experts" remain stuck on supposed agreements whose validity is so unreal that they are ignored by the White House and the Congress. What good does it do us to believe that Puerto Rico is not under the Territorial Clause when those in the colonial power are quite convinced of the opposite—especially when Puerto Rico's revolving-door administrations validate Congress's position by submitting themselves to the committees in charge of territories?

The twenty-first century requires clear definitions and practical models based on a new political, economic, and social structure with the inherent powers that sovereignty can provide.

The Hispanic Effect and Statehood

April 29, 2010

The 47.8 million Hispanics living in the United States have become its largest minority group; they now constitute 15.5 percent of the US population. It is projected that by the year 2050 the percentage of Hispanics will reach 24.4 percent.

Some statehooders believe this is a great opportunity for Puerto Rico to become the fifty-first state of that nation.

However, not all that shines is gold. . . .

Hispanics produce half the population growth in the United States. The growth of the Hispanic population in 2006 (24.3 percent) was almost four times that of the population as a whole (6.1 percent).

This rate of growth has a negative effect on the majority group in the United States, the Caucasian population, which sees its predominance evaporating. Can anyone imagine Caucasians welcoming [their] becoming a minority group? They are already taking aggressive action to protect their dominant position. The blogs of the conservative Tea Party group (www.teapartypatriots.org) have become tools for the protection of their hegemony.

[The Tea Party's] recent capture of the seat held by the late Senator Edward Kennedy, a liberal, in the only state that did not vote for Nixon in 1972 has energized the group.

Pat Buchanan, a political commentator and former US presidential candidate, says in his book *State of Emergency* [2006], "America faces an existential crisis. If we do not get control of our borders, by 2050 Americans of European descent will be a minority in the nation their ancestors

223

created and built. No nation has ever undergone so radical a demographic transformation and survived."

Most of the Hispanics come from five Latin American nations: Mexico (65.7 percent), Puerto Rico (8.9 percent), Cuba (3.5 percent), El Salvador (3.3 percent), and the Dominican Republic (2.8 percent). Unlike the minority group they have displaced—African Americans—Hispanics are not a homogeneous group. Each Hispanic group has its own agenda and priorities.

In 2008, 56 percent of the Hispanic population lived in three states: California, Texas, and Florida. Seventy-four percent lived in seven states: the three just named plus New York, Illinois, Arizona, and New Jersey. This means that in forty-three US states put together, the Hispanic population is nonexistent or numerically less than a million citizens.

Whereas the Hispanic vote is important in the House of Representatives, it is not in the Senate, the most exclusive and the most powerful government body in the American nation. The Senate is not a very democratic body because the senators' position and power bear no relation to the number of voters they represent. For example, the two senators from California, who represent 37 million inhabitants, have no more power than the two senators from Wyoming, who represent 533,000 inhabitants.

This means that for eighty-six of the one hundred senators, the Hispanic vote has no electoral importance, and, thus, diluting their power by expanding their own numbers would not serve their best interests.

Moreover, in those states with a strong Hispanic presence, such as Arizona, the Hispanic factor does not necessarily affect its senators' vote. Thus, a senator from that state, John McCain, in spite of a petition from his fellow party member Luis Fortuño, recently voted against the appointment of Sonia Sotomayor as the first Hispanic member of the Supreme Court.

On the specific matter of statehood for Puerto Rico, in a column published in 1998, "Let Puerto Rico remain Puerto Rico," Buchanan said that the United States should not try to absorb, assimilate, and Americanize a people whose hearts will forever belong to their Puerto Rican nation.

The dramatic growth of the Hispanic population in the United States, rather than favoring the annexationist movement in Puerto Rico, is becoming a poison pill for efforts to make Puerto Rico the fifty-first state of that union.

The Flight of the Pharmaceuticals and Commonwealth

May 27, 2010

News of the expiration of the patent for Lipitor (Pfizer), the prescription medicine with the greatest sales in history, and the consequent loss of thousands of direct and indirect jobs are an event that has been known to all and expected for years but ignored by the revolving-door governments of Puerto Rico's two main political parties.

The pharmaceutical industry is the cornerstone of Puerto Rico's industrial program. Some forty-five pharmaceutical companies operating in Puerto Rico are estimated to generate directly more than 20,000 well-paid jobs (36,500 in 2002) and indirectly some 50,000 more. Thirteen of the twenty most popular prescription medications sold in the United States are manufactured here.

Exclusivity in producing these medications rests on the duration of their patents. Once the patents expire, any corporation may manufacture the medications anyplace in the world as generic drugs.

It is estimated that in the next five years the pharmaceutical industry worldwide will lose $100 billion in sales due to the expiration of patents on medicines. The chief executive officer of the largest pharmaceutical company in the United Kingdom, Glaxo Smith Kline, recently remarked that for the industry to survive it would have to reinvent itself and diversify.

The current economic model of the Commonwealth of Puerto Rico was established in 1947 with Operation Bootstrap, based on a plan conceived by the American economic planner Harvey S. Perloff to attract foreign investment. The plan fed on the postwar chaos produced by the destruction of Europe and Japan. This new economic-development strategy displaced the one that had been followed by the last American governor, Rexford G. Tugwell, who supported the development of local industries and agriculture and warned against the dangers of an economy dependent on foreign investment.

While Europe and Japan were being rebuilt, Puerto Rico was being reinvented with the petrochemical industry, the remains of which today are a mere "ghost town" along Puerto Rico's south coast in Guayanilla.

In the 1970s, Puerto Rico got a fresh breath of air with the arrival of the pharmaceutical industry and the implementation of Section 936 [of the US Internal Revenue Code], and it also increased its dependency on food stamps. At the end of the 1990s, the US Congress, using its plenary powers over the territory of Puerto Rico, eliminated Section 936, which caused the flight of funds attracted to Puerto Rico under Section 936 and the beginning of the withdrawal of the pharmaceutical industry. In 1996, when it was decided that Section 936 would be terminated after a ten-year phase-out period, there were more than 156,000 workers in the manufacturing sector. Today, that figure has dropped to 90,400.

The principal strategy used by both the Popular Democratic Party and the New Progressive Party to replace the revenues that were generated under Section 936 was the issuance of public debt complemented by increased federal transfers. In 1972, Puerto Rico's public debt was $2.7 billion; today it exceeds $60 billion.

While the pharmaceutical companies reinvented themselves, Puerto Rico's lack of power to generate opportunities in the globalized economy of the twenty-first century meant that it could not reinvent itself, as have such successful sovereign countries as Singapore and Ireland. Sovereignty is not a magic wand that solves problems, but it is a first step in obtaining the powers and tools with which, along with good government, to maximize opportunities.

For the years 2011 to 2014, the Economist Intelligence Unit has projected a growth for Singapore of between 4.6 and 5.2 percent. In the case of Ireland, it projects growth of between 0.9 and 2.4 percent. Projections for Puerto Rico for the year 2011 are no more than −3.4 percent, and there are no numbers for the following years.

While some politicians spend their time on sterile status processes and others spend theirs defending structures from the past that are irrelevant in the world of the twenty-first century, Puerto Rico is missing the opportunities for prosperity and social justice that already exist in successful sovereign countries similar to it in size.

JOBS, JOBS, JOBS . . .

August 21, 2010

The key to overcoming an economic crisis and being able to structure a new country is the creation of jobs.

That was the strategy followed by President Franklin D. Roosevelt, elected in 1932, to reinvent his country, which was submerged in a monumental economic crisis with an unemployment rate of greater than 20 percent, a country controlled by financial magnates, a country lacking in social justice.

Some of this American approach spattered Puerto Rico under the leadership of the last American governor, Rexford G. Tugwell, with the active support of the US Armed Forces and the recently founded Popular Democratic Party led by Luis Muñoz Marín.

The Puerto Rico of the 1930s was up to its ears in a severe economic depression and a social crisis. The principal strategy for creating a new country, just as in the United States, included the creation of public and private employment as well as programs aimed at attaining social justice.

Foreign investors were encouraged to establish operations in Puerto Rico that would create jobs. At the same time, jobs were generated in public works, education, social services, research, cultural affairs, and other sectors.

The terms *employment* and *unemployment* are usually found in statistical writing employed by economists. But jobs have a direct effect on all citizens' daily lives.

Workers generate income for the government through the taxes they pay. Workers often free the state from having to provide education and health services. Workers create other jobs because they have an effect on the businesses they patronize in such areas as transportation, food, and clothing.

Unemployment is the worst-case scenario for the state not only because of the costs it generates in the form of unemployment benefits, but also because of the loss of a productive resource.

The unemployed are also harmed emotionally: their self-esteem is affected, and they may become depressed, with terrible consequences for the family, often leading to domestic violence.

A lack of employment affects a new generation as it faces the harsh reality of a world in which bettering oneself through education does not necessarily lead to secure work. This may induce [those without work] to explore the dark world of drugs as an escape or as a way of making a living.

High unemployment, if sustained, may cause the unemployed to lose their skills, which affects their ability to find work again once the economy recovers. Rumor has it that in Puerto Rico there are cases of scientists laid off by pharmaceutical companies and faced with financial need who are using their skills in the illicit world of producing synthetic drugs.

The few fortunate graduates who do manage to get a job in times when the labor market is tight begin their professional lives with the enormous disadvantage of earning low salaries, a situation that lasts throughout their working lives.

The creation of jobs, whether public or private, is the kind of medicine that has an immediate effect on a scenario such as the one in which Puerto Rico is living. In the past four years, we have lost 157,000 jobs (55,000 in the government, 102,000 in the private sector). The outlook is dreadful, given the imminent closing of pharmaceutical companies as their patents expire and given the multiplier effect of the closing of three Puerto Rican banks.

Even worse, Puerto Rico is implementing a strategy that in other places has failed to resolve economic and social crises. Public employees are being laid off, with the multiplier effect on private jobs; taxes are being increased; and the funding of the University of Puerto Rico, where the workers of the future are created, is being cut.

As long as we cannot manage to reverse Puerto Rico's massive unemployment, our economy and quality of life will continue in freefall.

Nobel Prize winner Paul Krugman has said that "failure to act on unemployment is not just cruel, it is short-sighted."

Asia Headed Toward the Lead

September 26, 2010

During most of its long recorded history, Asia led the world in terms of population and the economy. In the year 1000, the West's share of the world's gross domestic product was 8.7 percent, whereas Asia's was 70.3 percent.

The shift favoring the West began in 1820 with the onset of the Industrial Revolution. So growth in the Western world has proceeded at a dizzying pace during the past two hundred years. However, the twenty-first century is bringing about dramatic changes.

In its BRIC [Brazil, Russia, India, China] study, Goldman Sachs predicted that by the year 2050, three of the four principal world economies would be Asian. Its ranking was as follows: China, the United States, India, and Japan.

The future will once again be in the hands of the Asians. Though China is the leader, the region does not revolve around it because there are other strong contenders, such as India, Indonesia, Japan, Taiwan, Korea, Malaysia, and Vietnam.

Though [the Asians'] current dramatic growth is limited to manufacturing, their investment in education will put them in a position of leadership in technology and innovation.

In 2004, China graduated 600,000 engineers from its universities, the United States only 70,000.

This past June Beijing announced a national plan to develop and expand its talent bank from 114 million to 180 million by 2020. Beijing plans to import the best talent in the world and to prepare local talent to produce a new generation of political leaders, scientists, engineers, technicians, entrepreneurs, educators, agronomists, and social scientists.

According to the plan, this talent bank is essential to transform China from the principal manufacturing country in the world into a worldwide leader in innovation.

China is already showing the world its technological capacity in transportation with its ultramodern airports and high-speed trains that connect its cities and in bioscience with its Beijing Genomics Institute, which holds the greatest number of DNA sequences in the world and has thus positioned itself to launch its own genetic-engineering industry with stem cells. And China has just earmarked $15 billion to the automobile and battery industries to develop electric cars that will not depend on oil.

While China and Asia are leading the world into the twenty-first century, the United States is experiencing the highest deficit in its history, reporting high unemployment, and investing in military adventures in Iraq and Afghanistan without any chance of winning.

In the case of Puerto Rico, the two main political parties have driven the public debt to more than $67 billion, and the economy is in freefall as the island's leaders look to failed economic models (neoliberalism) for solutions.

Singapore is the Asian model that is most relevant to Puerto Rico. Its island is fourteen times smaller than ours; it has no natural resources; and its population will soon be greater than 5 million. Yet Singapore's growth rate this year is expected to be 15 percent—the highest in the world—with enviable quality of life for its inhabitants.

In 1965, when Singapore attained sovereignty, it realized that its future could not be one of dependence on Great Britain; its people were going to have to depend on themselves.

While Puerto Rico is adjusting the funding formula to appropriate more funds for the University of Puerto Rico, which is facing budget deficits and cuts in academic offerings, Singapore has announced that it will be opening its fourth public university, this one associated with MIT and dedicated to the study of technology and design. And it has reached an agreement with Yale University to offer study in the liberal arts.

The sovereign state of Singapore has placed its bets for development and a high quality of life in the twenty-first century, whereas the unincorporated territory of Puerto Rico has bet on outdated approaches and increasing dependency on the United States, with a consequent decline in the quality of life for Puerto Ricans.

A Decade Lost: 2000–2010

January 27, 2011

The first decade of the twenty-first century began in 2000, with the Popular Democratic Party (PDP) in control of the three branches of [Puerto Rico's] government and headed by the first woman governor, who had experience in government and the private sector.

Four years later, in 2004, a shared government was elected: the PDP in control of the governor's office and the judicial branch, and the New Progressive Party (NPP) in control of the resident commissioner's office in Washington and the Puerto Rico legislature.

In 2008, the NPP took control of the three branches of government and threw Puerto Rico into freefall while the opposition was ineffective, lacking in vision and obsessed with retaking power.

What happened in this decade in which we were governed by the PDP/NPP in different combinations of control?

Unemployment in 2000 was 11 percent, and in 2010 it was 16 percent. The lack of opportunity continues to force many of our university graduates to join the nearly half-million Puerto Ricans who have abandoned their country over the past decade. Our recently graduated physicians and engineers are also leaving for lack of opportunity.

Puerto Rico's economic growth rate in 2000 was 3.0 percent; by 2010, it had fallen to −3.6 percent.

In 2000, 41 percent of the working-age population was part of the labor force. By 2010, that figure had decreased to 36 percent. During the same decade, 52,900 manufacturing jobs were lost. In 2000, the Puerto Rico Electric Power Authority had 1,986 industrial customers; in 2010, it had approximately 808.

234

In 2000, the public debt was $24.2 billion; by 2010, it had increased to $62.2 billion.

In 2000, 28 percent of the population received food stamps; by 2010, that figure had increased to 35 percent. More than 40 percent of Puerto Ricans now live below the poverty line.

The Retirement System of the Government of Puerto Rico has unfunded liabilities in the amount of $17.1 billion; for the Teachers Retirement System, the figure is $6.6 billion.

The Puerto Rico Stock Index in 2000 was $6,930; by 2010, it was $2,028. This reduction dramatizes the evaporation of local capital in local corporations on the stock market. The economic crisis in Puerto Rico has affected all social classes.

To these figures, we need to add the dizzying increase in the incidence of murder, crime, and drug addiction. Can anyone in his right mind think that the public-safety programs enforced by these political parties have provided our society with a safe environment? Are these political parties capable of accepting that drug trafficking is the primary source of criminality and that the most effective way to fight the problem is by treating drug addicts as sick people and not as criminals?

Why have these parties permitted only 8 percent of drug addicts to receive treatment and tolerated [the fact] that in the controlled scenario of prison almost half the inmates are addicts?

Mental diseases have increased dramatically in this decade. The front pages of newspapers dramatize the chaotic situation of the country every day. Domestic violence and the abuse of women, children, and the elderly are signs that our society is deteriorating.

At the beginning of the second decade of the twenty-first century, the question we need to ask is: Are we better off in 2011 than we were in 2001?

At this historic moment, the country cannot afford the luxury of merely supporting the lesser of two evils. We need to explore other options, new options whose purpose is to rescue the country from career politicians and to offer honest government that will focus on prosperity, social justice, and a new, dignified, and decolonizing relationship with the United States, one that is in harmony with the twenty-first century.

Obama's 238 Minutes in Puerto Rico

June 23, 2011

After a wait of half a century, finally a president of the United States has officially visited Puerto Rico, its unincorporated territory. The last visit was in 1961 and lasted two days; this one lasted barely 238 minutes and ended one hour earlier than anticipated.

Half of the time of President Barack Obama's visit to Puerto Rico this past June 14 was spent raising funds for his campaign. The other important issue addressed was the way he comes across to Puerto Rican voters in the United States, particularly in Florida. With this in mind, Marc Anthony, a renowned New Yorker performer of Puerto Rican parentage, and a group of Puerto Ricans residing in Florida were also invited.

Puerto Ricans reacted euphorically when Obama mentioned *arroz con gandules* and *boricuas* in his speech. His use of such expressions was parodied and mocked on television in the United States.

Both those who protested against his visit and those who waved the American flag in front of the capitol were ignored by the visitor.

This is the sixth official visit of a US president to Puerto Rico. The others were by Theodore Roosevelt in 1906, Franklin D. Roosevelt in 1934, Harry S. Truman in 1948, Dwight D. Eisenhower in 1960, and John F. Kennedy in 1961.

Presidents Herbert Hoover (in 1931) and Gerald Ford (in 1976) visited the island on vacation and an international meeting, respectively. President Lyndon B. Johnson made a private visit to the federal air base, Ramey, in Aguadilla in 1968.

Of the five official visits, except for the Eisenhower visit, which was a technical stop made on his way to and from a trip through South America,

236

all the others were related to the role Puerto Rico played for the United States in military matters.

Theodore Roosevelt was returning from inspecting his new Panama Canal, whose Caribbean access is protected by Puerto Rico. He started his visit in Ponce and traveled through Cayey, Aibonito, Caguas, Río Piedras, San Juan, Arecibo, Utuado, and Adjuntas.

Franklin D. Roosevelt, who like his relative Theodore had been undersecretary of the navy, inspected his territory, which would afterward be militarily fortified for its participation in the Second World War. Franklin arrived in Mayagüez, then visited Ponce, Juana Díaz, San Juan, Cayey, and Caguas.

Harry S. Truman discussed with Governor Jesús T. Piñero return of the lands temporarily occupied by the military during the Second World War. He visited San Juan, Bayamón, and Aguas Buenas.

John F. Kennedy, during a stopover en route to Venezuela and Colombia, met with Governor Luis Muñoz Marín to discuss the request by the US Department of Defense that the whole of Vieques Island be acquired and that both the living and the dead be removed.

Obama's visit is the first presidential visit that has no relation to Puerto Rico's military past. The Cold War is over, and the geopolitical stage on which the twenty-first century will play out is the Middle East and Asia.

Although the purpose of the visit had to do with Obama's electoral interests—that is, his campaign for reelection—his visit once again inserted the colonial power into Puerto Rico's own elections.

This open intervention is consistent with what has happened in the past three elections [in Puerto Rico]. In the year 2000, the federal prosecutor's office filed charges of corruption against several members of the governor's cabinet to the benefit of the opposition party. In 2004, the Federal Appeals Court in Boston decided who had won the elections. In 2008, right in the middle of the electoral campaign, the federal prosecutor's office filed charges against the governor then in office, adversely affecting his chances.

During his visit, Obama had lunch in a public cafeteria with a candidate for the governorship, an opponent of Obama's host, the current governor. Several hours later the White House posted the photograph of that lunch on its Web site as the "Photo of the Day."

As the late political analyst [Juan Manuel] García Passalacqua would say, "The American has spoken." Now let's see what Puerto Ricans say in November 2012.

The Thirty-Eighth Parallel and Commonwealth Status

August 25, 2011

The Thirty-Eighth Parallel on the Korean Peninsula and the status of the Commonwealth of Puerto Rico have something in common: both are relics of the Cold War.

The Thirty-Eighth Parallel on the Korean Peninsula is the dividing line between (Communist) North Korea and (capitalist) South Korea. When the Second World War ended in 1945, Japan lost the Korean colony it had held since 1910, and the Soviets and the Americans forced the division of the country into two states.

The division caused a war. In 1950, North Korea invaded South Korea and managed to occupy Seoul and practically all of South Korea.

The Korean War turned the Cold War into a "hot" one and extended its perimeter from Europe into Asia.

More than 60,000 Puerto Ricans participated in the war, and 764 of them died. The participation of the Puerto Rican soldiers was worthy and brave. However, the arbitrary elimination of the Sixty-Fifth Infantry Regiment, the unfair court-martial proceedings brought against Puerto Rican soldiers, and the participation of Puerto Rico's legal representative, Abe Fortas, and the Muñoz-Marín administration in that process constitute a rather dishonorable chapter in the history of the governments of Puerto Rico and the United States.

Chinese troops with massive Soviet military support managed to help North Korea stop the advances of the United Nations troops under the leadership of the legendary General Douglas MacArthur.

For the armistice negotiated in 1953, both sides returned to the Thirty-Eighth Parallel and established a demilitarized zone. That zone, designed for military containment, remains hostile territory and unpopulated. It measures 4 kilometers in width by 238 kilometers in length.

In the middle of this zone lies Panmunjom, where the armistice was signed (the peace treaty has still not been signed). The zone is strictly regulated; taking photographs is prohibited; and there is a high level of tension. To visit the zone is to enter a scene from the Cold War.

The zone is administered by soldiers of the United Nations, North Korea, and South Korea, separated from each other by only a few meters, who keep a watchful eye on one another constantly as if at any moment the conflict might start once again.

It is like entering a time capsule. Contrary to the Checkpoint Charlie Museum in Berlin, which is testimony to the division of Berlin during the Cold War, Panmunjom is a dramatic representation of past reality made present, although the Cold War has ended, the Soviet Union no longer exists, and China owns the largest percent of the US public debt.

This Asian relic of the Cold War resembles Puerto Rico's current status, which is frozen in the 1950s. The US Navy promoted commonwealth status as part of a military strategy of the Cold War and to pretend that the United States was in compliance with the Atlantic Charter, which supported decolonization, in light of which it was unacceptable to maintain a classical colony such as Puerto Rico.

The Popular Democratic Party administration [in Puerto Rico] developed the new variation on a colony and attained extraordinary economic and social development, but at the cost of generating a high degree of dependency on the colonial power.

The difference between Korea and Puerto Rico is that the first knows that its final destiny is the union of its two states, as happened with Germany and Vietnam. They already have a modern train station in the demilitarized zone, Dorasan, ready to connect the two countries once China and the United States decide to end the conflict.

In the case of Puerto Rico, because it is not a priority for the colonial power, we are limited to fantasizing about a supposed pact, which

Congress and the White House completely disregard, and statehood, which the the United States does not want. Meanwhile, the country continues in a free-fall, controlled by two political parties whose goal is to win elections and control the government budget.

Stagnation and the Lack of *Indignados*

September 29, 2011

The days pass by, and we resign ourselves to witnessing a Puerto Rico in a free-fall.

Thousands of jobs have been lost in the private sector; there are only a few job openings for university graduates; inequality increases; criminality surges ahead triumphantly while federal authorities point to abuses and ineptitude in our police force; property values decrease; the Puerto Rico Stock Index dramatically drops, making local capital vanish; megastores displace local merchants; commercial credit for establishing new businesses is scarce; natural resources are destroyed; high energy costs strangle consumers and businesses alike; the quality of health and public education is substandard; university resources that are essential for the future are diminishing; the infrastructure deteriorates; and agriculture continues to be abandoned and forgotten.

Much of our best talent has to leave the country because of the lack of opportunities and the quality of life.

This chaotic situation in any other part of the world would have caused thousands of indignant marchers to hurl themselves into the streets. Spain, Chile, and Israel are recent examples.

The elements that prevent protest marches are the increase in government dependency (federal and local), the new funds generated with public debt that is to be paid by future generations, the underground economy, and the ease with which we can immigrate to the colonial power.

The two political parties that have taken turns in or shared power since 1968 are responsible for this situation. Both have devoted themselves

242

to maintaining the status quo, managing commonwealth status, and blaming the previous administration for all of our problems.

Both avoid discussing the cause of these problems, which lies in the lack of definition and the lack of powers under the current status. Without such powers, we cannot create a new economic model to maximize our resources in a global economy.

In 1970, forty-one years ago, a former governor and public-administration professor at the University of Puerto Rico, Roberto Sánchez-Vilella, remarked that "commonwealth status in its present form cannot answer for economic development or democratic institutions, political dignity or Puerto Rican cultural identity. . . . What has happened to commonwealth status? It has simply not had the powers that this country needs to solve its problems. . . . Today [1970], commonwealth status is essentially as it was the day it was born. Its history of eighteen years has consisted of political stagnation, which has damaged its constitutional dignity. Given its paralysis, it is destined to relapse into a colonial state."

Since Sánchez-Vilella uttered those words in 1970, commonwealth status has continued just as it was, which explains our country's current situation.

We live in a world without a Cold War, with China in unstoppable economic expansion, with the US hegemony falling, with a historic deficit and the economy globalized in a world of networks interconnected by high technology.

Some people think that the current status can be improved by seeking, as previously, new tax benefits from Congress. They forget that Washington is submerged in a serious political crisis and that Puerto Rico's primary protector and supporter, the US Navy, has left the island.

The success achieved by the Tea Party with its racist arguments and policies against government dependency should be considered a good indicator of the new scenario in Washington.

The solution to the political status problem will not be attained through failed formulas such as plebiscites, congressional hearings, executive-branch reports, lobbying, or political contributions.

The most effective mechanism to solve it is a constitutional assembly on the status of Puerto Rico, with delegates elected by the people and agreements that are eventually to be approved or rejected by the people in a referendum.

We have already tried all the other approaches, and they all have failed. As a wise proverb says, the biggest mistake is not to learn from our mistakes.

Suggested Reading

Contributors

Index

Suggested Reading

Ayala, César J., and Rafael Bernabe. *Puerto Rico in the American Century: A History since 1898*. Chapel Hill: Univ. of North Carolina Press, 2007.

Berberoglu, Berch, ed. *The National Question: Nationalism, Ethnic Conflict, and Self-Determination in the 20th Century*. Philadelphia: Temple Univ. Press, 1995.

Bosque-Pérez, Ramón, and José Javier Colón-Morera, eds. *Puerto Rico under Colonial Rule: Political Persecution and the Quest for Human Rights*. Albany: State Univ. of New York Press, 2006.

Burnett, Christian Duffy, and Burke Marshall, eds. *Foreign in a Domestic Sense: Puerto Rico, American Expansion, and the Constitution*. Durham, NC: Duke Univ. Press, 2001.

Cabranes, José. *Citizenship and the American Empire: Notes on the Legislative History of the United States Citizenship of Puerto Ricans*. New Haven, CT: Yale Univ. Press, 1979.

Carrión, Juan Manuel, ed. *Ethnicity, Race, and Nationality in the Caribbean*. Río Piedras, Puerto Rico: Institute of Caribbean Studies, 1997.

Collins, Susan M., Barry P. Bosworth, and Miguel Soto-Class, eds. *The Economy of Puerto Rico: Restoring Growth*. Washington, DC: Brookings Institution Press, 2006.

Copaken, Richard D. *Target Culebra: How 743 Islanders Took on the Entire U.S. Navy and Won*. Río Piedras: Editorial Universidad de Puerto Rico, 2009.

Dávila, Arlene M. *Sponsored Identities: Cultural Politics in Puerto Rico*. Philadelphia: Temple Univ. Press, 1997.

Dietz, James L. *Puerto Rico: Negotiating Development and Change*. Boulder, CO: Lynne Rienner, 2003.

Diffie, Bailey W., and Justine Whitfield. *Porto Rico: A Broken Pledge*. New York: Vanguard Press, 1931.

Duany, Jorge. *The Puerto Rican Nation on the Move: Identities on the Island and in the United States*. Chapel Hill: Univ. of North Carolina Press, 2002.

Fernández, Ronald. *The Disenchanted Island: Puerto Rico and the United States in the Twentieth Century.* New York: Praeger, 1992.

———. *Prisoners of Colonialism: The Struggle for Justice in Puerto Rico.* Monroe, ME: Common Courage Press, 1994.

Friedrich, Carl J. *Puerto Rico: Middle Road to Freedom.* New York: Rinehart, 1959.

González, Juan. *Harvest of Empire: A History of Latinos in America.* New York: Penguin, 2000.

Grosfoguel, Ramón. *Colonial Subjects: Puerto Ricans in a Global Perspective.* Berkeley and Los Angeles: Univ. of California Press, 2003.

Hunter, Stephen, and John Bainbridge Jr. *American Gunfight: The Plot to Kill Harry Truman and the Shoot-Out That Stopped It.* New York: Simon and Schuster, 2005.

Leibowitz, Arnold H. *Colonial Emancipation in the Pacific and the Caribbean: A Legal and Political Analysis.* New York: Praeger, 1976.

———. *Defining Status: A Comprehensive Analysis of United States Territorial Relations.* Dordrecht, Netherlands: Martinus Nijhoff, 1989.

López Baralt, José. *The Policy of the United States Towards Its Territories, with Special Reference to Puerto Rico.* San Juan: Editorial de la Universidad de Puerto Rico, 1999.

Mahan, Alfred T. *Lessons of the War with Spain and Other Articles.* London: Sampson, Low, Marston, 1899.

Maingot, Anthony P. *The United States and the Caribbean.* Boulder, CO: Westview, 1994.

Maldonado Denis, Manuel. *Puerto Rico: A Socio-Historic Interpretation.* New York: Random House, 1972.

Mathews, Thomas. *Puerto Rican Politics and the New Deal.* Gainesville: Univ. of Florida Press, 1960.

Mintz, Sidney W. *Worker in the Cane: A Puerto Rican Life History.* New Haven, CT: Yale Univ. Press, 1960.

Morales Carrión, Arturo. *Puerto Rico: A Political and Cultural History.* New York: W. W. Norton, 1983.

———. *Puerto Rico and the United States: The Quest for a New Encounter.* San Juan, Puerto Rico: Editorial Académica, 1990.

Morris, Nancy. *Puerto Rico: Culture, Politics, and Identity.* Westport, CT: Praeger, 1995.

Pastor, Robert. *Whirlpool: U.S. Foreign Policy Toward Latin America and the Caribbean.* Princeton, NJ: Princeton Univ. Press, 1992.

Perloff, Harvey S. *Puerto Rico's Economic Future: A Study in Planned Development.* Chicago: Univ. of Chicago Press, 1950.

Ramos, Aaron Gamaliel, and Ángel Israel Rivera, eds. *Islands at the Crossroads: Politics in the Non-Independent Caribbean*. Kingston, Jamaica: Ian Randle, 2001.

Rivera Ramos, Efrén. *The Legal Construction of Identity: The Judicial and Social Legacy of American Colonialism in Puerto Rico*. Washington, DC: American Psychological Association, 2001.

Rodríguez Beruff, Jorge. *Strategy as Politics: Puerto Rico on the Eve of the Second World War*. San Juan: Editorial Universidad de Puerto Rico, 2007.

Rodríguez Beruff, Jorge, J. Peter Figueroa, and J. Edward Greene, eds. *Conflict, Peace, and Development in the Caribbean*. London: Macmillan, 1991.

Rodríguez Beruff, Jorge, and Humberto García Muñiz, eds. *Security Problems and Policies in the Post–Cold War Caribbean*. London: Macmillan, 1996.

Torruella, Juan R. *The Supreme Court and Puerto Rico: The Doctrine of Separate and Unequal*. Río Piedras: Editorial Universidad de Puerto Rico, 1988.

Trías Monge, José. *Puerto Rico: The Trials of the Oldest Colony in the World*. New Haven, CT: Yale Univ. Press, 1997.

Tugwell, Rexford G. *The Stricken Land: The Story of Puerto Rico*. New York: Doubleday, 1947.

Wells, Henry. *The Modernization of Puerto Rico: A Political Study of Changing Values and Institutions*. Cambridge, MA: Harvard Univ. Press, 1971.

Contributors

Francisco Catalá-Oliveras attained his bachelor's and master's degrees at the University of Puerto Rico and his doctorate in economics at Georgetown University. For many years, he worked as a professor of economics at the Río Piedras Campus of the University of Puerto Rico, where he taught both undergraduate and graduate courses. He has published numerous papers with the Economic Research Unit of the University of Puerto Rico and in international journals such as *El Trimestre Económico* (Mexico). He has also published three books: *Democracia obrera ¿Autogestión o privatización?* (1996); *El callejón del sapo: Teoría y gestión del cooperativismo* (2004); and *Elogio de la imperfección* (2007). Catalá-Oliveras's professional experience has focused on cooperatives and labor unions.

Juan Lara is a professor of economics at the University of Puerto Rico, Río Piedras, where he has devoted eighteen years to teaching and research. He previously taught economics at the University of Puerto Rico at Mayagüez, Temple University, and Haverford College. He obtained his doctorate in economics from the State University of New York, Stony Brook. He also holds a bachelor's degree with a major in economics from the University of Puerto Rico, Río Piedras.

In addition to his teaching career, Lara has more than twenty-five years of experience as an economic consultant and practicing professional economist. He was the director of the Latin American Service for Wharton Econometric Forecasting Associates, a Philadelphia firm dedicated to making economic forecasts using econometric models. He also served as the senior economist for Mexico Services with the same firm.

251

His most recent publications include a chapter coauthored with Robert Z. Lawrence in the book *Restoring Growth in Puerto Rico* (2006) as well as a chapter in the book *Globalización y desarrollo: Desafíos de Puerto Rico frente al siglo XXI* (2005).

Index

Italic page numbers denote illustrations and tables.